POWER
TO
BURN

POWER
TO
BURN

MICHAEL OVITZ
AND THE
NEW BUSINESS OF
SHOW BUSINESS

STEPHEN SINGULAR

A BIRCH LANE PRESS BOOK

PUBLISHED BY CAROL PUBLISHING GROUP

To Eric

A Birch Lane Press Book
Published by Carol Publishing Group
Birch Lane Press is a registered trademark of Carol Communications, Inc.
Editorial, sales and distribution, rights and permissions inquiries should be addressed to Carol Publishing Group, 120 Enterprise Avenue, Secaucus, N.J. 07094.

In Canada: Canadian Manda Group, One Atlantic Avenue, Suite 105, Toronto, Ontario M6K 3E7

Carol Publishing Group books are available at special discounts for bulk purchases, sales promotion, fund-raising, or educational purposes. Special editions can be created to specifications. For details, contact Special Sales Department, Carol Publishing Group, 120 Enterprise Avenue, Secaucus, N.J. 07094.

Manufactured in the United States of America
10 9 8 7 6 5 4 3 2 1

Library of Congress Cataloging-in-Publication Data

Singular, Stephen.
    Power to burn : Michael Ovitz and the new business of show
business / Stephen Singular.
        p.   cm.
    "A Birch Lane Press book."
    ISBN 1–55972–335–1 (hardcover)
    1. Ovitz, Michael.   2. Theatrical agents—United States—
Biography.   3. Executives—United States—Biography.   4. Creative
Artists Agency—History.   5. Theatrical agencies—United States—
History.   I. Title.
PN2287.O77S56   1996
659.2'9791'092—dc20
    [B]   95–47830
                                                              CIP

CONTENTS

All warfare is based on deception. Therefore, when capable, feign incapacity; when active, inactivity. When near, make it appear that you are far away; when far away, that you are near. Offer the enemy a bait to lure him; feign disorder and strike him.

—Sun Tzu, *The Art of War*, 2500 B.C.

PREFACE

From August of 1994 until the end of the O. J. Simpson double-murder trial in October of 1995, I dealt with some of the major figures in that infamous case: defense attorneys Johnnie Cochran and Carl Douglas, prosecutor Christopher Darden, and several others. Back then, I was living in Denver, but during the course of that legal ordeal, I got to know something about the city of Los Angeles—about its racial dynamics, its political environment, its social landscape, its angers and fears. I was well aware that lawyers involved in prominent homicide cases are paranoid, especially when it comes to talking with journalists. They neither trust nor like reporters; maybe they have good reason not to. So I was not at all surprised that I had great difficulty interacting with these criminal attorneys. They were very skeptical, tough people engaged in a serious business, and it would have been naive on my part to expect them to behave differently.

I say all that as prelude to the spring of 1995, when I began working on this book about Michael Ovitz. My experience of dealing with high-powered people in Los Angeles during the Simpson case, I felt certain, would serve me well in the new project. I was, after all, writing about another famous person in L.A. Ovitz lived quite near Simpson in the fashionable neighborhood of Brentwood, almost within waving distance. Simpson was a national, to some extent international, celebrity, while Ovitz was mostly a local one. O.J. had been accused of butchering two people, while Ovitz had gained fame and notoriety as the most powerful talent agent and best dealmaker in Hollywood. Surely, I told myself, there was nothing in the entertainment business that could rival the fear and nastiness surrounding the super-ugly trial of a man charged with ending two young lives. Surely, having confronted Cochran, Darden, and Douglas, I was well prepared to take on show biz executives and Hollywood agents.

In the summer of 1995, I wrote a letter telling Ovitz that I'd been commissioned to write a "business biography" of him and seeking his cooperation with the book. I explained that I had not been asked to delve deeply into his personal history, his childhood, his relationship with his wife and kids, or his other private affairs, nor did I want to. My basic question for him was: How, in less than a decade, had he turned Creative Artists Agency, a company with virtually no assets and few visible resources, into the most successful talent agency in the world?

"I'm interested in documenting," my letter said, "how you and a handful of others started CAA; how your company grew; what has made it so successful; how it has changed the way things are done in the entertainment business; and what gave you the vision to begin and carry out this enterprise."

Simply put, I wanted to write the story of the triumph of CAA. I was well aware that Ovitz had a reputation for ducking journalists, but I thought that the avoidance of his personal life in this book might offer some appeal.

At the end of the letter, I said that I hoped to be able to interview him in the near future. "You are the source of the business," I wrote, "and have more to say about it than anyone else."

Two weeks later, the phone rang, and a young woman told me that Mr. Ovitz was on the line. Very graciously and quietly, he said that if he ever wanted to work on a book about his business with someone, I was certainly the kind of person he would be looking for. But at the moment, he just wasn't interested in such an undertaking. For the next several minutes, I attempted to tell him why the overwhelming success of CAA from 1975 to 1995 was, in the opinion of many well-informed people, the most significant event in show business during the past two decades. If he would agree to talk with me, I said, it would add an enormous amount to the book I was going to write.

Firmly and very politely, he again said no, thank you. It was the nicest way I'd ever heard anyone slam a door. I said I would call him later to see if he'd changed his mind, and then we hung up.

Six weeks passed, and I phoned his office, repeating my request to a female secretary. A few days went by before a young man called and said that he was Mr. Ovitz's assistant. At this time, he said, Mr. Ovitz was traveling, and unfortunately he would not be able to speak with me now—or in the future. The caller was gracious but as immovable as his boss had been.

"This sort of thing," the young man told me, "just isn't his cup of tea."

I was not very disappointed. I'd never fully expected Ovitz to talk to me, but I'd wanted to give him the opportunity at the outset. Now I felt freer to move in other directions.

Several months later, near the end of 1995, I was speaking with a television executive when I confessed that I'd once believed that my dealings with Johnnie Cochran and Christopher Darden would prepare me for writing about Michael Ovitz. This network vice president burst into laughter.

"You're kidding me, aren't you?" he said. "Cochran and Darden are rank amateurs compared to the people who run the world of entertainment. With those lawyers, you can smell their bullshit from a distance. You can hear and see what they're doing. Everything is obvious. With people like Ovitz, you never know anything. They don't talk to anyone they don't have to, they are five steps ahead of everyone else, and they are masters of controlling things through fear and some very subtle mechanisms. They are the best negotiators on the planet, and they make even good defense attorneys look like children."

By now, I'd begun to agree with this man. In over two decades as a journalist, I'd never seen or felt anything like the kind of resistance I was encountering in trying to talk to people about Ovitz. I'd attempted to interview studio honchos, other talent agents, and some of the biggest names in the film industry, but all of them had said the same thing: No, they would not talk on the record about Mr. Ovitz. Period.

The Biz, as the entertainment world is called in Los Angeles, did not want its business known, at least not to an outsider like myself.

Tony Fantozzi, a senior partner at the William Morris Agency in Beverly Hills, was a show business veteran when Ovitz went to work at the Morris office in Los Angeles in the late 1960s. The young Ovitz had once fetched coffee for the partner.

"I won't say anything bad about him," Fantozzi replied, when asked to be interviewed.

"Will you say something good about him?" I said.

"No."

"Why not?"

"I don't want to talk about it."

"Why not?"

"That's all I have to say."

Herbert Allen, one of the leading investment bankers in New York City and the single most important financial adviser in the field of entertainment, also refused to be interviewed.

"Mr. Allen," his secretary said, with the same polite but iron-fisted tone used by Ovitz's man, "will not talk to you unless Mr. Ovitz is speaking with you. We've called Mr. Ovitz, and because he isn't speaking with you, we must decline your offer."

Howard West, the co–executive producer of *Seinfeld*, the most successful television comedy show in recent years, had once taught Ovitz the TV-packaging business when the young man worked under him at William Morris.

"What does Michael have to say about your book?" West asked me in something like hushed tones, when I told him that I'd like to talk with him about this project.

I said that Ovitz was reluctant to speak to me.

"If he won't cooperate with you," West said, "then I won't, either."

When I phoned Bertram Fields, perhaps the most potent and renowned entertainment lawyer in L.A., and asked to talk with him about Ovitz, he would not return my calls. The same thing happened with the actress Sally Field, who'd gone to high school with Ovitz and become a CAA client.

Seven years earlier, I'd sold the rights to my first book to Oliver Stone, another CAA client. In 1988, he made the movie *Talk Radio*, which was partly based on my book. I thought this might give me a better shot with him.

Stone, of course, has directed some of the most controversial American movies ever made. He routinely takes on the political and economic establishment, the U.S. military, the reputations and the families of famous citizens, and other powerful elements in our society. Some people believe that nothing can intimidate him.

"Mr. Stone," one of his associates told me, when I called his office and asked for an interview, "can't speak to you about Mr. Ovitz."

"Why not?"

"Mr. Stone is a personal friend of Mr. Ovitz, and he knows that Mr. Ovitz does not like it when other people talk about him. So Mr. Stone won't do that."

"But—"

"The answer is no."

In private, off the record, countless folks in Hollywood will speak about Ovitz and CAA. They will complain about the man's strong-arm negotiating tactics, his driving up the costs of movie productions, his ruthless competitive streak, and his profound desire to win. They will vent their frustrations and they will make broad accusations against him. When I told one network vice president that I'd recently been writing about O. J. Simpson and Michael Ovitz, he said jokingly, "Well, I can see that you're only writing about dangerous people now."

Yet if you push these same people a little, they will usually acknowledge that CAA succeeded not because it had bad intentions or a questionable agenda. It succeeded because, as one executive put it, it "simply did not make mistakes. I can be as critical of Ovitz as anyone is, but the truth is that CAA did everything right."

By the end of 1995, I'd moved to Los Angeles to continue my research and get closer to this story. I'd come to Hollywood to write about success, but what I was discovering was mostly about anxiety and secrecy and fear. I was constantly amazed that highly accomplished adults with independent minds and great wealth and power would not allow themselves to have a public opinion about one of the most important figures in their business. I told many of them that my questions about Ovitz were not going to concentrate on personal matters and that I was not looking for scandals or dirt. My inquiries were more about trying to understand what had made the man and his company so phenomenally good at their jobs.

Nothing I said to these people mattered; like Tony Fantozzi, they did not want to talk about it. I'd entered the realm of awe and terror, and in this place silence was everything.

In time, I approached Ron Meyer, another CAA founding partner, but he also declined to speak with me. Fortunately, the other three men who'd created the agency along with Ovitz and Meyer were somewhat more accessible, yet they were still edgy. Once, when I asked Bill Haber if I could have thirty minutes for an interview about his thirty years in the business, he sounded shocked that I would make such an outlandish demand on his busy schedule. It was as though I'd asked to move into his home for the winter to bombard him with questions day and night.

When I traveled to a small airport just outside Santa Rosa, California, to meet with Mike Rosenfeld (who kept a private plane there), he would not talk to me until I'd shown him my driver's license, which proved that I was indeed who I said I was and not a secret agent from the CIA or some other nefarious agency. He studied my license for at least two full minutes before he was satisfied that I was not an impostor.

The other founding partner, Rowland Perkins, was pleasant and helpful, but when I asked him about what had happened ten or fifteen or twenty years earlier at CAA, he seemed curiously uninterested. The events I was questioning him about were far in the past; why would anyone want to talk about them now, when he was working on some new and exciting projects at his own production company? Perkins, like the other men who'd started CAA, had made his mark as an agent, not an actor or writer or director or historian. Agents live intensely in the present, anxious to make their next phone call and cut their next deal. And for many people in Hollywood, the deal, as the saying goes, is the sex while the movie is just the cigarette.

The people I was approaching might have spoken more easily to someone inside their industry, but my instincts told me they would not have. The reason was simple: I was not offering them anything tangible. I was not going to pay them for information, I was not going to help them put together their next deal, and I was not going to introduce them to Someone Very Famous; for all of these reasons, they were unmotivated to talk. In the lingo of the business, you're either a "buyer" (working at a network or a studio) or a "seller" (working at an agency and representing talent). Since I was neither of these, I was in a strange position indeed.

There were, however, some individuals who were close to CAA who held a different point of view. They possessed a quality that the others did not: they were capable of seeing the value of the CAA story itself, and they understood that, regardless of whether one liked or disliked everything that Ovitz and his partners had done, the rise of CAA is a remarkable tale of success in one of the most competitive and difficult industries in the country. It is well worth talking about, and there are lessons inside this story for anyone starting or running a business. The people who eventually did speak to me—and they included screenwriters, producers, network executives, studio employees, actors, agents, mailroom trainees from CAA, caterers, secretaries, attorneys, and others—agreed to open up, but on the condition of absolute anonymity.

Any reporter would prefer to identify his sources, and this case is no exception. On the other hand, as the months unfolded and my research continued, I began to feel that what I was picking up from my interview subjects was a significant part of this book. To grasp the entertainment business is to understand the overwhelming sense of insecurity and fragility that underlies it. The industry runs on frayed nerves, wild expectations, irritability, and constant hope. It is chaotic to a degree that no outsider can ever appreciate when watching a polished movie up there on the big screen. And anyone who can organize a little of that chaos or that insecurity and move with it in a new and productive way can probably make millions of dollars.

I'd originally come to L.A. looking for the key to Ovitz's success. As time went on, it occurred to me that perhaps the answer had been sitting there all along, right under my nose, in the great gaps of silence and the bottomless fear that Ovitz had inspired in others in the business.

In mid-January of 1996, halfway through this project, the phone rang one evening, and when I answered it a young woman told me that Mr. Ovitz was on the line. I was having a bout of the flu, and my voice was nearly gone. Ovitz inquired at length about my health and said he would be more than willing to call back later, when I was feeling better. I wanted to talk now.

He said that from our earlier conversation, he hadn't really believed that I was serious about writing a book on him and CAA.

I told him that I was continuing my research and the book was well underway.

"I would like," he then said, in a very soft voice, "to reopen our discussion."

I said that would be fine, and he replied that he would call me back a few days later, after my health had returned. I hung up, very surprised that he'd phoned and wondering what would happen next.

We then became engaged in a strange ritual that was difficult to understand. Ovitz's secretary began calling my office and saying that her boss was going to phone me soon and tell me his intentions regarding speaking with me about this project. I would ask when to expect his call, and she would say she didn't know. Then she would ask when I was available, and I would give her several specific times for each day. When I asked if those were good times for Mr. Ovitz, she said she had no idea if they were or not. When I asked what was a good time for him, she said she didn't know. After we'd had seven or eight of these conversations, I was reminded of the character of Major Major in Joseph Heller's novel *Catch-22*, who would always jump out the window of his office when someone was coming in the front door for an appointment.

Six weeks passed in this manner, and Ovitz and I never reconnected. By now, I'd given up believing that he would ever call. Then, one morning in late February, he did, and we resumed talking about whether he wanted to talk to me or not. And I'd once thought that the O. J. Simpson double-murder case was complicated.

During our discussion, Ovitz asked me questions about myself, about the publisher of this book, about my agent, and about several other things. Many people had already told me that to this man knowledge was power—he had to know everything about everything and weigh every factor before he bought an accessory for his home or office, let alone before he made an important business decision. Now I was getting the classic Ovitzian treatment, and as we talked, I could hear him taking notes in the background.

He wanted me to fax him a letter stating my "agenda" for the book and the questions I intended to ask him. Two hours later, this was done. The next afternoon, a Tuesday, his secretary called and said that Mr. Ovitz was traveling but would phone me soon.

On the evening of Thursday, February 29, I was watching the six o'clock national news on CBS when I saw a shot of the interior of the White House and a group of men sitting at a large table. On President Bill Clinton's right was Vice President Al Gore. On his left was Michael Ovitz. The gathering also included former film studio heads Barry Diller and Jeffrey Katzenberg, plus cable company and network executives. They'd all come to Washington for a historic meeting with the president, during which the television industry agreed to formulate a long-awaited ratings system for its programs. The industry was also backing "V-chip" technology, which would give parents more control over their children's television viewing. Not everyone in the entertainment business was happy about this development, but Ovitz had come forward as a strong advocate of these measures.

The news ended at six-thirty, and half an hour later the phone rang. Ovitz was calling from his apartment in New York. He said that he'd just gotten there from Washington, the heater in his building wasn't working, it was twenty degrees in Manhattan, and he was cold. After I expressed my sympathies, he said that he was "leaning toward" talking with me now, but he wanted me to do one more thing before he made up his mind.

"What's that?" I asked a little hesitantly, as I was now under deadline pressure to get the book done.

Make a list, he said, of everything I'd read since I'd begun doing research on him, almost a year earlier. When I replied that that would be a daunting and time-consuming task, he told me just to write out a list of the periodicals and books I'd perused and to fax it to his office in L.A. the following day.

"Don't make it complicated," he said.

At this point I was tempted to make a remark about complexity, but I let the impulse go.

The next morning I complied with his request and went back to work, wondering when the phone would ring again. Eight days later, Ovitz called, and we had the best and most complete discussion yet. He said that he'd given what I was doing a great deal of thought, that he'd let this situation go on too long, and that it would be difficult for him to accomplish much by getting involved at this late date. He wanted me to know that he'd done considerable research into the questions he'd posed to me earlier and that he was worried about "sensationalized journalism" and its effects not just on him but on the nation as a whole.

This was the fifth time I'd talked with the man on the phone. Whenever we'd spoken in the past, it had been clear to me that he'd chosen every word very carefully. Each syllable had seemed calculated. On this occasion, near the end of our conversation, I made a remark about his incredible achievements and the success of CAA. Unexpectedly, I hit a nerve.

"Look, Stephen," he said, his tone suddenly passionate and uncalculated and heartfelt, "we've made it a sin to be successful in this country. That's why we have a crisis on our hands—in politics, in government, and in other areas. That's why people don't want to come forward and be leaders. If you become successful, you get attacked by the media. I'm very concerned about this. Journalists act as if you haven't done anything to achieve what you have, or haven't done the work to get where you are. This has kept us from becoming fantastic."

Then he paused and said, "But that's another story."

PART ONE

THE BEGINNING
OF THE END

There are some roads not to follow; some troops not to strike; some cities not to assault; and some ground which should not be contested.

—The Art of War

I

The handsome screening room at Creative Artists Agency in Beverly Hills was crowded on this Monday morning, and the buzz in the air was thicker than usual. The hundred or so people who'd gathered here were not talking about the films they'd seen over the weekend or the restaurants they'd visited or the trips they'd taken out of town. They weren't discussing contracts or commissions or packaging fees for network television programs. They were whispering among themselves and glancing around, asking questions and looking at one another expectantly, nervously, even fearfully. In the next few minutes, when the staff meeting began at nine-thirty, something very dramatic was going to happen—or not happen.

If it did happen, long-standing plans would be shattered and careers would instantly be altered—for better or worse. People in this spacious, carpeted room, where CAA employees regularly came to watch movies, would suddenly be richer or poorer. Some would have new jobs, and others would be looking for work. Far beyond these walls, the lives of many film superstars would never again be quite the same, and the ripples that would travel outward from this meeting would affect business not just in Hollywood but on Wall Street and Madison Avenue, inside the nationwide telecommunications industry, and on the other side of the globe. On this morning, June 5, 1995, after twenty years of running the entertainment industry's most powerful talent agency, Michael Ovitz was going to leave CAA to become president of the MCA/Universal studio—or he wasn't. Rumors, expectations, and tensions had been building and building. A few minutes from now, something had to give.

Emotions in the screening room were ragged. Some of the

younger agents looked at Ovitz as an all-providing parent and felt certain that without his leadership CAA would soon lose its reputation and its clout. The agency would not be able to hold on to many of its stars, who made up a roster of the biggest names in the movie business: Tom Hanks, Kevin Costner, Demi Moore, Sylvester Stallone, Tom Cruise, Whoopi Goldberg, Robin Williams, Brad Pitt (plus twelve hundred other clients). The ninety agents at CAA represented not just the stars on the screen but also the directors who made the films: Steven Spielberg, Oliver Stone, Martin Scorsese, Ron Howard, Robert Zemeckis, among others. The agency represented megaselling authors, like Michael Crichton and Anne Rice, who'd written the books or the scripts the directors had used to create films that in some cases had generated more than a billion dollars. CAA also had a music department, and Ovitz and his people had negotiated huge contracts for Barbra Streisand, Michael Jackson, and Madonna.

The company's influence went far beyond acting, directing, and music, however. In recent years, Ovitz and his CAA team (nearly everything at the agency involved teamwork) had helped broker the sale of Columbia Pictures to the Sony Corporation; had played an even larger role in the purchase of MCA/Universal by the huge Japanese conglomerate known as the Matsushita Electric Industrial Company; and had been involved in the bailout of the MGM/United Artists studio by the French bank Credit Lyonnais. Ovitz had annoyed some investment banking firms in New York and Boston by taking over their role and brokering the sale of these studios. In 1991, he irritated and shocked the world of marketing by luring the Coca-Cola Classic account away from several of Madison Avenue's venerable advertising agencies. CAA was responsible for the ubiquitous slogan "Always Coca-Cola" and for filling American TV screens with images of cute, animated polar bears knocking back bottles of Coke.

Ovitz, once the power broker to the Hollywood stars, was becoming the power broker not just to the nation but to worldwide markets as well.

His success was peculiarly intriguing. He created nothing tangible. He had never directed a film or written a script or appeared in front of a movie camera. He had not manufactured or bought or sold a product, in the conventional sense. And he remained, despite his overwhelming clout inside the industry, virtually unknown beyond the relatively small circle of people who made all the crucial decisions regarding what Americans were offered as entertainment. Ovitz had achieved something truly extraordinary: he had convinced people—across town, across the country, and across the oceans—that he knew more than anyone else in Hollywood, that his knowledge could be turned into huge amounts of cash and that he could be trusted. Those who had believed him had often grown very rich. Yet even when he was wrong, people kept returning to him for advice and paying him colossal sums to deliver it.

In spite of all that, not every agent in the screening room looked at the man as a benevolent parent; or if they did, it was with the conviction that there comes a time when the father must step aside so the sons can assume more control (in CAA's case, "sons" is the appropriate word; women could do fairly well at the agency, but they did not reach the top). For the past two decades, CAA had been a family, a close-knit group that had lived by rules so unbending that it had inevitably conjured up images of the Cosa Nostra. Exactly three people in the organization were allowed to speak to the media. If anyone other than CAA founding partners Mike Ovitz, Ron Meyer, or Bill Haber, talked to the press for attribution, there were no second chances. In recent weeks, a female agent had violated this dictate, and she was no longer on the premises.

Agents, mailroom trainees, secretaries, and even the security personnel who watched the CAA lobby were taught how to dress, what to say, and the proper manner in which to behave throughout their shifts. If they didn't want to abide by these guidelines, they all knew they were expendable. If one wanted to see a floor-walker dressed in Armani, he could go the corner of Little Santa Monica and Wilshire boulevards in Beverly Hills, enter the glass front door of the spectacularly handsome building designed by the world-renowned architect I. M. Pei, and loiter for a few moments in the lobby. The security guard would very quickly appear and start asking questions. After showing an unwelcome visitor to the door, he would resume straightening the edges of the latest edition of the *Hollywood Reporter* on the lobby's coffee table.

Some people compared the management of CAA to a dictatorship. Some went much further than that—and into the far reaches of absurdity. An insider once told *Vanity Fair* magazine that being Ovitz's assistant meant working in "the Michael torture chamber" and likened Jay Moloney and David O'Connor to "Auschwitz survivors." Of course, that was an outrageous overstatement, but it made the point: one did things Mike's way at CAA because Ovitz had made untold millions for the company and for some of its employees.

Everyone could argue about the methods CAA's leader had used to build Hollywood's most respected and feared talent agency, but the results of those methods were unassailable. No one outside the organization knew how much money the privately held business earned annually, but when knowledgeable people guessed at the figure they started at around $80 million and moved up. Some of the agents in the screening room this morning were making a million dollars a year; others, more. Some received huge bonuses at the end of each year, and others got yelled at for not bringing in more business. It was not an enterprise for those with delicate sensibilities or those who were captivated by obscure, noncommercial works of art.

If there were people in the room who badly wanted Ovitz to stay, there were others who wanted him to step aside and take Meyer and Haber with him. Just below the three senior partners at CAA were two other layers of management, and they were seriously at odds with one another. One group, which included Jack Rapke, Rick Nicita, Lee Gabler, and Tom Ross, had been with CAA for years, some of them starting not long after the agency's founding in 1975. They weren't that much younger than the forty-eight-year-old Ovitz, and they'd worked very hard and waited very patiently to advance and become a part of CAA's power structure. Except for the three men at the top, the company had no set hierarchy, and ownership was shared with no one else. Ovitz held 55 percent of the business, while Haber and Meyer each had 22.5 percent. The other agents did not even have working titles. Some people liked this arrangement better than others. Some wanted a title, some wanted more money, and some wanted partnership.

The other layer of management at CAA was more troublesome.

They'd been gaining notoriety lately and were now referred to in the Hollywood media as the Young Turks. The Turks—Jay Moloney, David "Doc" O'Connor, Kevin Huvane, Richard Lovett, and Bryan Lourd—were all male, all in their thirties, and all highly ambitious agents. Not only had the company made them rich, but in recent years Ovitz had increasingly tried to keep them happy by giving them more control over some of CAA's most prestigious clients: Keanu Reeves, Michael Douglas, Woody Harrelson, Meryl Streep, Hugh Grant, Chris O'Donnell, and Robert Redford. The Turks were building momentum, not so much as five individuals but as a gathering force that would soon blow away whatever stood in its path.

The Young Turks, people around town were saying, were dissatisfied. Despite all that CAA had done for them, they believed they'd done just as much for the agency, and they didn't want to wait until Ovitz, Meyer, and Haber had moved on—and then wait another decade or two until Rapke, Nicita, and the others had run CAA before they got their chance. The Turks were a new generation, different from the last one. They'd had great success early on and were impatient, if not downright disrepectful, toward their elders. People said they'd recently made a pact together and were planning a revolt: they were going to demand more power, and if Ovitz said no, they would bolt the agency and strike out on their own.

The Turks had at least some sense of the history of agenting. They knew that twenty years earlier Ovitz, Meyer, Haber, Rowland Perkins, and Mike Rosenfeld—five discontented young agents at William Morris—had started CAA with roughly the same feelings and ambitions that they now possessed. Hadn't things turned out brilliantly for those men? Wasn't it time for another great change in the business? Could the Young Turks make it on their own, without the golden hand of Michael Ovitz to guide them? How could they answer that question unless they took the opportunity to break away and work for themselves?

If a lot was going on inside the CAA screening room this morning, just as much was going on outside it. In 1989, when Ovitz had counseled the Japanese at the Sony Corporation about buying Columbia

Pictures, there'd been rumors that he wanted to leave his agency and run the Columbia studio. Nothing had come of that gossip. In 1990, when Ovitz was orchestrating Matsushita's purchase of MCA/Universal, people said that he was preparing himself to run that studio, but this Hollywood scuttlebutt had never become reality, either. Yet now, five years later, things were different. Early in 1995, Ovitz had flown to Osaka, Japan, to advise the leaders of Matsushita to sell MCA to his longtime friend, thirty-nine-year-old Edgar Bronfman Jr., who headed Seagram's $6-billion-a-year spirits-and-beverage empire. Ovitz had not only helped bring this buyer and seller together, he'd also advised Bronfman on how to bow in front of the older Japanese gentlemen who ran Matsushita.

In addition, the agent had done something that in entertainment circles bordered on treason. He'd traveled to Osaka and spoken to Matsushita without telling the two longtime heads of MCA, Lew Wasserman and Sidney Sheinberg, what he was up to. If Ovitz was the king of Hollywood, Wasserman could only be described as the Supreme Being of show biz. In the 1930s, he'd gone to work for the Music Corporation of America, the largest band-booking agency in the country, just as MCA was expanding into the motion picture business (later, it would expand again, into television). Wasserman got his first million-dollar contract for a rising young star named Ronald Reagan. By 1946, Wasserman had become president of MCA, and four years later he instituted the concept of the "back-end deal," whereby an actor gets paid both a fee for his or her performance and a percentage of the take based on film receipts. The actor in this precedent-setting case was Jimmy Stewart, the movie was *Winchester 73*, and the concept was worth millions.

MCA eventually became known as "the Octopus," because it had a tentacle in virtually every corner of the entertainment world. In 1962, the federal government, as part of an antitrust strategy, forced the corporation to get out of agenting, but thirty years later, the Octopus was still heavily involved in movies, television, music, and theme parks. In 1995, Wasserman, at age eighty-two, remained at the pinnacle of the Hollywood game. No one else could run a fund-raiser the way he could. No one else commanded so much deference and respect. Nobody ever publicly insulted the man or went behind his back. Until now.

In mid-January of 1995, Ovitz had quietly gone to Osaka and indicated to Matsushita executives that change was in order and that selling MCA to Seagram would be a good idea. This would mean Wasserman and Sheinberg (only in his sixties) would be out of their jobs, but such sentimental considerations were secondary to the deal. In Hollywood, 1995 would be a time of transition and great upheaval; Ovitz had foreseen that and wanted to be out in front of the prevailing winds. After delivering his opinion to the Matsushita brass, he boarded a plane and flew home to Los Angeles. The following day, an earthquake hit Osaka, destroying 400,000 homes and leaving 5,500 people dead. Timing, as they say in show business, is everything.

That was now five months ago. The results of Ovitz's trip to Osaka were going to culminate this June morning in CAA's screening room—or not.

Regardless of what happened next, the Oedipal dynamics in Hollywood had grown intense: younger men were getting ready to push the older ones aside. The Turks at CAA bore the same relation to Ovitz that Ovitz now bore to Lew Wasserman. For years people had been saying that Ovitz would never leave his agency unless he could assume Wasserman's role at MCA and become the next godfather of the industry. That opportunity had finally arrived. Not only had Ovitz helped Seagram buy MCA—the deal had been done last April—but Wasserman and Sheinberg had now been removed from the picture, and Edgar Bronfman had offered Ovitz Lew Wasserman's chair. The stage was set for one of the biggest coups in the history of Hollywood. But on the morning of June 5, at a few minutes before nine-thirty, almost no one knew what Ovitz's next move would be.

A few miles north of CAA, just over some hills next to the San Fernando Valley, MCA executives were hovering near their phones or pacing the halls in fretful anticipation (some pundits had already compared this scene to the faithful waiting for the puff of smoke from the College of Cardinals in Rome that heralds the announcement of a new pope). Few believed that if Ovitz came to MCA he would come alone. Meyer and Haber might come with him; perhaps his right-hand man, Sandy Climan, would make the move as well. Ovitz's chief financial officer, Robert Goldman, might also be leaving CAA for the Valley, along with Robert Kavner, the former AT&T executive who was now working with Ovitz to deliver entertainment through the phone company. All of these men would likely assume prominent jobs at MCA/Universal, and inside that corporation there was growing fear and resentment that their business was about to be taken over by a group of people who'd never spent one day running a conglomerate that produced entertainment.

The situation on June 5 held some even more byzantine wrinkles. For the past two decades, Steven Spielberg had been making extremely profitable movies—*Jaws*, *E.T.*, *Jurassic Park*, and *Schindler's List*—for the Universal studio. Spielberg's mentor at MCA was Sid Sheinberg, and if anyone insulted the prickly mogul, he was in danger of insulting and alienating the gifted Spielberg too. Ovitz's recent behavior had been more than an insult: his trip to Osaka had been a slap in Sheinberg's face.

To complicate matters even further, Spielberg was Ovitz's client. Eight months earlier, in October 1994, Spielberg, along with Jeffrey Katzenberg, the recently deposed head of the Walt Disney studio, and billionaire music executive David Geffen had created SKG DreamWorks, a new production company that was about to get into the business of making films. Ovitz got along with Spielberg well enough, but the same thing could not be said for his relationship with Katzenberg or Geffen. While at Disney, Katzenberg had felt that Ovitz's negotiating tactics had driven movie production costs through the ceiling; on occasion, he'd let his opinions be known. Geffen and Ovitz had publicly quarreled in the past, and the music producer did not always pass up the chance to take a swipe at the superagent (they'd also been known to compete vigorously for buying expensive works of art). SKG DreamWorks wanted MCA to distribute its films, but if Ovitz took over the studio, most people felt, this marriage of fragile emotions and outsized egos would simply not work.

If Bronfman hired Ovitz to run his newly purchased corporation, would Steven Spielberg, the company's biggest cash cow, walk away from MCA?

Studio people weren't the only ones stewing this morning. Talent agents at the other powerhouse Hollywood agencies—William Morris, International Creative Management, and the United Talent Agency—were also waiting by their phones and getting ready to pounce. While Ovitz was running Creative Artists, the unwritten rule was that his clients would not leave CAA without confronting dire consequences; it could even hurt their careers. Agents at other companies would not dare approach his clients or try to steal them without feeling the wrath of Mike. But all of this etiquette would vanish the moment Ovitz departed CAA, and every major agency in town would scramble to sign the stars who no longer wanted to be associated with a company that had been abandoned by its leader.

On the other hand, it would be a grave mistake to jump at these clients too soon. So the rival agents had to make certain Ovitz really was leaving CAA before making their moves. Naturally, William Morris, ICM, and UTA were also following this morning's developments as closely as they could.

Hollywood was watching a cliffhanger.

For the past week and a half, Ovitz's people had been negotiating with Seagram's attorneys in the Manhattan law offices of Simpson, Thacher, & Bartlett. Representing Ovitz was Los Angeles lawyer Ron Olson, of Munger, Tolles, and Olson, while Kenneth Edgar of the Simpson, Thacher firm was speaking for the Montreal-based Seagram empire. Ovitz himself had stayed in Los Angeles, as if to indicate that he was interested in the job but it wasn't worth flying across the country for. Scraps of information had been leaking out of the negotiations, but no one beyond the tiny circle of key players really knew what was going on. Speculation centered around the belief that Ovitz was asking for a vast amount of money—a quarter of a billion dollars, people said—and he was also asking Edgar Bronfman for virtual autonomy to run MCA. He wanted a fortune and to preserve his freedom too.

That was just like Ovitz, followers of the negotiations were saying; he'd always expected to have it both ways at once. Talent agents were historically known as serving the cause of one client on a film project: you got the best deal you could for your screen-writer or your director or actor or producer. Ovitz had become the most potent figure in Hollywood by perfecting the concept of "packaging": CAA assembled and represented virtually all of the creative elements for a movie and then used its muscle to force the studios to accept each of those elements—or the agency would withhold the services of its stars. When the studio said yes to the picture, CAA collected 10 percent on every one of its clients.

Some critics had long questioned the whole idea of packaging. Could Ovitz really serve the best interest of one actor if he was ne-gotiating for several who were appearing in the same film? What if one of his stars didn't want to be packaged with another one? What if that adversely affected the quality of the movie? Was it right for a talent agent to be dictating these things to major studios?

As Ovitz became more powerful, the conflict-of-interest ques-tions grew. How could he advise a company on buying a movie stu-dio as well as offer counsel to the studio it wanted to acquire, as he'd done with Sony and Columbia in 1989? And how could he fairly advise Matsushita to buy MCA in 1990, when people were al-ready saying that his real agenda was to nudge Lew Wasserman aside and take over his job?

Conflict of interest or not, Ovitz had changed the nature of the business and generated extraordinary wealth for many of his clients (as well as for himself). In June 1995, why shouldn't he have ex-pected to be able to dictate any terms he wanted to the House of Seagram? Why shouldn't he have been able to bend them to his will, just as he'd bent the film executives in Hollywood?

Bronfman liked Ovitz and had accepted his counsel on many things, but he'd never negotiated with anyone like him before. This man asked for everything and did it with impunity. The moon wasn't enough for him: you had to throw in some stars and the light they cast across the heavens and a colorful planet or two and several comets with long, illuminated tails and . . .

Shortly after nine-thirty, Ovitz stepped forward to address his as-sembled agents and other employees. The room was now quiet, and everyone was focused on the man who was about to speak. He was impeccably dressed, as always, in a dark Italian suit, but at first glance he did not cut a particularly impressive figure. He had a trim physique, and when he stood next to President Clinton, for example, one could see he was nearly a head shorter than the chief executive. His expressions tended toward the impenetrable or the bland, and his fierceness, just like the hardness of his well-trained body, was quite well hidden. Many reporters had described him as having a boyish face, and almost all of them had mentioned his sandy hair and the gap between his front teeth. That gap was very misleading, because it appeared to dilute some of the will, intelligence, and shrewdness that lay just behind his eyes.

People said that Michael Ovitz calculated everything: every sentence, every gesture, every silence, every mannerism, every nuance of speech. They said that when he was standing a few feet away from a studio executive on whom he wanted to get the upper hand, he spoke in a virtual whisper, so the exec had to lean toward him to hear. The exec was now literally off balance, and Ovitz in the power position. From there, it was always easier to negotiate or make demands.

People said that Ovitz never made a knee-jerk movement. When he raised his hand it was for effect, and when he aimed a finger at someone it was because he had a very serious point to make. When he walked he didn't swing his arms, because that would imply that something about him was out of control, and he wanted to make clear to everyone that nothing could be further from the truth. When he focused his stare right on you, some highly successful business leaders and entertainment people said, you felt like the most important person on earth.

Slowly and quietly, Ovitz began talking to his staff, telling them how wonderful the past few years had been at CAA and how much he'd enjoyed working with all of them. He punctuated the words with small, shy smiles, one of his trademark expressions. For someone who never showed his feelings in public, this was virtually an emotional outburst, and it took a number of people by surprise. He looked a little fragile and almost . . . vulnerable. His employees began to touch hands with one another, and some of them later said they felt tears starting to well up.

He told them that he was certain that CAA could carry on and prosper without him. The building was full of extremely talented, gifted people who did their jobs wonderfully and deserved as much credit for CAA's success as he did, if not more. It was teamwork that had brought them to this place and teamwork that would always move the organization forward.

As he spoke, his appearance conjured up a series of contradictions. From certain angles, he looked passive and delicate, yet he had a black belt in the martial art of aikido. His demeanor suggested a quietness at his center, yet his employees knew that he could be very loud when he felt it was necessary. In public, he looked painfully wary of the spotlight, but for decades he'd thrust himself into the celebrity-making business—and then seemed shocked when he himself became a celebrity. He was so antipublicity that he regularly bought up existing photos of himself so that they could not be used again.

His eyes contained a sense of wonder, as though he were astonished at the things he'd accomplished, but they also hinted that he'd never—not even for a moment—doubted that he would do all of these things and more. For two decades now, veterans in the entertainment field had been saying that they'd never met anyone with quite his level of confidence and self-assurance. Mike Ovitz, people claimed, always knew exactly where he was going.

Yet this morning, the confidence in his face was muted, and a flash of uncertainty played around his mouth. His voice was even faltering a little. He hadn't expected the meeting to be so emotional.

Ovitz had tried to keep his negotiations with Seagram's quiet, as he'd always done when negotiating in the past, but this time he hadn't been able to. The deal was too big, and too many people were involved. Because of this, the agents inside his own building were gossiping about him, and that was worrisome. A few days earlier, an unnamed CAA employee had spoken to the trade paper *Daily Variety* and given the publication the kind of quote that the Ovitz-watching public loved but that the man himself could not tolerate.

"Many of us," this person had said, "believe that the deal is done, and we're just not being told. They stand there and tell us—in what everyone has come to realize are very carefully selected words—and we're all thinking that very shortly they are going to tell us that it's done. And they are going to say they didn't lie to us."

Ovitz looked out across the crowded screening room and smiled, saying that while it was true that he'd been in negotiations for another job, he would not be leaving CAA. He would be staying right there and running the agency, just as he always had.

The staff spontaneously rose to its feet and broke into loud applause. People were now hugging and cheering, and the tears had begun to flow. Ovitz himself seemed shaken by the response, as though he didn't quite know how to receive it. No one, according to some longtime CAA observers, had ever seen such an outpouring of feeling in this office before.

Phones commenced ringing, and faxes beeped all over town. Hollywood's world had tilted but not spun off its axis. At MCA, one could almost detect the outpouring of relief from those studio executives who would keep their jobs. Wasserman and Sheinberg were also said to be delighted when they received the news. At William Morris, ICM, and UTA, the reaction was just the opposite; these rival agents were not going to pick up their receivers and try to lure clients away from CAA. The old order remained intact.

In the days ahead, the *Los Angeles Times* and the *New York Times* would report that the negotiations between Seagram's and Ovitz's people had broken down in New York at two A.M. on Monday, just a few hours before this meeting was held in Beverly Hills. The details of the breakdown were sketchy and would not become much clearer with time. Some people said that Bronfman had ultimately turned his back on Ovitz's unrelenting demands, while others declared that the agent himself had walked away from the job offer. Wall Street made its own statement about the failure of the deal: following the announcement that Ovitz was not coming to MCA, Seagram's stock, which was trading at thirty dollars a share, fell fifty cents on the New York Stock Exchange.

The next morning, Ovitz was back at work and conducting business as usual. Disappointed studio executives, who'd thought that he might be leaving agenting and giving up some of his power, had already begun grumbling about him again. One exec told the *Los Angeles Times* that while Ovitz had missed a beat or two in recent days, because of all the distractions surrounding the MCA job, he would be "terrorizing everyone within a week."

Many observers felt that Ovitz, the master negotiator, might have finally overplayed his hand with Seagram's. Edgar Bronfman apparently agreed with them. In its August 1995 issue, *Los Angeles Magazine* would report that Bronfman had told his friends that courting the agent for the MCA job was "like being possessed by a demon." He'd also told them that the collapse of the deal had left him feeling like "the luckiest Jew in America."

PART TWO

THE BEGINNING

Nothing is more difficult than the art of maneuver. What is difficult about maneuver is to make the devious route the most direct and to turn misfortune to advantage.

—*The Art of War*

2

In retrospect, some periods of time are clearly more pregnant with possibility than others. Looking back twenty years, it's now obvious that late 1974 and early 1975 were special months in the history of the talent agent business. No one, of course, knew quite what was coming, and often what appeared to be the most important event of the day turned out to be relatively insignificant—and vice versa.

On December 30, 1974, Marvin Josephson, the owner of the International Famous Agency, bought out Creative Management Associates, which was headed by Freddie Fields, Hollywood's superagent at the time. Fields's client list included Robert Redford, Paul Newman, and Steve McQueen, while others at CMA represented Al Pacino, Dustin Hoffman, Barbra Streisand, and James Caan. Josephson merged IFA and CMA into a huge new agency called International Creative Management. ICM could compete with the indomitable William Morris agency as an equal, and one of ICM's most ambitious employees, the flamboyant Sue Mengers, would soon replace Fields as the hottest agent in town.

The merger had reduced the number of large agencies in Hollywood from three to two. Astute followers of the business side of entertainment have often said that the industry needs at least three big agencies to keep everything in balance and running smoothly. With only two, regardless of their size, power becomes too concentrated, and competition isn't as sharp.

At the end of 1974, the merger was very much in the trade papers and the public eye, while other stories were being played out with little fanfare. Nobody even noticed when several young men at the Morris agency began talking about leaving and starting their own business.

In the mid-1970s, three men in William Morris's Manhattan office dealt directly with the New York television network brass. Larry Auerbach, Lou Weiss, and Sol Leon were the agents responsible for servicing ABC, CBS, and NBC. In that capacity, they went to lunch with the networks' executives and discussed that season's programming, they talked about the TV talent pool, and they handled numerous business negotiations.

They were busy men, but not as busy as they used to be. In decades past, most of the big decisions involving the Morris television department had been made on the East Coast. In the 1950s, when a single sponsor such as Procter & Gamble purchased all the advertising spots for an entire one-hour show, Morris agents often worked closely with Madison Avenue on ad campaigns. By the seventies, ads were so costly that sponsors were buying only single sixty-second spots on an individual program; thus a large part of the agent's job evaporated.

More important, the production of TV shows had long since moved to the West Coast. Day-to-day decisions and the countless details and phone calls regarding programming were now being handled in Los Angeles. In many cases, all that Auerbach, Weiss, and Leon could do in Manhattan was second-guess what the fellows out on the other coast had already set in motion. Since the New York agents were the senior executives in the company and were supposed to have more clout, this naturally created tension.

In Beverly Hills, three men in their thirties and early forties—Rowland Perkins, Bill Haber, and Mike Rosenfeld—were the William Morris connections with CBS, NBC, and ABC, respectively. The trio were young, smart, ambitious, and somewhat defiant.

"We couldn't call them up and tell them every time we were going to the bathroom," says Rosenfeld. "When issues came up, we had to act and think for ourselves. We were in the trenches, and they were in Manhattan."

The threesome had already spent many years in television, and they didn't like taking orders or waiting for others to make decisions. They didn't enjoy being monitored by New York. They felt they knew as much, if not more, about the television business as their East Coast superiors did.

"We were working harder at William Morris than anyone," says Rowland Perkins. "If there were three lights burning in the agency late at night, you could be certain that those lights were in our offices."

While the men strongly believed that they should be given more freedom, money, and power to do their jobs, they were also keenly aware that before they could advance up the Morris ladder, several layers of management would have to step aside. That was a serious problem. Executives at William Morris were not quick to retire, regardless of their age.

"Old agents," went the office joke, "don't fade away, they just die." But in the early 1970s, nobody was either fading away or dying.

"It was like walking into a restaurant and seeing twenty-five people waiting for two open tables," Rosenfeld says. "No one at the agency mistreated us, but the situation was upsetting."

The Morris honchos in New York had a reasonably good idea that a rebellion was fomenting out west. Their solution for quelling the disturbance was not to promote Perkins or Rosenfeld or Haber but to go in the opposite direction. They sent Larry Auerbach out to California to ride herd on the younger men. As anyone close to the situation might have expected, this did not sit very well with the upstarts.

"Sending out Auerbach was too little too late," says Rosenfeld. "We were big boys now."

If Auerbach's arrival did not endear the New York office to Perkins, Haber, and Rosenfeld, it deeply annoyed their mentor, a crusty, stern-looking veteran Morris agent named Phil Weltman. Many people compared Weltman to a Marine Corps sergeant, which wasn't far off the mark. In fact he'd been in the army in World War II, served in five battlefield campaigns, and won the Croix de Guerre. Fifty years after his discharge, he still wore a military haircut, had a direct manner of speaking, and conveyed an underlying toughness that could be felt across a room. He had represented Fanny Brice, Edward G. Robinson, Walter Brennan, and

Tallulah Bankhead, and he liked to lean back in his chair, smile proudly, and say, "I had my share of 'em."

By 1974, his deal-making days were mostly behind him, and his job consisted largely of training younger agents in the Morris TV department in L.A. He ran things with a fair yet firm hand and was determined to give talent agents a better image.

There have long been insulting lawyer jokes, and just as mean-spirited were agent jokes, which did not create a flattering picture of those who negotiated contracts and cut deals in the entertainment business. Agents were routinely called ten percenters, flesh peddlers, bloodsuckers, and worse. In some circles, they were viewed as people without talent who took away one-tenth of a performer's income for doing nothing more than making a few calls and signing a few papers. This was rarely true, but the image of the flashily dressed, fast-talking, slick-haired hustler with his hand rummaging through someone's pocket was always there in the background of show business, undermining the very notion of honest, mutually beneficial, long-term relationships between agents and the people they represented. Phil Weltman wanted to abolish that perception forever.

He told his agents to have a clean, crisp appearance at all times and to shave every morning. He told them to wear dark, tasteful suits, dark shoes, white shirts, and subdued ties. "I want my boys to look sharp and impeccable," Weltman often said. "I want them to look like bankers or other business executives."

He told his protégés that they could drink coffee at his Thursday morning staff meetings, but they could not eat danish or bagels or other food that might make noise or smudge their appearance.

He told them that they could never get in trouble telling the truth, because when you told people the truth, you didn't have difficulty later on remembering what you'd said. "I taught them never to lie to a client," he said. "Never try to soften the message. Give it to 'em straight and it will help both of you."

He told them to write down every phone call they received during the course of a day and to return each one before leaving the office that night—and if they couldn't do that, then their assistant was to phone the other party and say that they would be returning the call tomorrow morning. "God help you," Weltman once said, "if a client ever called me and said he couldn't reach his agent. You can make a mistake once, but don't ever make it again."

He told them to write down all the details of a business transaction. Just talking about these things wasn't good enough. Get it in writing, he told them, and then get the buyer to sign a piece of paper before he had a chance to go home that evening, sleep on his decision, and change his mind.

Weltman drove into them that it was the movie stars who deserved all the adulation and attention; agents were to stay inconspicuous and behind the scenes. His men practiced this faithfully for many years—until some of them became famous themselves.

Weltman told them that when negotiating, they were to aim exceedingly high. Almost forty years after the fact, he liked telling the story of how he nearly fired one young agent who could not bring himself to ask a network executive, who was paying a TV actor $750 a week, for a $9,250-a-week raise for this performer.

"I taught my boys," he said, when he was well past eighty and fervently recalling the men he'd trained over the years, "that when you go out to make a deal, never negotiate from a position of weakness. You've got to believe that your client is the best person in the world for the job. And don't be afraid to reach for the moon. I want the buyer to say to me, 'You're crazy, you're ridiculous.' You can always come down later on, and when you do, the other guy thinks he's getting a deal." (When Weltman finally left the entertainment business, network execs all over town began sighing with relief. "God, I'm glad he's gone," a vice president once said. "Phil was impossible to negotiate with.")

Weltman was exceedingly proud of his protégés, and he had every reason to be. He'd trained Barry Diller, who became the head of Paramount Pictures. He'd trained Joe Wizan, who became president of Fox. He'd trained Bob Shapiro, who became president of Warner Bros. For decades he'd been doing things the same way, using the same gruff manner, and it had produced unparalleled results.

He'd also helped train Rowland Perkins, Mike Rosenfeld, and Bill Haber, and this generation of younger men looked up to Weltman. "He could scare the shit out of you," says Rosenfeld, "but he had a good heart."

By mid-1974, when Perkins, Haber, and Rosenfeld were working late at night, their office windows glowing above the streets of Beverly Hills, the trio occasionally talked about leaving William Morris together and attempting something risky and new. They discussed taking some of the principles they'd learned from Weltman and using them to run their own agency. If they were committed to working this hard, they really ought to be working for themselves. . . .

It was exciting to speak this way in private, but it also felt treasonous, almost like plotting revenge against an all-powerful parent. William Morris was the biggest name in agenting and had been for decades. The three men had all started their careers in the legendary Morris mailroom. They'd essentially spent their entire working lives at the agency. The thought of leaving was disconcerting. Overall, the Morris office had been good to them, but it had also made a lot of demands. And more than anything else, it had demanded loyalty.

Into the autumn, they kept talking about the possibility of change—talking when they sat at their desks and when they met in the halls and when they went out to lunch together. They wouldn't quit the agency right now, of course, but maybe later on, when they had a little more experience and money in the bank. They definitely wouldn't want to leave this winter, because that was the middle of the television season and they had obligations to fulfill, but maybe they should think about departing next April or May, in the spring of 1975, when the TV season was finished. That might be a good time to make the break.

In one of these conversations, Haber said that it was very dangerous to talk this way, because once they'd had these thoughts and put them into words, everything they were talking about was going to come true. That was how things worked, he said. Perkins and Rosenfeld thought he was joking.

3

B y early December 1974, the three agents had begun speaking with two younger men at William Morris, Ron Meyer and Michael Ovitz. One evening, the five of them went out to dinner and quickly realized that they'd all been pondering the same thing. Meyer and Ovitz were thinking of starting their own company, but they had far less experience than Perkins, Haber, and Rosenfeld did. Was it possible that they could all combine their interests and work together to create something new? A sixth agent, Fred Westheimer, was also dissatisfied and possibly ready to leave the Morris agency, but he was uncertain whether he could actually go through with it. The quintet who'd gone to dinner told Westheimer that he was welcome to join them, and they then began making some tentative plans. They needed a line of credit and some good advice, so Rosenfeld said he would call a knowledgeable attorney in New York and ask a few questions.

By now, the five men collectively had a considerable history of working as agents. Rowland Perkins, a forty-year-old native of Los Angeles, had been a Morris employee for fifteen years (his initial hiring into the mailroom had been facilitated by a kind word from the aunt of one of his friends; the aunt's name was Loretta Young). Perkins had risen to become the head of the TV Talent Department, and in that capacity he ran the TV-packaging operation on the West Coast. (TV packaging involved using various clients from the Morris agency to put together a television game show or series.) In one year alone, Perkins had overseen the development of sixty-three TV projects, twenty-one of which were produced as pilots, and seven of which became on-air series. Of the five men, he was regarded by Morris executives as the most likely to achieve real success. Tall and bone thin, he was personable, unfailingly polite, and quietly aggressive, and he got things done. He had the combination of classiness and efficiency the agency was looking for.

Mike Rosenfeld, also forty, came from Philadelphia and had started his career in the late 1950s in the New York William Morris office. In Manhattan, he developed various contacts with book publishers and editors and worked on the motion picture side of the business before turning to television. His most successful TV show was *Barney Miller*, which he'd developed with Michael Eisner, a young network executive who was the head of comedy development at ABC. Rosenfeld was short and had the forearms of a butcher. He gave the impression that he could handle himself just fine in a scrap. In college at Penn State, he'd played the piano and written musicals; he saw himself as more creative and more literate than most talent agents (in later years, he would joke that what distinguished him among the five men who'd founded CAA was that he was the one who could read). By the mid-seventies, Rosenfeld, like Perkins, had a family to support. For nearly two decades, he'd known only the comfort and security of working for a stable, celebrated, hugely profitable talent agency. The other four men may have concealed or denied some of their feelings about bolting William Morris, but Rosenfeld did not. He acknowledged, at least to himself, that the thought frightened him.

Bill Haber, a Californian in his mid-thirties, was also married and had children. When people talked about him, the first thing they said was that he was an outstanding talent in the business: he was brilliant at TV packaging and had a gift for generating—and spending—money. The second thing they said was that he was eccentric, at times volatile, and much less predictable than the other men. He had a fanciful streak and a mischievous light in his eyes, and he liked to speak his mind. His eccentricity was seldom on display at William Morris; under Phil Weltman's tutelage, agents were expected to subdue themselves in order to serve the needs of the company and its clients, and Haber had attempted to do just that. Only later, when he'd moved on to CAA and become his own boss, would he indulge his penchant for colorful behavior.

Ron Meyer, who was single but about to get married, was in his late twenties and an ex-marine. He'd grown up in a tough West L.A. neighborhood and had dropped out of high school. In the mid-seventies, he wore his hair fashionably big—blown dry and puffed up on top of his head. With his handsome features, stylish

clothes, and big glasses, he inevitably drew comparisons with Warren Beatty's character in the hit movie *Shampoo.*

Normally, being a dropout would have eliminated him from
contention for employment at William Morris, but when Meyer arrived there in 1970, he'd already put in five years at the Paul
Kohner Agency, where he'd learned the business. Weltman instantly liked the young man and felt he could be a great asset to
the company. There was something about Meyer that people were
naturally drawn to. He was good-looking, he was sincere, he was
approachable. He had a way of making people feel comfortable
around him. The adjective "nice" does not have the best reputation, but when people applied it to him (and everyone did), it carried a very positive ring. The other men were often referred to by
their last names, but everyone who knew Meyer called him "Ronnie"—even after he became one of the most powerful agents in
the business.

The fifth member of the group was the youngest: Mike Ovitz,
who was twenty-seven years old in the fall of 1974. In the mid-
sixties he'd attended UCLA, where he'd studied psychology and
planned to go on to medical school. He'd put himself through college by working as a tour guide at Universal Studios, and while
there he'd observed a number of interesting things about the entertainment field. Movies were fascinating, and the stars who appeared in them were captivating, but behind all the films and the
celebrities were business people putting together the deals and the
financing that drove the entire machine. Sometimes when he was
on the job at Universal, he noticed men in dark suits hanging
around the sets, talking quietly and earnestly but always remaining
in the background.

An inveterate inquirer, Ovitz asked about these men and
learned that they were talent agents, hired by the stars to negotiate the terms of their employment. They did their work away from
the spotlight, did it subtly, stealthily, without press conferences.
Ovitz liked that. He himself was never going to be a movie star, but
this . . . this was interesting and secretive, this was possible and
might even be fun. Unlike many others in Hollywood, he did not
want to draw attention to himself; he wanted to stay inaudible and
invisible so that he could maneuver without being detected.

After college, Ovitz had gone through the Morris training program, but he'd left the agency to return to UCLA and study law. Graduate school was challenging, but time was passing, and nothing about the legal system was quite as intriguing as the things he'd observed and thought about while working at Universal. There were millions of attorneys, and most were drudges. The lure of the smaller, more glamorous entertainment industry brought him back to William Morris. Being commonplace was what he was determined to escape.

Michael Ovitz was born in Chicago in December 1946. His father, a wholesale liquor salesman, soon moved the family to southern California. The Ovitzes settled in the Los Angeles suburb of Encino, in the San Fernando Valley, where in the postwar years of movement and growth and optimism virtually everyone wanted a tract house, a new car, and a secure financial future. Their neighborhood was working class, but it was aggressively aspiring upward. In the San Fernando Valley in the 1950s, the American Dream of stepping into the middle class was becoming the new reality. The American Dream was fine, but young Mike Ovitz had bigger things in mind.

In later years, he would movingly praise his father's hard work and the efforts he'd made on behalf of their family. Ovitz would say that from a very young age he had been encouraged to become an achiever, if not an overachiever. He would say that he had always been led to believe that he could become a success. His love for his family would be obvious, but what he wouldn't say was that as much as he admired his parents and appreciated his upbringing, he was committed to leaving that environment behind.

He wanted more money, but he was also interested in things that went beyond finances. He was hungry for knowledge, culture, and worldliness—all of which were not so easy to find in the much-joked-about San Fernando Valley (in Los Angeles, the Valley has long been regarded as a wasteland of shopping malls and smog, populated by airheads). Ovitz wanted to know about art, music, and philosophy. He wanted to master whatever subject he turned his attention to. And he could only do that, he believed, by gorging himself on information. So information became power, and he craved it.

"The thing you have to understand about Mike," says one of his associates, "is that he was not from New York and he was not from Los Angeles. He was from the San Fernando Valley. He wasn't born into an intellectual environment, and he didn't come from a sophisticated background. He didn't grow up around the affluence or the kind of nonchalant, superior attitude you find among a lot of people in Beverly Hills. He couldn't take anything for granted, so his insecurity was always real.

"If he wanted to learn about something or accomplish something, he had to do it on his own, and he discovered the value of that early on. He didn't ask other people for their approval. He didn't look outside of himself for validation. He just went ahead and did things. As with many other aspects of his life, he took what could have been a disadvantage and turned it into an asset.

"People always want to know where his ambition and his relentless drive came from. You don't have to look any further than the San Fernando Valley. He never wanted to go back to where he'd been."

In earlier years, Ovitz would have gone to high school in Van Nuys, but in the postwar baby-boom era, there was a shortage of classrooms, so he ended up attending Birmingham High, a makeshift school that had been created out of some abandoned army barracks. They were anything but posh and generated something of an attitude among those who matriculated there. Ovitz and several of his classmates, including the future actress Sally Field and the future junk-bond king turned criminal Michael Milken, decided that not going to the best-looking school in the Valley would not stop them from aspiring to greatness. Ovitz, already setting the pattern for his adult life, didn't wait to start building his reputation. He became Birmingham's student body president.

At UCLA he joined the Zeta Beta Tau fraternity and studied psychology. For a while, he didn't call attention to himself, and his frat brothers didn't pay much attention to the smallish, quiet young man. On the campus at Westwood, as when he'd entered high school, he observed everything, absorbed everything, gathered all the information he could, set his goals, and surveyed the competition. He decided that he wanted to play on the fraternity football team (he was too undersized, people said), he wanted to date Judy Reich, the official "sweetheart of Zeta Beta Tau," and he wanted to be president of the fraternity. Then he went to work.

Before graduating from college in 1968, he became a gridiron stalwart at the frat and one of the most heralded presidents of his house. A year after graduating, he married Reich, and they would eventually have three children. In the UCLA yearbook, he became known to posterity as "King Mike." While Ovitz had attended college in southern California during the tumultuous 1960s, he was unaffected by the upheaval taking place all around him. He was not a war protester or a drug user or a rock 'n roll fan. In fact, in some ways the young man bypassed the sixties and seventies altogether and prepared himself early on for the success-oriented, materialistic, business-driven eighties in America. His identity was shaped well before the war in Vietnam shook up the nation and its youth. Nothing in the sixties put a dent in his ambition.

The experience of working at Universal Studios during college had convinced Ovitz to apply for a job as a trainee at William Morris. He was accepted into the program and then given the very unglamorous tasks of sorting mail, waiting hand and foot on his superiors, and running their tedious errands. The idea, of course, was to wash out anyone who was not fully committed to becoming an agent and giving permanent, heartfelt loyalty to the Morris office. Roughly two-thirds of the trainees didn't make it. Ovitz did, but then left for law school after only a year on the job. As far as the agency's brass was concerned, that was the end of his career in show business. Once you'd said good-bye to William Morris, after you'd wasted their time and resources to train you, you were officially persona non grata.

When Ovitz quit law school and tried to come back to the agency, there was great opposition from above. Sam Weisbord, who ran the West Coast TV department and was Phil Weltman's boss, was adamantly opposed to the idea. He reminded Weltman that people simply could not come and go as they pleased at William Morris. Weltman and a successful TV-packaging agent named Howard West told Weisbord that Ovitz wasn't a bad kid and suggested they give him another chance. West needed a secretary, and he thought the young man was ready to work on his desk and learn the packaging business. Reluctantly, Weisbord agreed.

Ovitz went to work for Howard West. In that capacity he got to listen in on phone negotiating sessions between West and buyers at the networks, but he was not allowed to talk. After a while, he began assisting Elliott Kozak, the head of daytime TV packaging at Morris. When they started, Kozak was handling two of the networks and Ovitz one. Before long, the numbers had flip-flopped. Ovitz was soon representing Chuck Barris, Bob Barker, and Merv Griffin. He was also booking guests on *The Carol Burnett Show.*

Despite his success, he was not considered a rising star at the agency. He excelled at negotiating, but he was quiet the rest of the time, almost surreptitious. He was the young man over in the corner reading financial magazines and business reports, perusing guild agreements and the fine print of contracts when others were out having boisterous lunches or drinks after work. He wanted to know everything there was to know about agenting, and he always appeared to be thinking about something, but Ovitz kept most of his thoughts to himself.

"At that time," says a veteran Morris agent, "we were hardly aware of him in the office. No one believed he had much of a future in the business."

Over the next several years, Ovitz perfected the details of TV packaging and began working with new clients, such as Rich Little and the Jackson Five. One thing Ovitz had noticed was that the entertainment business was not the most highly organized industry around. At the center of it was something like chaos—who could ever really know where the next star or the next blockbuster TV show or the next hit film was coming from? Show business could never be as predictable as cornflakes or tires, but was that necessarily a bad thing? Or was this chaos an opportunity waiting to be exploited? And were there other opportunities that no one had really explored yet?

Near the end of 1974, when Ovitz and Ron Meyer learned that

Perkins, Haber, and Rosenfeld were thinking of leaving William Morris and starting their own agency, Ovitz was very interested in joining them. He realized that if he and Meyer left alone, they would face overwhelming obstacles. The three older men were more seasoned and knew people all over town. They had more clients, more good contacts, more resources. If Ovitz and Meyer could merge with them, who knew what was possible?

Haber, Rosenfeld, and Perkins had a few reservations about hooking up with the younger men. They all liked Meyer; everyone liked Ronnie and trusted him. You just wanted to do business with the man. But they didn't quite know what to make of Ovitz, the one with the least experience as an agent among them. Hadn't he bolted the Morris office once before and then talked his way back in? Wasn't he somewhat hard to read? Didn't he have a look in his eye and a small, elusive smile that were unfathomable?

Also, astute observers had noticed, he had a confidence about him that surpassed all the other men's. It seemed almost out of place on someone so young. And there was one other thing about him: in some basic way, he appeared to be freer than the older agents. This quality was alluring but somewhat disconcerting.

4

Sam Weisbord grew up in the same Brooklyn neighborhood as Phil Weltman, and they became teenage friends. In the late 1930s, Weltman went to work at the Morris agency, where Weisbord was already employed. Over the next twenty years the two bachelors were inseparable. They were like brothers, but then, in the mid-1960s, Weltman got married, and things between them were never quite the same. It was almost as though Phil had betrayed Sammy by taking a wife.

Weisbord had risen higher in the agency than Weltman had; Sam was more of a company man—spending time each day with Abe Lastfogel, the venerable head of William Morris—while Phil was more outspoken, paid less attention to the boss, and was more willing to let the younger guys have some of the glory. By the mid-1970s, he thought the aging Morris management badly needed some fresh blood, and in the TV department he was known for giving lucrative deals to promising upstarts.

One afternoon in the first week of December 1974, after working at the Morris agency for thirty-five years, Weltman glanced up and saw Weisbord come into his office. Their company was now computerized, and the numbers that were fed into the machines showed precisely how much money each client—and each agent—was generating for the business. Weisbord, who'd been studying those numbers closely, walked up to Weltman and made a remark that would echo far into the past and across the future of agenting. "You were put in the computer," Sammy told Phil, his old Brooklyn sidekick and companion of nearly half a decade, "and found wanting." It took Weltman a little while to figure out that he'd just been fired.

"Sam was the best man at my wedding, and we were so close," Weltman said twenty years after being shown the door at William Morris, "but the sonofabitch had no balls at all. He was always kissing Mr. Lastfogel's ass, and I didn't do that. 'Put in the computer and found wanting.' I still can't believe he said that to me."

When the news of Weltman's firing spread to five of his men in the TV department, they told their mentor something they hadn't been able to admit to him until now: they'd been thinking of leaving the agency and going off on their own. They hadn't mentioned this before because they thought that it might hurt Weltman's feelings, but now there was nothing to hide.

A few days later, the younger men gave the older one a farewell dinner and presented him with a plaque that read:

TO PHIL WELTMAN
With gratitude and appreciation from his team
December 6, 1974

The five agents were now more committed than ever to make their break from William Morris, but their timetable remained intact: they would depart next spring, after the current television season had expired, and after they'd had time to secure financing and a new place to work, and after they were more certain of what they were doing. They still had a few months in which to solidify their plans.

In recent days, Mike Rosenfeld had been waking up very early, and at precisely six A.M. he'd been calling an attorney friend of his in New York, where it was nine. Rosenfeld wanted advice about quitting the Morris office and starting a talent agency. He had financial questions, legal questions, and queries about other professional matters. He'd been speaking with this lawyer for weeks, but when he phoned him on the morning of Tuesday, January 7, 1975, he heard something that gave him a nasty shock.

"I just want you to know," the man told him, "that the William Morris brass is aware of what's going on."

"What do you mean?" Rosenfeld asked.

"They know you're leaving."

There was a pause on the California end of the line. "They do?"

"Yes, they do."

When Rosenfeld tried to find out how they knew this, the attorney would reveal nothing more. But the agent had heard enough.

"Now the toboggan was heading downhill," he would say years later, when describing that moment in January 1975, "down toward the scary bottom, and all I could do was hang on for dear life."

He wanted to tell the other men as quickly as possible, but Haber was out of the office, Ovitz was off skiing, and Meyer was at home, sick with the flu. Rosenfeld didn't call him right away. When he saw Perkins that morning, he told him what had happened and said that he should expect a call from Weisbord. Perkins said he would deny their departure plans, but his fellow agent was not convinced that would do any good; the brass probably knew more about their rebellion than Rosenfeld had been told. The five men, who had developed no strategy for an emergency, were caught completely off guard.

Early that afternoon, Perkins and Rosenfeld had a lunch date with some representatives of a West Coast literary agency called Adams, Ray, and Rosenberg. The two men asked these agents if they would be interested in merging and forming a company together—soon—but the literary reps were wary and noncommittal. Although Perkins and Rosenfeld tried to hide their reaction during the lunch, this response to their offer felt like another blow.

When Perkins got back to the office, a message from Weisbord was on his desk. The older man wanted to see him immediately. Weisbord asked him to come outside, and they began walking up and down the quiet residential streets of Beverly Hills, where the Morris agency was located. They went around and around the blocks south of Wilshire Boulevard, Weisbord moving faster and asking harder questions and trying to control his temper but gradually speaking with more heat.

"Sam walked five to ten miles a day," Rosenfeld says. "That was his form of exercise, and he was in good shape. If you went walking with him, you didn't want to have on good loafers but sturdy tennis shoes. With loafers, you'd have blisters for a week."

Weisbord was steaming now, walking even faster and demanding that Perkins tell him everything he knew. The younger man was taller but had to hustle to keep up. He was also hustling to think of something to say.

At first, Perkins tried to avoid facing the situation, but when he realized this was impossible, he confessed to his boss that yes, some of the younger fellows were thinking of leaving William Morris and had intended to speak to him about this soon. They wanted to do this in the appropriate manner, but the timing just hadn't been right, at least not yet.

Weisbord stopped walking and exploded into a series of angry questions: Hadn't he been Perkins's champion at the agency? Hadn't he always stood up for him in the past? Hadn't he been preparing him for a wonderful position in the organization?

Yes, of course he had, but—

Was Perkins crazy? Did he really believe he could leave the best talent agency on earth and have any future at all in this business? Did he?

Well, they—

No one treated the William Morris agency this way, and by God . . .

When the older man had calmed down a little, he insisted that Perkins name the others who were in on the plans. Since he could no longer evade the truth, Perkins complied, mentioning four individuals (the potential sixth man, Fred Westheimer, had decided to stay at William Morris).

Weisbord exploded again.

Later that afternoon, Rosenfeld was called into Weisbord's office and given the same chewing out that Perkins had received: the Morris agency, Weisbord told him, had trained these agents and provided them with a stable financial future, with prestige and connections and a great position in the entertainment business. How could they be so stupid and so ungrateful?

"When Sam asked me if I were leaving," Rosenfeld recalls, "I couldn't answer the question. I opened my mouth to speak and nothing came out. The umbilical cord that had been nurturing me for seventeen years was about to be cut."

Rosenfeld tried to reason with Weisbord, to tell him that the company had indeed trained them brilliantly and treated them well, but the time had come for them to try something different. They were still young and ambitious, and not all of their desires could be satisfied by working in the highly structured environment of William Morris. They were tired of waiting for something more, and what was happening right now was a natural development between senior and junior people in a corporate organzation.

Weisbord was too hurt and too angry to hear the speech with any emotional clarity. He just fumed, asking again and again if the renegades intended to raid the Morris client list and take some stars with them. When Rosenfeld tried to assure him they wouldn't do this, Weisbord didn't believe him and kept on railing.

"Sam was like a machine," says Rosenfeld, "and it was always tough to get close to him. The problem was that he didn't have a heart."

The five ingrates, Weisbord told Rosenfeld, weren't just going to start a new agency; they were going to harm William Morris.

"I shook my head and replied that there was no way we could hurt the Morris agency," Rosenfeld says. "I told him that if we attempted to do that, it would be like a flea shitting on an elephant. I thought that was a wonderful phrase, but, of course, he didn't appreciate it."

After Rosenfeld had left his office, Weisbord phoned Meyer at home and demanded to know if he too was planning on leaving the agency. Between his illness and his emotion over what he was hearing, Meyer could barely speak, but he managed to say yes.

Before the day's end, Haber would also be called into the office, but when Weisbord began to castigate him, the agent did not quietly absorb the assault. For every insult he was given about being a troublemaker who'd exploited the agency for his own benefit, he leaned closer to Weisbord and criticized him in return, harsh word for harsh word, telling him that William Morris had become too old and too staid and too stale, and that since it was unwilling to promote younger employees and make the changes that would help ensure its success in the future, the agents had little choice but to act on their own.

"Bill had guts," says Rosenfeld. "We all did, but his were different."

Because of his ski trip, Ovitz missed his confrontation with Weisbord. That evening, Rosenfeld drove to the young man's home in Sherman Oaks in the Valley and left a note on his kitchen door. It was short and to the point: he was no longer an employee at William Morris.

Ovitz returned from skiing, Meyer got well enough to come to the office, and for the next two days the five men were debriefed by company executives. They had to clean out their desks and tell the execs what deals they were working on and anything else that was pertinent to their business affairs. By now feelings on both sides had settled down, and the departure was carried out with civility. It was in everyone's interest to make the separation as peaceful and swift as possible. By Friday, January 10, they were gone.

"The thing about leaving a job," says a longtime Morris agent, "is that you really want people to miss you. You want them to feel bad that you're going away. We didn't feel that bad about losing these men. They were decent guys and hardworking, but we didn't think any of them had that great a future in the business. They were just agents and could be replaced."

The most important thing about the quintet who now found themselves out on the street was that they had an attitude, right from the start. That attitude was there when they began congregating in the Morris agency late at night and talking about making their break. It was there when they decided to pool their resources and become one group of five, instead of two groups of three and two. It was there at the end, when they were being lambasted by Sam Weisbord, and there when they walked out of the Morris office for the last time.

The attitude was "us against them"—"us against the world." They had a quiet defiance and a belief that they could run their own business and compete with their former superiors. It was all for one and one for all, and the devil take anyone who was disloyal to the cause. They weren't just starting a company now, they were taking a stand against the biggest (with more than a hundred agents) and the best talent agency that had ever been created. Executives at William Morris had told them that they were beyond foolish to leave and that they would soon be back working at another agency—for less money and with less prestige. Career-wise, they'd been informed, what they were doing was suicide.

"They told us," says Rosenfeld, "that we would drive one another completely crazy. They said we'd start killing each other within six months."

5

In Hollywood, "the favor" is everything. You either owe one to somebody or are owed one by somebody. Career opportunities rise and fall on handing them out and calling them in. It is not uncommon to hear an older entertainment executive say, "I did that guy his first favor, and he owes me his entire career. No, he owes me his life." At William Morris, the five agents had done many favors for others, carrying out at least some of them with an eye toward their own future when they might be working for themselves. Now they could ask for a couple in return.

Rosenfeld phoned Irwin Russell, the right-hand man for David Wolper, who'd been the producer on the hit TV show *Chico and the Man*. Some of the William Morris defectors had worked with Wolper in the past, and they thought he might let them use office space in his building for a couple of weeks, until they could figure out what to do next. Rosenfeld asked Russell to ask Wolper for the favor. Wolper sent back the message that he had to call Lou Weiss, Morris's East Coast TV honcho, before he could say yes. Favors could be executed, but not if they offended those higher up on the favor chain.

"Weiss did not put the kibosh on this," Rosenfeld says. "He acted like a gentleman, and then Wolper told us we could move in. My one phone call got us an office."

Security Pacific Bank extended the men a $100,000 line of credit (the leak to their erstwhile William Morris bosses that they were laying plans to depart the agency, Rosenfeld says, may have come from a loan officer at this bank, whom some of the agents had spoken to earlier). The quintet had gotten access to money and a makeshift office; now they needed a name. They quickly settled on something that was to the point—Creative Artists Agency—and that also lent itself to shorthand: CAA. Whether coming up with a name or making other decisions, they soon discovered that five was a good number of partners; it gave them a diversity of opinion and experience, and they could not have a tie when taking a vote. If four men were for something and one was against, the one who lost the vote would be less inclined to mope about it, because he had no allies. If the vote was three to two, they all had to learn to live with the democratic process.

"In the beginning," says Rowland Perkins, "we were each given an ultimate veto for any issue, and we made the agreement that we could use it just once and never again. It could be applied to any situation, but strangely enough, nobody ever used it."

Once they were installed in Wolper's building, Rosenfeld contacted a real estate agent in Beverly Hills, telling him that they needed office space in the neighborhood, something big enough for five men and a receptionist and with a conference room. The agent soon found an acceptable lease arrangement in the Hong Kong Bank Building, at 9300 Wilshire Boulevard, not far from the Morris agency. The CAA founders didn't care how close they were to their past, and in fact they didn't mind running into their former employers.

"The brass at William Morris used to eat lunch at the Hillcrest Country Club," says a longtime Hollywood entertainment lawyer. "When Ovitz and the others started CAA, they went to Hillcrest and ate lunch too. They would sit near the Morris people and be very friendly, but very visible. That impressed me. It was like they were saying, 'Here we are and we're not going away.' "

Rosenfeld purchased a $169 conference table in the San Fernando Valley and rounded up some other used furniture from business associates. All the men hauled in card tables and folding chairs from home. They installed telephones, and their wives took turns being the receptionist. When an inspector from the state labor commission came over one afternoon to look at their new digs, he eyed the agents suspiciously. Something about the office seemed a little cheesy. The place looked, Rosenfeld once told the *Los Angeles Times*, more like a bookie's den than a talent-booking agency. The inspector asked a few questions and uneasily left.

Only one of their cars would comfortably hold all of them— Perkins's Cadillac de Ville—so it became their office away from 9300 Wilshire Boulevard. After setting up appointments with network people they'd known in the past, they threw their briefcases in the trunk and hit the road. They were where they'd long wanted to be: in business for themselves.

"For a year," says Haber, "we just pretended that we had something to sell."

"We worked around the clock," says Rosenfeld. "We talked to people all day and had staff meetings all night."

"We ran on adrenaline," says Perkins, "and it was the most exciting time we'd ever had. Sometimes we ate two business breakfasts if we wanted to meet two different clients during the same morning. Sometimes we ate two dinners for the same reason. We did whatever was necessary to let people know that we were no longer at William Morris."

In the beginning, the men agreed not to take a salary for the first twelve months, just in case there was no money in the till in December 1975. They could live that long on savings or borrow money to see themselves through. They needed to ignore some of their financial worries, make a commitment to the new venture, and go to work—at least for a year. If nothing happened by then, they could reevaluate the situation and look at their options.

While the abruptness of their exit from William Morris had initially felt like the worst thing that could have happened to their plans, it turned out to be the best. It galvanized them into action and heightened their fervor for the cause.

When things unfolded as they did, Ovitz was the most prepared to move forward without hesitation. He'd been quietly nurturing his ideas and his leadership qualities for years: when he was at Birmingham High School; when he was seeking the presidency of his fraternity at UCLA; when he was walking the halls of the Morris agency and observing how things were done. He'd learned a great deal in the past ten years and from a number of different, and often surprising, sources.

The Tao of Physics by Fritjof Capra, published in 1975, contends that the ancient spirituality of the Far East and the new understandings of Western physics are leading both Eastern mystics and Western scientists to reach similar conclusions about the nature of matter and how our universe really functions. In the 1990s, the highly popular writings of Deepak Chopra have delved into the roles of Eastern religion and Western medicine in achieving good mental and physical health. The business world, however, has paid less attention to the growing synergy between East and West.

In college, Michael Ovitz was exposed to two things from very different cultures that he would later combine in the realm of entertainment, with startling results. On his own, he read Oriental philosophy and studied the ancient Sun Tzu text *The Art of War*, a classic military handbook that advocates deception, maximum flexibility, rapid action by elite shock troops, supreme loyalty of one's troops toward their leader, and turning an opponent's weakness against himself. The book is a series of subtle aphorisms that take for granted that war is a necessary and very significant part of life. Because of this, one must be fully prepared for combat before blood is ever spilled. And the most essential part of that preparation is the ability to cripple your opponent, mentally and emotionally, before the fighting has begun.

The Art of War is the first example in human history of how psychological manipulation can be used to destroy an adversary on the field of battle. It embodies a state of mind that believes human conflict is inevitable and you need every weapon at your disposal to triumph over your enemy. If you can control his mind, you can guide his actions and lure him into disaster. The goal is not to kill for the sake of killing but to learn how to kill and win efficiently.

At UCLA, Ovitz liked team sports, and in later years he would talk to his employees at length about using basic athletic principles in their work at CAA. One adage of the sports world is that over a period of time a consistently applied "system" will beat a "non-system." In the 1960s, for example, the Dallas Cowboys invented their own system of play calling, and they appeared in five Super Bowls during the following decade. In the National Basketball Association, the Boston Celtics of the 1950s and '60s employed a system of tenacious team defense and won eight straight NBA titles, perhaps the most brilliant example of this concept in the history of professional sports.

Closer to home for Ovitz was the UCLA basketball team of the 1960s, which came to prominence just as he was entering school on the Westwood campus. John Wooden, the UCLA coach, preached team basketball as opposed to individual achievement, and from 1964 to 1975 his squads won ten national championships, a record that will likely never be touched.

Anyone sitting on the sidelines at UCLA games during those years was able to see an important concept in action: cooperation works, and it generates more intelligence, energy, and opportunities than do individuals working alone. One plus one can equal more than two. Or as Mike Rosenfeld once put it when discussing CAA, "Three plus two equaled twenty."

Ovitz fervently believed in teamwork and in other, more subtle ideas that were highly valued in the East. He'd become president of his high school and his college fraternity by building relationships with people. He understood that these relationships had to be nurtured over time; only then would people come to trust you and want to cooperate.

From reading ancient philosophy, he'd grasped that beneath all the words and all the thoughts and all the actions, human beings were comprised of emotions. Money and contracts naturally pushed deals along, but emotions ultimately drove everything.

The primary emotion in the field of entertainment, Ovitz had noticed, was fear. It was everywhere, and it made everyone feel insecure. In his own past at William Morris, people had tried to use fear to motivate him or to rein him in, but he'd resisted this strategy and had always resented it. On one occasion, an older agent had criticized him because Ovitz was trying to put together a deal that the senior agent believed him unqualified to do. Ovitz walked up to the man, pulled his tie, and suggested that he never again tell him what his limitations were.

Now that he had his own agency, Ovitz wanted to play a new game. From now on, fear was something that belonged to other people but not to him. He wasn't going to be controlled by it, and if those he was doing business with were afraid, he was going to turn that weakness against them and use it to his own advantage. The time had come to see if Sun Tzu's ancient strategy could be applied in the Western world of entertainment.

If the young man really wasn't fearless and was subject to the same doubts and insecurities as everyone else, that didn't matter, just as long as he created the impression that he could not be manipulated by others. Attitude, he had come to believe, was everything. Attitude was a tool, and he was about to reveal himself as the greatest tool user in the history of Hollywood.

In later years, Ovitz would enjoy telling people that, in Hollywood, illusion is reality. By then, he was a master of that concept. He knew better than anyone else that if people believed you held all the power, and if you acted as though you did, then you did indeed hold power over them. If others were not in control of themselves, he had no compunction about controlling them.

"When we left William Morris," says Mike Rosenfeld, "the rest of us were concerned about the future, but Ovitz never was. He never doubted for a moment that we would make it."

6

Before they were let go, the five men had been doing plenty of deals at the Morris office, but they could take neither the commissions nor the talent with them—at least not until the clients' contracts had run out and they were free to go elsewhere. At William Morris, they'd been working with Sally Struthers and Rob Reiner of the smash CBS-TV comedy *All in the Family*, which was the top program for the fourth straight year in the Nielsen ratings. They'd also been working with some lesser properties, such as daytime quiz shows, nighttime series, TV actor Chad Everett, and the singing group the Jackson Five, not a great list of clients. They had connections in the entertainment world but no immediate cash flow.

Creative Artists started with the intention of becoming a full-service agency for TV and eventually film talent, meaning that it would serve actors, directors, producers, and writers. By representing all of these elements, it could put together its own TV packages and sell them to the networks. When presenting their packaging concept to potential buyers, the CAA men said one thing that was highly appealing.

The standard agency commission had always been 10 percent. William Morris had clung to this figure through good times and bad, its management stringently refusing to lower the figure when stars insisted that they should. In addition to these fees, for a typical TV-packaging deal, the Morris agency had devised a complicated formula that allowed it to receive more than 10 percent on each of its clients. The agency charged a package commission, payable as follows: 5 percent up front from the network license fee; 5 percent deferred, which would be paid by the producer or production company to the agency from the revenues earned from off-network distribution, including international sales, and then later, home video, cable, or other sources; *plus* a 10 percent commission on the domestic syndication revenues earned by the producers. This form of packaging was known around Hollywood as "five, five, and ten."

All of these revenue streams fed the agency, but syndication was the great bonanza. For example, the megahit *The Cosby Show* brought the Morris Agency an estimated $50 million—just in syndication monies alone from the mid-eighties to the mid-nineties.

When CAA began, it told potential buyers that its packaging fee would be only 6 percent: half up front and the other half from future profits. Other than lowering the numbers, the concept was essentially the same. Around town, a CAA deal was referred to as "three, three, and six." But while the new agency could negotiate new deals with flexibility, William Morris was locked in to long-term contracts with its buyers. Morris agents were being undercut, and there was nothing much they could do about it.

"We just felt," says Rosenfeld, "that taking 10 percent was being too greedy. The costs of producing TV shows kept going up and up, so agencies were taking more and more of a percentage of those costs. How big of a pig could you be? We decided to offer people something that was more attractive. That was one important reason that buyers were rooting for us, right from the start."

At their late-night staff meetings, the agents talked not only about finding single projects for potential clients but also about each person's long-range career objectives. Ovitz, especially, was always looking well into the future and encouraged the others to think the same way. For years he'd been plotting out his own existence in neat fragments of time—deciding where he wanted to be when he was thirty, thirty-five, and forty. Why couldn't CAA do the same thing for other people? Perhaps it could, but that might involve making some difficult decisions when the business was young.

"One of our first big breakthroughs came with Chad Everett," says Rowland Perkins. "We were all sitting around the office one day, and a TV script came in for a movie-of-the-week. Everett was looking for work, and we thought this might be a really good opportunity for him. Ron Meyer had already seen the script, and he told us that there was good news and bad news. The good news was that the part was worth $50,000. That meant that our commission was $5,000, and we really needed the money. All of us could see that $5,000 right in front of us, and it looked very good.

"The bad news, Ronnie said, was that the movie stinks. After talking it over, we all decided that despite the $5,000, playing this part would not be a wise career move for Everett. We couldn't let him do this, so we turned it down. After a while, something better came along for him. We learned that if we could say no when we really needed money, then in the long run we would be all right."

At William Morris, the more powerful agents had their own "boutiques" within the company; they handled their stars separately from everyone else, and sometimes in secret. CAA began with the notion that all the agents would represent every client and all would share whatever information they had. They would also share in the monies generated by each new signing and commission. If, over time, an actor or writer or director naturally gravitated toward one agent more than the others, that was fine. But cooperation, teamwork, and openness were essential if they were going to survive.

"Our attitude among ourselves," says Perkins, "and then later when we started hiring people, was that you should never be afraid to ask for help. At William Morris, we saw agents and trainees who were fearful of asking questions; they didn't want to look stupid to management. At CAA, we thought that the people who asked for help were the smart ones. If you needed assistance in closing a deal, just ask for it. We wanted to operate as a whole unit and an egalitarian company."

Perkins, the most experienced of the five, became CAA's first president. The initial idea was that each man would serve in that capacity for two years. Ovitz was the second president in line. Once he assumed that office, the plan flew out the window.

"He liked being president so much," says Perkins jokingly, "that we just let him keep it. Seriously, Mike had the vision and we all knew that, so there was no reason to keep changing presidents. The mantle fit."

It was Ovitz who suggested that when the men went out at night to drum up business they go not as individuals, visiting five different places, but as a quintet who were coming en masse to one location. They were five agents going to a sound stage at ABC to shake Michael Eisner's hand and watch a comedy pilot being shot, or five agents showing up at the film opening of *New York, New York,* or five agents dining out at the legendary Chasen's in Beverly Hills, the celebrity restaurant that for years had served Elizabeth Taylor her favorite bowl of chili.

They were five agents dressed in handsome, dark business suits and dark ties, precisely how Phil Weltman had taught them to dress. Yet they were no longer exactly as Weltman had told them to be. Their hair was now falling over their ears, Rosenfeld was wearing a big beard, and their ties were as wide and clunky as other fashion statements were from the mid-1970s. Ovitz maintained the neatest look of any of them, but when his sandy-colored locks began to creep over his earlobes, he looked younger and somewhat mischievous.

When they went out on the town, the men were no longer five separate people but the new company called CAA. Five men doing something together looked more impressive than one or two. Five men with a similar purpose and moving in the same direction called attention to themselves. Five men pooling their physical and mental powers might achieve something known in scientific circles as critical mass. When enough energy was concentrated in one area over a long enough period of time, explosions sometimes occurred. New waves of energy were created and released. And five people could reach critical mass much faster than two or three.

"We quickly learned to set aside our very distinct and disparate personalities, so that we could work together as a group," says Bill Haber. "That was the key to our success. Each man played a distinct role. Rosenfeld was our wise rabbi. Perkins was our hard-working Calvinist Protestant. Meyer was the nicest and most decent man on the planet. I was the humanist, who did things more with his heart than his head. Ovitz was the leader. He was the most driven executive in the United States and he was—and still is—one hundred times more driven than anyone else."

They were now generating not just energy but also a little money. They'd landed some television bookings for the Jackson Five and Rich Little and had put together a game show package for ABC called *Rhyme and Reason*. Michael Eisner had told his people at that network to meet with the new agency and come up with something they could all do together—so they had. The word about CAA was spreading, and the men barely had time to sleep.

"The hours they worked were extraordinary," says Ellen Meyer, a Hollywood casting director who became Ron Meyer's wife soon after the new agency was formed (they are no longer married). "Creating a new business is like having your own child. You will do things for your baby that you wouldn't do for any other human being on the planet. You will stay up very late and get up very early. You will do whatever has to be done. That's the way they approached CAA.

"The five men paid attention to all the details. Phone calls were always returned, no matter how important, or nonimportant, the caller. They put things in writing. They cared about their appearance and about what they said and did in public. They were very meticulous and very conscious of what they were doing.

"In the really heady years, when they were launching CAA, the scales were heavily balanced toward the men's professional lives, versus their personal lives. When you're an agent, your job lends itself to working all night, reading scripts on the weekends, and traveling to locations when things are being produced. You want to be near your actors and directors. You're on a treadmill going one hundred miles an hour, and it doesn't stop. Once you sign someone, the work has just begun. You have to find that person a project and then keep them happy. That's a whole new challenge."

"Making your client feel loved is the heart of the job," says Rosenfeld.

"Being an agent isn't merely a job," says Perkins, "it's a way of life."

"We all worked very hard," says Rosenfeld, "but Ovitz was the one with the agenda. He was highly organized, and he set our goals. He would come into the office in the morning and say, 'Tonight we're going to such-and-such studio to see a TV pilot that's being shot,' or 'We're going to this screening at this location and this time,' or 'We're going to this party. We have to meet people and we have to be seen together. We need to get this producer and that actor, because they're hot.' So we went to these places and made our presence known. Right from the beginning, Mike had an intelligent, audacious plan, and nobody could argue with him because everything he said made sense.

"Even though he was the youngest, he knew how to synergize us. At William Morris, he'd quietly studied our strengths and weaknesses, and he saw how to use each man's talent for the good of the whole. He knew that Haber was better at one thing, but Perkins was better at something else. He knew that he himself had the best business background, and he knew that Meyer was very good at handling clients and public relations. He knew that when the time came to make new hires, I would be good at that. He subtly encouraged each of us to move in the best direction for the company. And when we weren't doing our jobs, he was the one who reminded us of that."

Ovitz was constantly making calls all over town, finding out which business managers and which lawyers represented which television actors, movie stars, producers, directors, and scriptwriters. While the other agents were working on specific deals, he was absorbing any piece of information that might be useful, taking notes on everything he encountered, and laying the groundwork for the future.

"We were TV agents," says Rosenfeld, "and Mike knew we

could build on that to start CAA. But he realized that if we were really going to be successful, we needed to be in the motion picture business. He set that goal for himself, but he pushed all of us to think bigger."

"We were in a meeting once with some literary agents," says Perkins, "and we were talking to them about doing a project with Robert Redford. They laughed at us and said we could never represent a star like Redford. We got up and walked out of the room. We didn't want anyone telling us what we couldn't do."

Ovitz's long-range approach to the film business was not to go after movie stars directly but to reach them through the attorneys and business people who were already involved with the actors and actresses. He would start by working the edges and gradually move closer to the target, using indirection, just as Sun Tzu had suggested. In addition to this, he began recruiting young, successful agents in William Morris's motion picture department because they were skillful and hungry and already had established relationships with some stars.

Ovitz also began planting favors all over town. He found out which network or studio executives were currently looking for jobs. Then he phoned them and said that perhaps he could help them find employment, if not now, then in the future. The upstart was as brash as he was aggressive. There was no one he was afraid to call.

When he contacted a rising William Morris employee, Ray Kurtzman, and invited him to come work at his new agency, the man resisted his efforts. Undaunted, Ovitz began sending flowers to Kurtzman's wife. When he contacted Bertram Fields, who was widely regarded as the most powerful entertainment lawyer in the business, the attorney was perplexed by Ovitz's confidence. The kid worked for a nickel talent agency but was acting as though he owned Hollywood. Ovitz gave Fields a token five-dollar retainer fee so that Fields was now his lawyer and would not take any future cases against CAA.

Occasionally, Ovitz's self-assurance and self-control were tested to the limit. "One day, I was having lunch with Mike, and he was trying to sell me on an afternoon program," says a former network executive about the early days of CAA. "I wasn't against doing the show, but I wasn't in a position where I could tell him that my people were ready to say yes to the project. I could tell that this really bothered him. He completely believed in what he was selling me, and he kept coming at me and coming at me from different directions. He asked a lot of questions and made a lot of suggestions, in order to find a way to close the deal. I would respond, and then he would take notes in the tiniest handwriting I've ever seen. Then he would ask some more questions.

"He finally made one last pitch, and I couldn't give him the answer he wanted to hear. He didn't say anything, and his expression didn't change, but he slowly got up out of his chair and began walking in a circle around the perimeter of the restaurant. It was a large room, and he walked around it very purposefully, looking straight ahead, making a full circle and then another. I watched him and thought this was very strange. He came back, sat down, thanked me, politely shook my hand, and that was end of our meeting. The walk had gotten rid of his anger and frustration. It was his way of controlling himself, and it was a lot better tactic than getting upset with me."

It was Ovitz who usually set the strategy for landing new clients. "In our first year there was almost nothing we wouldn't do to get business," Rosenfeld says. "I don't mean bad things, just creative ones. We talked about parachuting into a potential's client's backyard and thought of ourselves as the crew from the old TV show *Mission Impossible.* One afternoon, we invited a husband-and-wife writing team to the office. We took them into the conference room and sat them down at our $169 table, with the Formica top. All five of us made our pitch to them, one right after the other, but the couple were very reserved and cautious. They were drama writers, so they were pretty serious people. Nothing we'd told them was pushing them over the line to sign with us.

"Finally, one of us said, 'What do we have to do to impress you? Get up on the table and tap dance?' They just stared at us. Ovitz spontaneously got out of his chair, jumped up on the table, and began to dance in front of them. The funny thing was that he didn't know how to tap dance, but that didn't make any difference. He was not afraid to make a fool of himself, and these people found it irresistible. Ovitz had cut through their seriousness and taken exactly the right tack. They started to laugh, and then they signed with us. It was Mike who got up and did it."

While working in the Hong Kong Bank Building on Wilshire Boulevard, the CAA partners often ate lunch together and discussed their upcoming plans. On their way to one Beverly Hills eatery or another, they walked past the big plate-glass window of a Jaguar dealer. One day only four of the men left the office for their noontime meal, because they couldn't find Haber. As they strolled by the glass facade, they glanced inside and saw him sitting in the driver's seat of a top-of-the-line Jag, hands on the wheel, eyes on the make-believe road, immersed in his imaginary pleasure. It was typical of the man, who could be quite childlike and loved to fantasize about their future success. In time, he would hand out fat cash Christmas bonuses to some CAA employees, surprise one of his secretaries with a redecorated living room, and own a French château and fly to Paris on the weekends just for fun. But in 1975, when the men were counting dimes, such thoughts were nothing but fantasies.

Back then, when they ate lunch in Beverly Hills, the bill was frequently steep, and there was always a pause when the waiter or waitress dropped it on the table. None of them had a predictable income, and no one knew exactly where the next commission was coming from. "Don't worry about it," Haber would say to the others, as he reached for the tab and studied the numbers. "We work for a very rich company." It was a standing joke, and the men chuckled at it somewhat nervously while reaching for their wallets. Then they went back to work, motivated by professional hunger and a profound desire to prove themselves to their former employers.

They made lots of jokes in those days, but it was no laughing matter when they went to a restaurant one evening with actor Joe Bologna and his wife, actress Renee Taylor, two clients the agency had recently signed.

"Joe and his wife called and wanted to take all five of us and our wives out to dinner," says Rosenfeld. "We were to pick a room where we could do this in private. We thought this was a wonderful gesture on their part. We were struggling, and the thought of having them as clients and being taken out to dinner was very nice. We picked the Jade West, a Chinese restaurant in Century City, because it had a private room and I knew the owner. Prior to the dinner, Meyer and Ovitz had gone to the restaurant's maître d' and told him that when the bill arrived—we knew it would be several hundred dollars—the waiter was to give it to Mr. Bologna. We weren't trying to stick him, but he'd invited us to dinner, and we didn't want any confusion when the tab came.

"That evening, we were seated at a big square table, and Renee and her husband were on opposite sides of it. Seated next to Joe was Rowland Perkins's ex-wife, Diane. She was an upper-class sort of woman who believed that everything should be done by the book. Diane had a high-pitched, Billie Burke–type voice. Burke, you'll remember, was the good witch in *The Wizard of Oz.*

"Rowland was the senior member of CAA. He'd worked at William Morris for seventeen years, and his wife had enjoyed the benefits and the prestige that came with that job and with accompanying Rowland to many black-tie events. She'd seen him pick up a hundred checks. Somehow, it hadn't occurred to her that those conditions of his employment no longer applied. It had never crossed her mind that every dollar was now important to us.

"The dinner was good, and Joe and Renee were very funny and great company. When the meal was finished, he lit up a big cigar and told stories that had everyone laughing. It was terrific for our egos to be in this situation. We needed to know if we were making headway in the business, and this evening told us that we were. Finally, the waiter came over and sat the check down next to Joe. He just looked at it and puffed his cigar. At that moment, some bolt dropped out of Diane's brain. She grabbed the check, and in her best Billie Burke voice, she said, 'We never let our clients pay for dinner!' Ovitz and Meyer turned white.

"Diane, of course, had no intention of paying the bill. And Bologna never made a move toward it. He just kept puffing that big cigar. Diane passed the check to the next person, and it started bouncing around the table. It went from one person to the next, and when it got to Meyer, he reached into his pocket, pulled out a credit card, and put an end to the goddam thing. You had to be there to see the look of horror on all of our faces. Ovitz and Meyer were absolutely crazed.

"Nowadays, Mike spends that much money without blinking, but things were very different back then. CAA was not always the company it became."

7

C AA's letterhead promoted the young company as a "literary and talent agency." These words were carefully chosen, and from the beginning Ovitz wanted to be associated with a literary agency that would feed CAA manuscripts that would eventually become books; in time, Hollywood might then turn these books into TV shows or miniseries or feature films. Ovitz knew that actors were primarily interested in good stories, and if he had access to those stories, the talent would follow. CAA's early efforts to join forces with the literary firm of Adams, Ray, and Rosenberg had not worked out, but Ovitz had continued doing research in this area and found something with more potential: the Morton Janklow Literary Agency in New York. Janklow represented some of the most commercially successful writers in the nation—Judith Krantz, Danielle Steele, Jackie Collins, and Sidney Sheldon. If they did not create literature for the ages, they regularly churned out entertaining stories and generated vast amounts of money.

One day Ovitz called Janklow cold and said that he was twenty-eight years old and had recently opened a talent agency in Beverly Hills that within a decade would be the most powerful company of its kind in the world. The key to CAA's success, he went on, would be Morton Janklow's own firm. If Janklow would just allow him to represent a few of his properties in Hollywood, Ovitz would sell them, they would be in business together, and this would greatly benefit both agencies.

Janklow was noncomittal but amused; he'd never seen this kind of chutzpah before. He wondered if the kid would ever call back.

Ovitz phoned him again and again and then again. Janklow took the calls but remained lukewarm. Ovitz kept phoning. Finally, he asked if he could have half an hour of Janklow's time in person, and the answer was yes. Ovitz flew to New York, walked into the man's office, took off his watch and set it on Janklow's desk, talked for exactly thirty minutes, explaining how successful they were going to be together, jumped up, grabbed his watch, shook the man's hand, and left just like that.

Janklow was convinced that Ovitz was a brilliant speaker, but did he have any follow-through? The older man said he would think about the offer.

Ovitz went back to L.A. and kept working the phone. He told Janklow that he would call every Thursday morning at precisely ten-thirty in New York to ask if he was ready to give him a manuscript. Each Thursday at ten-thirty, the phone rang in Janklow's office and the young man was on the line from California. The employees in the Manhattan office could set their watches by this. This went on for more than a month.

Finally, the literary agent gave Ovitz a book that had been rejected at a number of places. Within a few weeks, Ovitz had sold it as a TV package in Hollywood. After that, he didn't have to make any more Thursday morning calls at ten-thirty. Janklow had become a believer and began feeding CAA material regularly. They would eventually work together on more than one hundred hours of TV programming made from the writings of Janklow's clients, including such miniseries as *Rage of Angels, Hollywood Wives, Mistral's Daughter,* and *Princess Daisy.*

By late December of CAA's first year, the company had used only $21,000 of its $100,000 line of credit and done $2.5 million in bookings. After the five men had subtracted their clients' percentage of the take and their own office expenses, they were left with $125,000. They split the profit, and each went home with $25,000. The agency was by no means well established, but the men would never again have to worry about working for nothing.

CAA had recently signed Debbie Reynolds, Ernest Borgnine, and Burgess Meredith—not hot stars perhaps, but people who'd had names in show business for a long time. Then they signed Buddy Hackett, William Conrad, Yvette Mimieux, Karen Valentine, Eva Marie Saint, and Angela Lansbury. More names, with more years in the industry.

By the summer of 1976, CAA had outgrown the Hong Kong Bank Building and needed a new office. They found space in Century City, just south and west of Beverly Hills, in the Tiger International Building, headquarters for Flying Tiger Airlines. In September of that year, CAA moved into the fourteenth floor. They were no longer working on card tables or folding chairs, and their wives were not answering the phones. The old conference table was gone, and CAA had taken on a very clean, efficient, professional demeanor. In the new conference room was a portrait of their mentor.

"To Phil Weltman," the plaque beneath the portrait read, "who taught us the meaning of integrity and self-respect. We dedicate this agency." They'd asked Weltman to join them, but he now worked alone and liked it that way.

Ovitz had replaced Perkins as president, and his office in the Tiger International Building was in one direction, while everyone else's was in another. He was clearly in charge now, CAA's TV accounts were bringing in money, and he was ready to tackle the movie business.

Ovitz approached Marty Baum, a veteran's veteran in the field of entertainment. He'd once been a talent agent at Baum and Newborn in New York, but by the late 1960s, he was working for ABC and producing feature films. As the head of the network's movie department, Baum had overseen Sam Peckinpah's *Straw Dogs* and Bob Fosse's *Cabaret.* He'd picked up an Oscar for producing *They Shoot Horses, Don't They?*, starring Gig Young and Jane Fonda. Bright, energetic, blunt, red-faced, and described by more than one person as "the toughest man in show business," Baum was like a character in a movie about the hard side of the glamor industry. He was nobody's fool, and he was knowledgeable about virtually every aspect of making motion pictures.

As an agent, he'd represented some genuine stars: Sidney Poitier, Julie Andrews, Richard Harris, and Joanne Woodward. As a producer, he'd made award-winning films. He knew the talent, both on camera and off, and he knew the people who handled the money. He knew where the movie crowd congregated and how to talk to them. And he had the one thing that Ovitz wanted most: credibility in the film business.

In October 1976, the young man made him a partner at CAA. Baum brought Poitier, Andrews, Harris, and Woodward plus actress Dyan Cannon, author James Clavell, and Carroll O'Connor, who'd become one of the most recognizable faces in America as Archie Bunker on *All in the Family.*

Although he'd known considerable success and was many years older than the other partners, Baum did not hesitate to join the fledgling organization. "In a business where duplicity and avarice are held to be the keys to the door," he once said, evoking the cadences of W. C. Fields, "these men stood out by their display of decency, their intelligence, and their sensitivity to their colleagues and clients. I knew they had a great future because of Mike Ovitz. When I met him, he was only twenty-nine, but his instincts for the business were remarkable. Being told no did not discourage him, because he knew there would eventually be enough yeses to overcome the nos.

"Mike had a way of getting to the point of an argument quickly, and in the early days of CAA, we had to move fast. People now like to talk about the influence of Eastern philosophy at the agency, but that didn't apply back then. The name of our philosophy in those days was survival and trying to make a buck. It had nothing to do with Japanese thinking."

Ovitz wanted to know everything Baum knew and meet everyone the older man could introduce him to. He relentlessly queried Baum about the film business. What were the fears and insecurities of the stars? What were the concerns of the directors and producers? Who were Hollywood's best people at casting a picture? What did the studio people worry about—and what would allay their worries? What was the difference between a good script and a bad one? How did you know from reading a screenplay if it had great commercial potential or not? How did the financial side of filmmaking work? Where did the money to make films come from? How was it spent? Who made all those decisions? What was the most difficult thing about getting a picture made? Who held the real power in the movie business?

Before becoming a CAA partner, Baum had worked with Blake Edwards, the director of the *Pink Panther* movies, which had starred Peter Sellers. One of Baum's first assignments at CAA put this connection to good use.

"Although we could ill afford to do it at that time," he says, "Mike sent me to the south of France to meet Peter Sellers, who was there working on a project. Blake Edwards was also there, and he made the introduction to Sellers for me. Fortunately, I was able to sign him."

Back in L.A., Ovitz was anxious to begin calling film heavies, but first things first. Phone etiquette in Hollywood is more of a science than an art. It has its own language and its own rules, as complex and elaborate as the mating ritual of sandhill cranes.

Says one longtime Hollywood secretary, "There is lying to your mother, and then there is lying for your boss on the phone in the entertainment industry. You just never tell people on the other end exactly what is going on, until you're told to do that, which is probably never."

In short, unless you are quite famous, you can't just pick up the receiver and call people in the movie business—with any serious hope of getting through—unless you attach your name to the name of someone who is more well known than you are. You'll never make contact on the first two or three calls; and while you might eventually wear the callee down and get a return call late on a Friday afternoon, it's a poor way to make an introduction.

However, if you phone and say, "Someone With Clout suggested I give you a call," you have a fighting chance to make a connection. Once you've accomplished that, you have thirty to forty-five seconds to say something that will hold the other party's attention and give him or her some hope of generating money with you.

"In the entertainment business," says Rowland Perkins, "the very best you can hope for is access to the right people. Once you have that, you're on your own."

Back in the sixties, Marty Baum had worked for Ted Ashley,

who'd run New York's Ashley Famous Talent Agency (later absorbed into ICM). Ashley had represented many stars, and Baum felt that Ovitz could greatly benefit from meeting him. Because Ashley was now the chairman of Warner Bros. studios, his name and his phone calls carried considerable weight in Hollywood.

"As a favor to me," says Baum, "Ted drove in from the Valley one day to our office on Century Park East. He sat with Mike and me for two hours. He heard us out and listened to what Mike wanted to do in the film business. Then he promised to help us make contacts throughout the motion picture community, and he did just that. We needed more entree, and he gave it to us."

Ashley called the other studios and made contact with some actors, directors, and producers who were less than happy with their agents. He told them about CAA. Baum and Ovitz made the follow-up calls. Baum also phoned the press agents or lawyers for other discontented actors. The movie crowd respected Baum, not just because he could speak their language, but because he had a brilliantly polished golden Oscar sitting in a glass case in his office. He took people to lunch or dinner and bought them drinks.

"We spent money," he says, "whether we had it or not."

Sometimes Ovitz went along with Baum on these excursions. They attended industry parties together and shook more hands. They weren't necessarily looking to sign people—or to steal them from other agencies—at least not right now. They were merely surveying the turf.

"One night there were TV and movie people at a gathering in L.A.," a network executive says, recalling this period of CAA's history. "The TV people were sitting in a group talking among themselves, and the film people were off in another corner. Mike came in, and I asked him to come over and have a drink with us; he'd been pitching a lot of TV shows to us lately, and I thought he would like the chance to sit down and join us. He just gave me a little smile and kept walking.

"He went over and began mingling with the movie crowd. It was as if he were saying to us, 'I've got bigger things to do now, and you're part of my past.' It was a subtle but unmistakable gesture. He had his eyes on much larger prizes than selling daytime TV game shows."

While Ovitz told everyone that CAA was moving into the film business, he didn't say that he would be doing this with a game plan that had essentially never been tried before. Not that anyone would have listened to him or cared, just as no one had cared two years earlier, when the men had started the agency. It was still too early for anyone to pay much attention to what CAA was doing.

Baum already had Joanne Woodward as a client, so he suggested to the partners that perhaps they should think about signing her husband, Paul Newman. After all, they had a natural in with him. The younger agents liked it when he said things like this; it gave them a rush of excitement. Why not go after a film legend like Newman? "Reach for the moon," Phil Weltman had always said. What did they have to lose? Maybe they should also go after Robert Redford.

Baum told them to pursue Diahnne Abbott, an actress who had a small part in the upcoming film *New York, New York*. She wasn't a star, of course, but she was married to Robert De Niro. If they signed her, they might get to know her husband. They put Abbott on their list. Maybe they should think about Dustin Hoffman, too.

Newman. Redford. De Niro. Hoffman. If they could land just one of those names, they would be well launched in the film industry. So they made a few overtures, a phone call here and there, but nothing that caused the other Hollywood agencies to feel concerned.

"Let me tell you something about the movie business," says an agent at William Morris. "You have a star client like a Dustin Hoffman, let's say, and he does a picture every two or three years. Sure, he makes money for you, but you have to service him the whole time he's not working. You have to fly him out to Hollywood for meetings so he can explore projects that he might be interested in. You have to put him up in a nice hotel. You have to feed him and give him a nice car to drive. Then he turns the deal down. He doesn't work for several years, while you're paying all these bills and pissing away thousands and thousands of dollars. I could tell you about actors.

"Then he finally finds something he likes and decides to do a picture. He gets his three million, and you get three hundred thousand dollars. That's not bad, but you've been spending money on him for the past few years. So three hundred grand is really a lot less than it looks like.

"Now let's say that you're in the TV business. You sell a show, it goes on the air, it starts making money, and you never have to service it again. A few years later, maybe it goes into syndication in the United States and a few other countries, and it makes money for you every time an episode goes on the air. You don't have to fly it anywhere, or check it into an expensive hotel, or provide it with a car, or feed it meals. You don't have to listen to it complain. You don't have to do anything except cash the checks. That's how you make money in the agency business. That's how William Morris was making lots and lots of money when CAA started.

"We heard that Ovitz and his boys were thinking of getting into the film business, but we just shrugged and said, 'So what? You want to try and keep Dustin Hoffman or some other star happy, go right ahead. And good luck.' We were content to keep cashing those TV syndication checks. We weren't worried about CAA. The thought of them going after a star like Hoffman didn't really bother us."

He paused for a moment, then said, "We were wrong."

8

Little by little, CAA was growing as a business. When the company decided to start hiring people and training them to be agents, Ovitz felt that Mike Rosenfeld would be the best one for the job. Rosenfeld was perceptive about people and good at seeing both sides of an issue; more than once Ovitz had used him to mediate a dispute between two of the partners. Rosenfeld was a balancing influence in the office, and Ovitz was a strong proponent of the Japanese concept of *wa*—creating harmony in a working or living environment.

After hiring new recruits, the CAA men instituted the same system of training that they'd been part of at William Morris. Competition in the Morris mailroom—which had produced such future entertainment moguls as Barry Diller and David Geffen—had been extremely intense, at times vicious. Fistfights had broken out between ambitious young men, and legends had been spawned about the frustrations that came with being on the lowest rung of the agency business.

There were stories of trainees getting into car wrecks while making a delivery across town and then continuing on with their missions—faces bloodied and noses broken, but spirits unbowed. There was the story of a trainee who couldn't take the stress of being yelled at or dictated to by his superiors anymore, so one afternoon, while conducting "dispatch"—carrying mail to the far side of town—he drove to the edge of a cliff of a well-known L.A. canyon and threw all the letters over the edge, tossing away his career in the business as well. There were stories of mailroom trainees steaming open letters, reading them, and then resealing them before they were delivered to the higher-ups. And stories that the successful older agents expected the trainees to do these things if they were to have any chance at all in this cutthroat enterprise.

There were stories of brash mailroom hopefuls taking the initiative and slipping scripts to famous actors on their own—and getting fired for their efforts. There were stories of trainees accidentally mentioning in public that one of their bosses was sleeping with a budding starlet—and being dismissed for this indiscretion, too.

CAA newcomers who were being groomed as future agents started out by sorting letters, running errands for older agents, and doing "coverage"—perusing scripts that came into the office and writing comments about them. One quick way of separating the comers from the losers in the Hollywood agenting business was to give a young person an unproduced screenplay with its title page removed. The reader would not know who wrote it and would have to rely on his own instincts to decide whether this was a commercial property or not; if he gave the wrong answer to his superiors, it could permanently hurt his chances for advancement.

Trainees delivered gifts and scripts to actors and directors all over town. They picked up dry cleaning for the partners and brought them their favorite snacks from the market. They worked seventy-five hours a week for minimum wage. They supplied their own cars. With overtime and doubletime, they could make twenty grand a year. The whole system conjured up a group of pledges being tortured in their first semester at a fraternity.

"When young people came to me and applied for a job," says Rosenfeld, "I would remind them that the partners at CAA never got sick, and if they did, they kept working anyway. At the end of our interview, I would make a speech to the kid so he could understand our work ethic. I'd say, 'Listen, there will be a morning when you get up and you have a headache and a sore throat and you just don't feel good. You'll think about calling in sick, but don't even entertain that idea. Drag yourself out of bed, brush your teeth, have some coffee, and head to the office. If, on the way in, you trip on the curb and fall down and think you've broken your leg, don't call for an ambulance. Pull yourself up and crawl on your hands and knees into my office. I'll decide if you're sick or if your leg is really broken.'

"They knew I was having fun with them, but they also got the message. This is not a clock-punching job. If you want to be in this business, you put in your time. No malingering here. The rewards will be there for you if you do the work and stay with it. And it has paid off for many of them."

One young man who was fired after nearly two years as a CAA trainee, when he'd already come to believe that he'd survived the cut, received the news that he was being dismissed, walked out into the parking lot, bent over, and vomited. "Working there," he says, "was very demanding and very difficult, and it was the best experience of my life. In the mailroom, you worked very closely with other trainees in a very small space. The people I went through that program with are still my best friends. The whole thing was incredibly dynamic and incredibly exhausting."

Says another trainee from that era, "You did not go to Sally Struthers's house and leave a package on her doorstep. That was not good enough, and you could be fired for doing it. You knocked on her door, and if Sally wasn't home, you put the package in someone else's hands and you said it was to be given to Ms.

Struthers. You made sure someone had it before leaving the premises. Then you could go back to the agency and say the job was done."

"One time," recalls a trainee from CAA's early days, "I forgot to write down on the phone log one call that had come in that day for my boss. He found out about this, and that night he made me get in my car, drive across town at three A.M., and put a ten-dollar bill under his front door. It was a very long drive from my house to his, and during the whole trip I had the opportunity to think about my mistake. I never made it again."

A former mailroom employee says, "The agency taught me the most valuable things I've ever learned: assume nothing and follow up on everything."

Trainees studied all the partners at close range, and Bill Haber generated the best anecdotes. "Haber was absolutely the most eccentric person in the agency," says an ex-CAA colleague. "In later years, he had a chandelier in his office, and a bidet. He also liked to practice the violin during working hours. He was a master at working the phones. He always rushed the net in telephone tennis. That means that he was never, ever on the defensive. In all the years I watched him, he never took a phone call. Not one. He always had his secretary say that he was busy or out. Then he called back after he'd had time to think about what he wanted to say and could go on the offensive.

"Sometimes, when he was working on his violin lessons in the office, the trainee who was supposed to be manning his desk would forget to answer the phone. Forget may be the wrong word. You know, people got really tired of listening to the sounds he was making. Bill would find the trainee and smash his bow in front of him and make him pay for a new one. It cost sixty-four dollars each time he broke one. But when Christmastime came around, he gave his trainees one-hundred-dollar bills as a bonus."

Another person who made it through the program says, "The thing they drove into you was not to talk about our business with anyone outside the agency. Period. You knew that that would get you fired faster than anything else. The secretiveness and the silence fostered a great sense of power at the top of CAA. But the whole idea of not talking to the press was not done to hide something, but so that we would not reveal things that could hurt us. After a while, everyone was afraid to break the code of silence."

"CAA now has a great aura of mystery around it, as if we did something very secretive in the mailroom and the conference rooms in order to achieve success," says Rowland Perkins. "There was no mystery to it. We were five guys who knew what we were doing and worked fifteen to eighteen hours a day in the beginning. It amazed all of us when our company eventually took on the aura that we all got up very early each morning, put on dark Armani suits, and behaved like sharks who were out to conquer the town.

"At first, we shunned publicity. After a while, we tried to talk to reporters and dispel the feeling surrounding CAA. But we learned that no matter what we did, everything they wrote only heightened our mystique."

By the late 1970s, CAA's work ethic was starting to pay off. In their fourth year in business, they did $90.2 million in gross sales. They were now aligned with Witt-Thomas, one of the leading television production companies in Hollywood, and with the help of literary agent Morton Janklow they were selling numerous TV packages to the networks. They were also involved in several movie projects, including *Urban Cowboy*, starring John Travolta; two Peter Sellers films, *Fu Manchu* and *The New Pink Panther*; and the Norman Jewison picture . . . *And Justice for All*.

"When they approached the motion picture people," says a CAA employee of that era, "Mike and the other men tried to give the impression that they were very, very rich, even when they were not. They all dressed well and began driving Jaguars. Ovitz had developed a passionate interest in art. He put fine paintings on the walls and made certain that everything, and everyone, looked good. Ovitz cherished the idea of perfection, and it came out in the physical environment he created at work. He wanted everything done perfectly, and he simply didn't understand it when someone told him that something couldn't be done. While at CAA, I removed the word 'no' from my vocabulary."

At the end of the decade, the company had nineteen agents and fifty-five employees overall, including trainees and secretaries. One recent standout hire was Steve Roth, who'd grown up with actor Michael Douglas, the son of film legend Kirk Douglas. Like Marty Baum, Roth was very familiar with the movie business. He had flash and style, he knew all the right people, he introduced Ovitz to more industry heavies, and he gave the agency more credibility.

Baum himself had lately been working on one of CAA's first lucrative film projects, Blake Edwards's *10*. "One week before the start of principal photography on this picture," Baum says, "George Segal dropped out of the starring role. In order to get the people at Orion who were financing the film to go along with Dudley Moore as the leading man, Blake Edwards and Julie Andrews gave up their salaries and gambled on making the money back in future profits. They were my clients, and when the movie came out and was a great success, CAA got a check for one million dollars."

When money came in, the spoils were divided evenly among the partners, regardless of who was most involved in generating cash flow. Ovitz's system of teamwork and cooperation was being applied at every level of the agency.

Power is a slippery game, and it can never be mastered easily. While Ovitz had clearly emerged as the head of CAA, his primary competitor inside the organization was Bill Haber, who worked as a TV agent and, according to most observers, brought in more money than anyone else. By his own admission, Haber felt that business decisions could be made at least as much with the heart as well as the head. Ovitz, on the other hand, was a strenuously calculating rationalist, who also handled the agency's financial affairs. Occasional conflict between the men was inevitable.

"There was a great sibling rivalry between Ovitz and Haber," says a CAA employee. "Bill was the queen, but Mike was the king. When they fought, Ronnie [Meyer] or Rosenfeld was the peacemaker. Bill wanted equal footing with Mike, but Mike just ignored that and kept leading the agency. If there was a serious battle, Ovitz was always going to win. He was a better strategist and more determined. Also, in terms of the big picture, he had a clearer sense of what was good for the company.

"Mike had great ways of signaling power. He would speak very quietly so you would have to listen extremely carefully to him, and that gave everything he said an air of importance. When he came into your office, he would sit down in your chair. Just take it over. He would have his secretary phone someone's office and tell that person that he was going to be calling in exactly thirty minutes. It was his way of freezing you next to the phone and saying, 'I'm going to call, so you better be there.'

"Haber kept some riding crops in his office. Sometimes Ovitz would come in and the two of them would stand up and duel with the crops. This never turned serious, but the duels had a wonderfully rich subtext.

"Mike forced Bill to deal with and sign some people he didn't want to. When these clients would call Haber on the phone, he would get unhappy and start beating the chairs in his office with one of the crops. He would beat them until the foam rubber popped out."

By 1980, Aaron Spelling had emerged as the biggest name in the TV producing business. In the sixties, he'd made the hit shows *Burke's Law* and *Mod Squad*, and in the seventies, he'd created *The Love Boat, Fantasy Island, Charlie's Angels*, and *Hart to Hart*. Later, he would go on to produce *Dynasty, Melrose Place*, and *Beverly Hills 90210*, among others, and his shows would eventually go into syndication in more than ninety markets around the world. He would open offices in London, Paris, Rome, Toronto, Sydney, Tokyo, and Rio de Janeiro. The Spelling Satellite Network would be seen in four million homes worldwide, and *Melrose Place* and *Beverly Hills 90210* would generate half a billion dollars in merchandising products, such as calendars, T-shirts, and perfume.

Spelling was often criticized for the unabashedly commercial content of his programs, but he was fond of saying that he did not make TV episodes for either media critics or those in Hollywood who liked to snipe at successful people. He knew that mass entertainment was for the masses, and everything the man touched turned into money. In 1981, he became a CAA client, and in time he built a 123-room mansion in Holmby Hills.

"Mike forced Bill to sign Spelling," says a former CAA employee, "because this greatly helped the agency. At first when Spelling began calling our office, Bill would stick his finger down his throat because Spelling had the reputation of making shows for idiots. But after a while, Bill's attitude changed, and I think he really grew to like and respect Spelling."

"Aaron Spelling was a phenomenal money-maker for CAA," says a network executive. "Ovitz, of course, understood that from the start, and he never let other things distract him from the task at hand."

This same executive mused, "The heart is a wonderful organ, but it can get in the way of executing a long-range business plan."

9

Upon starting CAA, its founders believed the day would eventually come when they would know they'd comfortably made it as a talent agency and as a force in the business; they were going to be successful, so now they could at last relax and enjoy themselves.

"It never happened," says Haber. "First we thought, if we can just get some decent furniture, we'll know we've arrived. We got the furniture, and then we wanted a better office. We got a better office, and then we wanted better cars. We got the cars, and then we wanted more clients. We got the clients, and we wanted more clients and bigger deals. Each breakthrough just led to the desire for more and more."

When they'd left the Morris agency, Nat Lefkowitz, the lawyer-accountant who headed the William Morris New York office, had derisively referred to them as "shoe-leather agents." He'd meant that none of them (including Rowland Perkins) was really executive material; in fact, they were little more than five guys out on the street trying to hustle up a deal.

"Lefkowitz intended for the remark to be an insult," says Perkins, "but when we heard about it, we took it as a compliment. He was right. We were shoe-leather agents who were always out looking for business."

CAA's presence, with its better office and flashier cars and growing client list, was starting to be felt around town, especially at the Morris agency. CAA's lower TV packaging fees were undermining William Morris, and Ovitz had made a run at a couple of its motion picture agents. In later years, the CAA partners would go out of their way to say that they did not begin with the intention of harming their former employer. They would publicly thank the Morris office for giving them such good training, repeating this almost as if it were a mantra. They said these things because there was truth in them and because they did not want to deepen any of the hard feelings that were slowly developing between the two companies.

"In the 1980s," says Perkins, "relations between CAA and William Morris became strained, but it really wasn't because of what we were doing. It was because they were asleep at the switch."

When CAA began, one long-standing Hollywood taboo was that while agencies could make a lot of money from packaging TV shows, the same concepts should not be applied to the movie business. Television and films were two different entities, with different sets of rules: TV was more profitable, but motion pictures were the status symbols of the entertainment world. One treated them with a certain deference and respect. They were a part of American cultural history and had a tradition going back to the first part of the century.

In decades past, the studios had dictated which talent they wanted for a motion picture, and no agent had ever wielded the kind of power that would allow him to tell Columbia or MGM whom it should hire as producer, director, screenwriter, and actors. No agent, including the redoubtable Lew Wasserman, had ever been in a position to have his way with the money people at the very top of the film business. The idea of a talent agency packaging movies had been talked about for years, and even tried a few times by Sam Cohn, a legendary dealmaker in New York who was associated with ICM, but movie packaging had never really become a part of the business. Even to attempt something like this took vision, a long-range strategy, and a lot of clout.

By the late 1950s, the old system had crumbled, and studios had lost the kind of power they'd once had in Hollywood. A kind of void existed in the business now. Stars had become more independent; they weren't tied to long-term contracts and could make pictures for a variety of employers. If the studios were still powerful, they were also increasingly vulnerable.

Ovitz saw that void and that vulnerability and decided to build his strategy around it. If he and his men could sign enough stars, writers, directors, and producers, they could replace the old system with something new. They could put together all the elements necessary to create a film and present the whole package to a studio. The more key elements CAA had in hand for a project, the harder it would be for a studio to turn the movie down. By representing the various creative parts, CAA would not only make more money (by collecting a 10 percent commission on each part), it would also be able to provide more work for its stable of clients. And the notion of future employment, for an actor, was basically irresistible.

"Become your own studio," Ovitz had once told Sally Field, his old high school classmate, after he had founded CAA and she had complained to him about the difficulties of landing a new film role. He meant that if she were in the business of producing her shows, as well as starring in them, she would not always find herself in such a position of dependency. She would no longer be the actress-as-victim-of-the-money-people.

At CAA, Ovitz did not want his agency to be dependent on others for its success. He wanted others to be dependent on him, and his plan stood the old "studio system" of filmmaking on its head. Put another way, he was more interested in acting like a buyer who was shopping around for a studio than like a mere seller who was trying to find a part for one of his actors. To carry out his strategy, Ovitz needed to build a more formidable power base than any that had come before.

His view of power, which he'd shaped over time, was very simple: one plus one equals more than two; two plus two equals more than four. In the movie business, people nowadays love to talk about "synergy." The term is used to describe bringing various people or talents together and creating something new and vital. In scientific terms, what Ovitz believed in and practiced is called resonance: combining two compatible energy streams with roughly the same frequencies releases a third stream that is more potent than the simple sum of the first two. The young leader of CAA had found this to be true inside his own agency, and he believed that the same principles could also be applied to the movie business.

When Ovitz looked at William Morris's motion picture department, he saw another vulnerability. By the late 1970s, that department had the leading movie agent in Hollywood, in the highly respected Stan Kamen, but if Kamen was known as a great signer and handler of talent, he was not known as a great administrator. He tended to do things on his own and, at times, without telling others at his own agency. Like many successful people, he felt that he had to take care of everything, and delegating responsibility did not come naturally to him. He and he alone represented Robert Redford, Chevy Chase, Jane Fonda, Goldie Hawn, and many others. Kamen's mentality was the direct opposite of Ovitz's team concept—and he was only one man against five or seven or ten or more.

Ovitz had quietly put out feelers to Rick Nicita, a very promising agent at William Morris who handled Eric Roberts, Christopher Walken, and Sissy Spacek, and to Jack Rapke, an agent in the Morris motion picture literary department, and he'd kept pressuring Ray Kurtzman to join his young firm. Ovitz told all three men that they had far more of a future at CAA than at the highly structured, hidebound Morris office. All three soon made the move.

The tactics that had helped Ovitz in high school and college, the same ones that he'd absorbed while reading *The Art of War,* were now being put to use in his agenting business. Relationship building, teamwork, resonance, stealth, indirection, and conducting warfare by turning an opponent's weakness and vulnerability against himself—all these things were gradually spreading outward from his corner office in the Tiger International Building on Century Park East. Though it would take years to see the results of his efforts, the spadework was just about done.

While almost no one was paying attention, a new creature was being born on the Hollywood scene. Ovitz's style would have many names, from "Shark" to "Samurai Agent" to "Crypto-Japanese Businessman."

"When Mike started CAA," says one longtime Ovitz observer in the industry, "he accessed the consciousness of an ancient warrior. That's who he is, that's how he thought, and that's where his strategy came from. It was just a matter of time before he was in the right place to carry out his plan.

"He'd read deeply in Eastern thought, and when CAA began, he looked at the terrain of the film business and asked the questions a warrior asks, 'What are my goals and aims? Whom am I going to do battle with? Who is going to try to stop me? What are their resources? What are mine?' He analyzed the people who would try to prevent him from reaching his goals, and he constantly looked for ways to block their strengths.

"His initial question was very basic: do I fight in obvious ways or do I go into a guerrilla mode and use more subtle means? If you have no money—and CAA had none when they started—then you become a guerrilla. That's why he never wanted to speak to the media. He might have leaked his strategy or tipped his hand to his competitors. So he kept quiet, and never gave away a resource that would undermine him later on. In times of combat, generals never talk to the press. They never tell reporters what their real objectives are.

"In order to win, you have to build alliances that attract people to the game you are playing. The ideal is to redefine the game and control the rules of the battle itself. The old game was just to land a big-name client. The new game for Ovitz was to build power in a variety of places and then tell the studios, 'Take it, leave it, or shove it up your ass.' He began amassing allies and leveraging power wherever he could. He made contacts with everyone, he returned every phone call, and he gave people a reason to believe that he could help them in the long run.

"More than anything else, he sold them the idea of having a long-term future with CAA. What everyone in the entertainment business—where you can't predict anything—wants is to have a more secure future. Mike intuited the insecurity of the industry better than anyone before him. Then he exploited that intuition relentlessly."

Says another executive in the business, "Look at Ovitz closely and you can see who he really is. In his face are elegance, grace, humor, and ruthlessness. He looks like a master of the martial arts training. You sense a very sharp mind, but also a man who is physically fit, agile, flexible, able to adapt very quickly to changing circumstances, able to quickly turn a disadvantage into an advantage. He is not large but has a great concentration of power in his body. His little smile is the only thing that gives him away and tells you that much, much more is going on behind his eyes than you can possibly see. He knows he is ahead of other people, but he doesn't want to tell anyone that and give the game away."

"Mike is ruthless," says another Ovitz watcher, "because he's always waging a kind of strategic warfare. He was built to do this, just like other military generals were, and if he couldn't do it, he would die. He has very conscious objectives, and people will get sacrificed in the pursuit of those objectives. If you take drugs in the office, you're gone. If you want to fool around at CAA late at night, you're fired. If you talk to the media, you're history. A cruel man will cut off your balls for sport. A ruthless man only does it when it's necessary. Ovitz is extremely good at setting clear boundaries and being able to control people who are out of control. That's how he got where he is.

"He strives for self-control, and when he explodes, it is usually for effect. Everything is a game, a play, and he's the lead actor, because everything he does is a calculated performance. He's attempted to master his emotions, and he knows how to mask them. He's a warrior twenty-four hours a day. People don't always love true leaders, and they don't love Mike, but he commands enormous respect.

"He is not the quiet guy who claims to be the power behind the throne. He is the throne itself. He saw his role as an agent as being the most potent role he could play over a long period of time in the entertainment community. It is more powerful than that of the actors, writers, directors, and producers who constantly come and go. He looked at the whole field and saw where he wanted to be, and then put his strategy into action.

"Day by day, week by week, and month by month, he defined and redefined his goals, building on each relationship as he went along. He's one of those rare people who is not only a visionary but knows how to execute on a daily basis. Visionaries often get lost in the ether, and then get blindsided by changing events. Ovitz kept his vision far enough in advance while keeping his daily calendar under control. He knew how to maximize power. If you do that and if you can control the resources of an entire industry, then you don't have to live with the fear that people are going to fuck you over."

10

By 1980, CAA was ready to strike. Ovitz and his partners had said they were willing to cut their commissions to roughly half of William Morris's (on the TV side, CAA was dropping its packaging fees from 10 to 6 percent; on the film side, the agency was said to be luring stars with the promise of taking only a 5 percent commission—or less). The agents had told the person whom they were targeting that they would be involved in solidifying, prolonging, and expanding that individual's entire career. Phil Weltman had taught his charges to have respect for talent: the CAA men didn't fawn when making a presentation to an actor, but they were deferential. CAA was a service business, the partners emphasized, and they were there to serve.

Ovitz had by now mastered his approach to actors he wanted to sign; only the details differed from one to the next. First, he did extensive research before meeting with the talent. He read about the actor's background, watched and critiqued his or her movies, and developed a sense of the arc of this person's working life. Its zenith had been here, he would acknowledge when speaking to the talent, and that was a great accomplishment indeed, but for the next plateau to be reached, something more was necessary.

To actors, the CAA approach wasn't like dealing with just another Hollywood agency or even a good business manager. As numerous people would say in the future, it was like dealing with someone who knew more about your professional existence than you did—and someone who cared about you and your whole body of work, not just the last picture you'd made.

Every artist holds a secret conception of what he has achieved or might achieve in the future. Every one of them cradles some hidden notion that one day he might just do something perfect. Every one of them feels that no one else can possibly understand what he or she has gone through. All of them feel trapped inside some vision or impulse they can't quite see or understand. Artists are self-involved people, whose passion is expressing something within themselves that wants to come out. Anything that stands in the way of that expression is a potential enemy. Anything that facilitates that expression is a great ally. And every artist is prone to self-doubt.

If all artists feel these things, then actors and actresses probably feel them more deeply than others. They display their talent on a stage or up on a screen, in which they are many times larger than normal people. They are praised or attacked in public by critics who may not have any insight into what they are doing and certainly were not involved in the creative process; actors are often castigated for things they have no control over. They are usually dependent on the work of writers, directors, and producers before they are even given the chance to be employed. And their gifts are not well understood. Mastering a musical instrument is one thing; but where does an actor's talent come from? And can't it just disappear one morning and never come back? How is it nurtured? What makes it blossom or wither away?

As a high school student, Ovitz had stood in the rear of the auditorium at Birmingham High and watched an aspiring actress named Sally Field rehearse a play. He'd lingered there in the shadows, not wanting to be seen, just observing carefully, in part because he found the young woman attractive, and in part because he was fascinated by the world of entertainment. He was also preparing himself for his career. In later years, people would say that he was a world-class negotiator, a superb businessman, and a great leader. By then, all of those things were well established, but what wasn't said so often was that he had a remarkable understanding of talent.

He knew that the core reality of every performer, director, or writer was uncertainty, regardless of their money or fame. He knew that they are worried about losing "it" and can't even define what that mysterious "it" is. He knew that what they really wanted was the feeling that they would be working in the future, so they could simply relax and forget about the business side of their career and focus on doing what they loved.

For many artists, money is merely the vehicle that allows them to keep working. Money is delightful, of course, but not as delightful as the freedom to engage your passion and see audiences respond. All talent agents have some grasp of these basic things, but Ovitz plumbed them more deeply than anyone before him.

When movie stars met him for the first time, they often came away feeling that they'd just encountered something very, very different. These were world-class performers who'd just met another sort of world-class performer, who claimed to be nothing more than a businessman. But who was the actor here and who was the agent? How was it possible that a man could set aside his feelings and his ego to the degree that Ovitz appeared to, so that he could focus all his attention on you? How did he know so much about your experience, and how did he know precisely what you wanted to hear? "When Mike speaks to you," more than one person in Hollywood has said, "you just feel very important."

In 1980, when Ovitz and the other CAA men spoke to Dustin Hoffman, Robert Redford, Paul Newman, and Bill Murray, the actors were ready to listen. CAA had been targeting Hoffman for years. Redford was Stan Kamen's client at William Morris, and Kamen was still the biggest agent in the business. He'd devoted months to signing the star, but keeping him satisfied was another matter. Redford wanted to direct films as well as appear in them, and CAA let him know that not only were they fully aware of his long-term goals, they would help him reach them. And there was another issue.

"The thing about Redford," says a Morris agent, "is that he never wanted to pay anyone a commission, and we wanted our 10 percent. He was easy for Ovitz to pick off. One thing that isn't talked about in our business is that some stars don't pay agents anything. The commission is simply budgeted into the film and the studio pays it. It goes on around here, no matter what anyone tells you."

Paul Newman had been working without an agent for years. He was such an established star that he didn't feel he needed one. However, he was getting older and entering a new phase of his career. His wife, Joanne Woodward, had good things to say about CAA, and Newman thought that perhaps he too should explore a relationship with the young agency.

To the CAA men, Bill Murray was more than just an odd-looking *Saturday Night Live* comic. He had film star potential, and it was just a matter of finding him the right picture.

Half a decade of schmoozing, planning, and spreading the message across Hollywood was about to pay off in a huge way. In May of 1980, Newman signed with CAA. In early July, Murray joined the agency. In late July, Dustin Hoffman became a client. Then Redford came aboard. For five years, Ovitz had been calling everyone in town and telling them that he was interested in being in the film business. Now CAA's phones were starting to ring, and other motion picture clients suddenly wanted to hear what they had to offer.

"By the middle of 1980," says one CAA staffer, "we already had just about the best client list in town. We would celebrate with each big signing. Not large celebrations, but just things that would let us know that we were making significant progress. Hey, it's really something when you land Paul Newman, and we did it when he was still Paul Newman."

In 1981, Sylvester Stallone, lying on a beach in Hawaii, was approached by a couple of men in their mid-thirties. Stallone had become famous by appearing in the *Rocky* movies but had recently appeared in two bombs—*Victory* and *Nighthawks*. There were reports that he was going through a period of confusion and self-doubt. He was a William Morris client, and the people surrounding him had told him that he should be particularly wary just now; the heads of CAA might try to lure him away in a time of frustration or weakness. The young agency was known for seducing disgruntled actors, who were fearful for their careers.

On the beach, Ron Meyer began talking with Stallone about his future in the film business, while Ovitz just listened. Meyer was the softer presence of the two, and this was a delicate situation. Maybe Stallone needed to think about making a change. Maybe a new agency could get him some better scripts and bigger deals. He was still a huge name in the business, and maybe a fresh start was all that was necessary to put him back on top. Maybe they could help him find a new direction . . .

Stallone soon became a CAA client. The agency's first effort on his behalf—casting him as a singing cab driver playing opposite Dolly Parton in *Rhinestone*—was not a success, but CAA then negotiated for him one of the most astounding deals in the history of Hollywood. Under an agreement with two new companies, MGM/UA Communications Co. and Carolco Pictures, Stallone was guaranteed $15 million for his next five "action" films. He was also guaranteed future monies for five other movies that he would produce but not appear in.

The year that CAA signed Stallone, Bill Murray appeared in the hit comedy *Stripes*, about a cynical loser whose life is turned around by a stint in the army. The director of *Stripes* was Ivan Reitman, and Murray's costar was Harold Ramis, both of whom were CAA clients. The agency had brought the three men together for this project.

Ovitz's concept of movie packaging was an idea whose time had come.

The following year, something occurred that would be discussed and written about (most notably in Frank Rose's *The Agency*, an excellent history of William Morris) for years to come. It was a non-event outside the film business, and in some circles within the industry, it was only a minor moment. But for those who were aware of what was taking place over in the Tiger International Building in Century City, it was a startling omen of the future.

As William Morris's leading agent, Stan Kamen had tried to sign director Sydney Pollack, without success. In 1982, Dustin Hoffman and Bill Murray were teamed up with CAA client Teri Garr in the film *Tootsie*, a Pollack-directed comedy about a gifted but cantankerous actor, played by Hoffman, who, disguised as a woman, tries out for a female part on a soap opera, lands it, and then becomes a national sensation because of "her" outspoken ways. Pollack himself, now a CAA client, appeared in the film as Hoffman's agent, and in a scene set in the agent's office, the camera gave viewers a glimpse of something that was increasingly familiar to people inside the film business: the CAA logo.

The film was a smash hit, and for those who liked symbols, this one was unmistakable. Michael Ovitz and his agency had definitely arrived.

PART THREE

DOMINANCE AND
INTIMIDATION

Subtle and insubstantial, the expert leaves no trace; divinely mysterious, he is inaudible. Thus he is master of his enemy's fate.

—*The Art of War*

11

In the mid-1980s, the long-standing joke at the William Morris Agency—that its older agents don't fade away, they just die—was no longer funny. Too many of them were now being buried. In September 1983, Nat Lefkowitz, the lawyer-accountant who had once headed Morris's New York office, passed away in Manhattan after heart surgery. He was seventy- eight. In December of that year, fifty-one-year-old Ed Bondy, a Morris agent whose client Lou Gossett Jr. had won an Oscar the previous spring for his work in *An Officer and a Gentleman,* died of a heart attack. In August 1984, Abe Lastfogel, the revered leader of the company for many decades, checked into Cedars-Sinai Medical Center in Los Angeles. A few days later, he was dead.

Nearly ten years earlier, Phil Weltman had tried to tell the agency's brass that they were aging quickly and needed to prepare some of the younger fellows for managerial jobs, but no one had listened. Now his words were proving to be alarmingly prophetic. Weltman, still bitter about being fired from William Morris, avoided the company's office in Beverly Hills, but he wasn't heartless, and he couldn't stay away from the Morris executives' funerals at Hillside Memorial Park.

In March 1986, Morris Stoller, who had been in charge of William Morris's financial affairs, died of stomach cancer. At the memorial service for Stoller, Sam Weisbord approached Weltman and attempted to say something to heal the wound that had separated them for more than a decade. Weltman refused to take his old friend's hand. Two months later, Weisbord died of lung cancer.

If each of these deaths adversely affected the agency, the most significant blow of all came early in 1986. In January of that year, Stan Kamen was said to have lymphoma, but people close to him knew that he was suffering from the advanced stages of AIDS. By the end of February, Kamen was dead. Although Ovitz and CAA had been raiding the Morris movie department for years, luring away both clients and talented agents, some very big names remained connected to that office. Now Kamen was gone, and so was the heart and soul of the operation.

No one at CAA had planned it this way, of course, but when Morris's motion picture division lost its leader, Ovitz and CAA were in the perfect position to take advantage of the new reality. CAA had already signed, or was about to sign, William Morris clients Gregory Hines, Rock Hudson, Farrah Fawcett, Burt Reynolds, Goldie Hawn, and Chevy Chase. They were working on even larger names. Months before his death, Jane Fonda had told Kamen that she was pursuing a new agency, one that was capable of getting her better roles than she'd recently been seeing from the Morris office. She needed to see more scripts and better ones, scripts about things other than romance, comedy, or melodrama. She wanted serious parts in movies with a political message, just as she'd had a few years earlier in *The China Syndrome*, a film about a near disaster at a nuclear power facility.

And there was one other reason for her to start shopping around. "Fonda is a good person and a fine actress," says a longtime Morris agent, "but when she came to us with all these complaints, what could we do to keep her? She said that we were wonderful people, but she wasn't going to pay any more agency commissions, or at least not the 10 percent we'd always charged and were going to keep charging in the future. She said that from now on all of her movie earnings were going to support Tom Hayden's political work, so she had to stop paying agency fees. We had a choice: cut our commissions or lose her. We could not let her dictate the terms of our business relationships with clients, so we had to let her go."

CAA was also courting another Morris megastar, Barbra Streisand. "In the early eighties," says a Morris agent, "Kamen was handling Streisand, and she passionately wanted to make *Yentl.*

This project was a personal thing for her, something she had to get done and get out of her system. She'd been trying for years to get the picture made and hadn't been successful. Under Kamen's guidance, the Morris office put the whole thing together for her. We helped her get financing for the film, we helped her work with the right people, and we helped her make her movie. Once it was over, she came to us and said that we'd done a terrific job, but she was going to CAA, because their commissions were less than ours. We all just looked at one another, in a state of shock. If we'd reminded her of all the effort we'd put out on her behalf to get *Yentl* made, she wouldn't have heard a word we said. It would have blown right past her."

While Kamen was dying, Ovitz had promised not to make advances on his clients, but it was the nature of the business that movie stars who felt their interests were being undermined by changing events would try to halt the damage. If Ovitz didn't phone them, they occasionally picked up the phone and dialed CAA. He was available to talk and willing to give them a few helpful suggestions. Or maybe he ran into them at a restaurant or on the set of a movie or at a film opening. With Kamen's death, CAA naturally looked more and more attractive to people who'd once pledged their unfailing allegiance to William Morris.

Morris employees had by now begun referring to the rival agency as "Ca-Ca."

"Loyalty is a very shifting thing in Hollywood," says a veteran independent producer, "and almost no one can hang on to it forever. It's always sad to see it slip away from people and entertainment companies, especially because of deaths, but when your career is on the line, money and new connections are the overriding factors. Some people think that makes us shallow. I think it makes us flexible."

As Kamen's life was ending at UCLA's Memorial Hospital, he heard reports about Ovitz schmoozing some of his clients. His anger erupted toward CAA. Two months before his death, he called Ovitz and said that it appeared there was no longer enough business for everyone in Hollywood, because CAA had to have it all. "It was just a very bad situation," says a Morris agent. "It wasn't

Stan's fault, and it really wasn't Mike's fault, either. We never saw what was happening to our agency for a long time, and when we finally did, it was too late."

What was happening to William Morris was a startling loss of clout and prestige in the film industry. In March 1987, just one year after Kamen's death, of the twenty actors and five directors who were competing for that spring's Academy Awards, nine were CAA clients, six were ICM clients, three were represented by a new agency called Triad Artists, and seven were represented elsewhere. None was a Morris client.

By the mid-1980s, CAA had become the most powerful agency in Hollywood—exactly as Ovitz had predicted to Morton Janklow ten years before. CAA had Robert Redford and Deborah Winger, plus director Ivan Reitman and the writing team of Jim Cash and Jack Epps Jr., working on the package deal that would eventually become the MCA film *Legal Eagles.* Redford earned $5 million for the picture, Winger earned $2.5 million, Reitman approximately $2.5 million, and the writers $750,000. In movie packaging, the agency does not collect a fee on the film's overall budget, as in TV packaging; it gets "just" a percentage of each client's take. By representing five key people in the *Legal Eagles* package, CAA earned huge commissions, and its display of muscle in negotiating better deals for all of its clients raised the production costs of the movie from the originally budgeted $25 million to $32 million. *Legal Eagles* was not a hit, and the additional $7 million was not recovered at the box office (although video rentals helped bail it, and many other films, out of the hole).

Through its film-packaging strategy, CAA was not only growing rich, it was also becoming a significant irritant to the other agencies by showing them just how well organized and potent it had become.

"In CAA's early days," says Mike Rosenfeld, "when there were only two big agencies and we were just starting out, people were cheering for us. They wanted us to succeed and take away some of the power from William Morris and ICM, because that would make the field more competitive."

"We changed the business by representing our clients to the fullest and using a team approach," says Rowland Perkins. "After we became successful, people began criticizing us for what we'd accomplished. Both things just kept growing—the success and the criticism—but once we began putting packages together and gaining momentum, no one at our agency wanted it to stop."

CAA's negotiating tactics when presenting a package—offering studios all-or-nothing deals—were gradually driving up the price of making movies. If Ovitz and his people could get millions and millions of dollars for their actors for one picture, this would inevitably force a theater owner in New Jersey or Nevada to bump the cost of his ticket another fifty cents or a dollar. The family of four sitting out there watching movies in Iowa was eventually going to feel the pinch.

As CAA's clout was expanding, a parallel development was taking place in professional athletics—with similar emotions attached to it. In the early 1970s, sports figures began hiring very aggressive agents, who negotiated larger and larger salaries for their clients (some of whom were not big stars). Over the next fifteen years, this trend produced anger and resentment on the part of fans. Many supporters of sports franchises now felt that agents had far too much power and were controlling the games and its stars; agents had loyalty to no one but themselves, and their strong-arm tactics were driving the cost of a ball game beyond the reach of people of average means. When baseball and football had lengthy, disruptive strikes over money issues, the players and their agents, fairly or unfairly, received most of the blame.

Grumblings had already begun about rising prices in the film industry and about too much concentration of power in one place. Stan Kamen's passing, people said, had signaled the end of an era. Agenting may have never been a gentleman's game, but in the past it sometimes pretended to be. Now it was only about money and numbers—about CAA agents convincing the talent that they could drive a harder bargain than anyone else and then proving that they could. Agenting had become a form of psychological combat, orchestrated by a man who handed out copies of *The Art of War* to his employees.

"Ovitz had created within CAA a class of samurai warrior ants," says an agent who works for another company. "They dressed alike, in Armani or Cerutti, they thought alike, and they acted like one another. They stayed up late at night studying the ancient ways of blindsiding the competition and destroying it. They were smart and ambitious. They looked great, and they went places in groups. They were quietly forceful, and they were spread out all over town now. I've heard more than one studio exec refer to that book as 'The Art of Bullshit,' but the truth is that the stuff in there worked."

The CAA warriors tended to be male heterosexuals.

"It was not a great idea to be a woman at the agency," says one female ex-employee. "There were times when it seemed that the higher-ups just wanted to be around men. Women asked too many questions and slowed them down. We don't fit as well into that samurai thing. Over the years, a number of very talented women have left the agency because they just didn't think it was female-friendly. Men like to sit around and tell one another stories. That's how they entertain each other and get pumped up to act. Women aren't as good at storytelling. We just want to know the facts and get to the point."

"If you were gay at CAA," says another former worker at the agency, "you went deep into the closet and stayed there. At some other agencies, they like their gay men to hold the hands of the aging female stars, but Ovitz didn't want that as part of his image. Maybe Stan Kamen's death had affected him in some way. Everything with him is about image, and he didn't want CAA associated with certain things. There were some gay people at CAA, but they made a point of not being effeminate and of keeping their mouths shut about their sexuality. Ovitz very much wanted his agents to be his version of normal: to be married and to be stable in their personal lives and to behave very well in public."

A male trainee from the mid-1980s says, "CAA always felt like a minicountry to me, and Ovitz was the figurehead. No one dared breathe a word about him in the office or challenge his basic ideas. You felt that the paintings had eyes and the walls had ears. There were rumors that he sent out his troops specifically to see if anyone was gossiping about him. People said that anyone caught talking about him would be consigned to TV residuals."

Outside the walls of CAA, harsh feelings toward the agency were building among its rivals, but that did nothing to curtail Ovitz's success.

"Everything was going right for CAA," says a Hollywood entertainment lawyer. "Not only were they making a lot of deals, but the business was exploding on all fronts. You had more production facilities, more cable outlets, more independent producers looking for projects, and the arrival and growth of the home video market in the early eighties also helped them a lot. It was just one more income stream for them to negotiate for their clients."

In 1984, CAA had Bill Murray, Dan Aykroyd, Harold Ramis, and Ivan Reitman appearing in *Ghostbusters*, which would become a smash. The agency had persuaded Cher to push her film career forward by taking a role in what would become the hit romantic comedy *Moonstruck*. CAA had put Paul Newman and Tom Cruise in *The Color of Money*, an updated version of Newman's classic early-sixties role of Fast Eddie Felson in *The Hustler*. CAA client Martin Scorsese directed the film, and guitarist/singer Robbie Robertson, also with CAA, created the movie's soundtrack. The agency had Dustin Hoffman and Tom Cruise working on *Rain Man*, a protracted and highly complicated project that would go through a series of writers and other film talent before it was finally completed—in time to clean up at the 1989 Academy Awards. CAA teamed up Gene Hackman and Willem Dafoe in *Mississippi Burning*. Ovitz had great talent in his stable; now it was mostly a matter of finding the right parts for the right people, and bringing stars together for film projects was one of his prevailing passions.

"Despite Michael's extraordinarily calculating mind," says an agent in Beverly Hills, "I think he put together these packages like a child puts together puzzles. You could just envision him sitting in his office taking his little notes and asking questions in his endless search for perfection: How do I get all the pieces that will fit just right? How do I move the pieces around and keep everybody happy? How does this thing work? Beneath everything else, there's something very childlike about Michael. An innocence or vulnerability that only comes out when the media start questioning him or people start criticizing his tactics."

In 1987, while pursuing his interest in the martial arts, Ovitz had met a handsome young man in his late thirties named Steven Seagal. Six feet, four inches tall, with naturally arching eyebrows, a magnificent jawline, and a long, dark ponytail, Seagal could throw human beings into the air with a twist of his oversized hands. Adept at both aikido and self-mythologizing, Seagal was fond of telling people that in the 1970s he'd lived in Japan and worked as a CIA operative on undercover missions in Asia. He still spoke in muffled tones, as if someone might always be surreptitiously listening in on his conversations.

After leaving Japan, he returned to the United States and began running a martial arts school, the Aikido Ten Shin Dojo in Los Angeles. Seagal was a startling physical presence, and when Ovitz first encountered him, he sensed that he'd just discovered a new movie star. By this stage of his career, the agent rarely got involved with promoting unpolished talent, but this case was exceptional.

Ovitz went to Terry Semel, the president of Warner Bros., and asked him to consider Seagal as a new leading man in an action thriller. Semel was cautious, but Ovitz kept calling him and repeating in his ear words to the effect of "Think of this guy, think of this guy, think of this guy." Eventually Seagal was given a screen test and the chance to show the Warner execs an aikido demonstration. Semel was impressed with the young man's undeniable charisma and agreed to give him a shot at stardom. Seagal expressed his gratitude to Ovitz by showing him some new martial arts moves (but he never, as was widely reported when Seagal first came into prominence, became Ovitz's aikido teacher).

Ronald Shusett, a screenwriter and CAA client, wrote a script for Seagal entitled *Above the Law*, about a Chicago cop whose investigation of political corruption leads him into the middle of a CIA-connected Central American drug ring. The film cost $7.5 million, made $20 million, and instantly brought Seagal into competition with the other big-screen vigilante heroes: Arnold Schwarzenegger, Clint Eastwood, Charles Bronson, and Chuck Norris. He would go on to make *Hard to Kill*, *Marked for Death*, *Out for Justice*, and his biggest box-office hit, *Under Siege*.

Seagal never forgot to whom he owed his success. "Michael and

I are very close—we love each other," he once told the *Los Angeles Times.* "I'm like a guru to him."

Ovitz had also begun looking at sports stars, and by 1988 he'd signed Magic Johnson of the Los Angeles Lakers. As part of his ongoing effort to sow and reap favors throughout the entertainment industry, Ovitz was now telling film executives that if they needed a contract negotiated or renegotiated, he would be happy to handle this for them. A few years later, in the early 1990s, he would put together deals for Joe Roth at Disney, Sherry Lansing at Paramount, and Mike Marcus, a former CAA agent who would take over the studio at MGM.

Ovitz would no more be limited to servicing film or TV talent than he would be constricted by the belief that a Hollywood agent could not venture outside the boundaries of L.A. and have any success. He was fond of telling people that each new achievement was not a final goal or an end in itself but merely a plateau that would lead to a higher level of achievement in the world of business later on. And by the late 1980s, it was clear that virtually every endeavor in America (including politicians' book deals and Olympic celebrities' appearances on TV to pitch household goods) was now a part of that world. Show business was expanding in every direction at once; why shouldn't a talent agent do the same thing?

If CAA's power was spreading because its leader was using his "samurai warrior ants" to apply some arcane principles from a distant time and another culture to modern-day America's free enterprise system, it was also growing for some much more basic reasons.

"L.A. was a fast, harsh place in the eighties," says a woman with more than twenty years' experience in the entertainment field. "Real estate prices were escalating like mad, and a lot of people could make a million dollars a year by falling out of bed in the morning. That caused some of them to get lazy and some of them to get mean. If you couldn't help me make money right now, then get out of here and leave me alone. It was all about 'What can you do for me?' Not 'What can I do for you?'

"During those years, CAA kept servicing people. They kept

handling the details. They kept following through. They kept treat-
ing their clients with respect. When you call people in New York,
they say they will get back to you, and they do. They might call you
a schmuck when they return your call, but they will return it.
When people in L.A. say they will get back to you, many of them
never do. CAA did. Always. That may sound like a very small thing,
but it's much more important than you realize. When Ovitz started
to become famous and to attract publicity, I think one reason that
he never talked to the media is that he didn't want anyone to figure out the simplicity of what he and his company were doing.
Then others might have started copying him.

"He never let things slide or lost sight of the fact that he had
to keep building new relationships and nurturing them over time.
He used old-fashioned, long-term romance and seduction to do
this with new contacts in L.A. and New York and with the Japanese. For most people, the eighties weren't about relationships;
they were about getting rich now and the hell with the future.
Ovitz was always working on things that would produce money
years later."

An L.A. screenwriter, who was never one of the agency's clients,
says, "CAA was a great place if you were on their team. They got
the best deals for their people, no question about it, but if you
weren't one of them, that could make things harder for you. They
were the power in town now, and they represented something that
a lot of people almost regarded as a dictatorship. This is when all
the fear started. You went through their office and used their talent, or it didn't get done. When Ronnie [Meyer] was winning, he
didn't mind letting the other guys win once in a while. But Mike
was always hungrier; he had more of a scorched-earth policy. He
was a great friend but a terrible enemy.

"And woe to anyone who was at CAA and tried to leave for another agency. Loyalty was everything to Ovitz and his men. It was
part of the whole Japanese warrior thing. If you violated the code,
watch out."

12

By 1985, CAA had outgrown the Tiger International Building, and the partners wanted a new home for their agency. Ovitz had no intention of being just another lessee in search of enormously inflated office space in Century City or Beverly Hills. He was ready to take a piece of his inner vision and give it physical form. He naturally gravitated toward things Far Eastern. He liked the aesthetic attention to detail that characterized Japanese and Chinese art and the formality and rituals of their cultures. By the 1980s, Japanese businessmen who had become stupendously rich were purchasing real estate and trophy hotels in Los Angeles and were looking to invest in the entertainment industry. Ovitz met and liked a number of them. He seemed to have things in common with them that many other Westerners did not.

"The Japanese can teach Americans a lot about the art of negotiating," says a real estate agent in Beverly Hills. "They are masters at not showing you their hand and at wearing you down. To us, time is money. To them, patience is money. They work in teams, and they will duck and dodge and do everything possible to avoid giving you a straight answer or revealing their long-term strategy, until they are absolutely ready to do so. By then, it's generally too late to implement your own plans.

"They want you to get angry and offer resistance to what they are doing. They want you to give in to them, and Americans usually do, because we just want to get the deal done and move on. Then they win and you lose. To deal with them requires more patience than most of us have."

Porter Bibb, the managing director of the New York brokerage house Ladenburg, Thalmann & Co. and a longtime observer of the entertainment business, says, "Ovitz studied the Japanese and learned a lot about their culture. When he started doing business with them, the fact that he was well informed about the Far East greatly impressed them. Many Americans treat the Japanese as little robotic people, but he respected them, and that made a big difference in all his future dealings with them."

Like Ovitz himself, the Japanese were very persistent in their desires and were not enamored of the word "no." In the mid-1980s, for example, a group of Asian businessmen were interested in purchasing the Bel Air Country Club, one of the most prestigious golf courses in L.A. The group made the club's shareholders a very generous offer, but Bel Air's leaders were not interested; they politely turned them down. Before long, the men came back with a better offer and received the same reply; the country club had no intention of selling itself to them, and the decision makers at Bel Air did not want to be approached on the matter again.

More time passed, and the group returned with an outlandish bid for the club—an offer that would have reportedly given each shareholder something in the neighborhood of a million dollars. Once more, the answer was no.

Undaunted, they went out and bought Pebble Beach.

Ovitz wanted to build a new headquarters for CAA—beyond anything the world of agenting had ever seen. The recently constructed William Morris office, located just behind the Beverly Wilshire Hotel, was more or less what one would have expected it to be: a modern-looking, rectangular, black glass box. Everything about it suggested efficiency, squareness, and masculinity. The lobby was rather cramped, the artwork was predictably decorative, and there was nothing imaginative in the architectural design. If the building was exceedingly functional, it did not make one think about the wonders of sunlight or the value of empty space or the effects of aesthetics on people in a working environment.

Ovitz was after something more rarified. He was a perfectionist, particularly when it came to surfaces and appearances. One could easily see that by examining his clothes, which always made a subdued, well-matched, and very costly statement. The white shirts were crisp, the dark pants expertly tailored, the creases firm, and the belt brought everything above and everything below it together, just the way it was supposed to. Even his casual clothes had a striking richness about them. Everything he wore seemed to have been chosen with a highly conscious intention: looking successful helped you become more successful, especially in L.A. But beyond that, he liked everything to be very attractive and very orderly.

Visual things had always been important to the man, but now they were becoming even more so. In the early days of CAA, while the other agents were writing contracts or talking on the phone, he occasionally sat in his office and indulged his passion for reading about and looking at works of art: from Africa, Europe, America, and the Far East. Now that he'd become successful and had money to spend, he was in a position to do something more than gaze. Barbara Guggenheim, an art consultant who worked on both coasts and the wife of L.A. entertainment lawyer Bertram Fields, helped give Ovitz entree to Manhattan's art-buying scene (she has no connection with New York's Guggenheim Museum). She informed him about gallery owners, and told him who the up-and-coming painters were, made introductions, and suggested which artists were creating pieces that would make good long-term investments.

Just as Marty Baum and Steve Roth had once walked Ovitz through the moviemaking business, Guggenheim was now teaching him the nuances and financial aspects of the world of contemporary art. He studied the subject tirelessly, voraciously, absorbing the history of art and learning about modern painters: Rothko, Dubuffett, Lichtenstein, Schnabel, Dine, Irwin, Reinhardt, and others. He began building a collection that would one day include not just the latest recommended investments but four-hundred-year-old Chinese furniture, Rembrandt etchings, and elegant African works from distant centuries.

In New York, Morton Janklow introduced Ovitz to Arnold Glimcher, the highly successful owner of Manhattan's Pace Galleries. Glimcher furthered his knowledge about buying aesthetic objects (while Ovitz returned "the favor" by helping Glimcher expand his business into Los Angeles). Like others before him who were first encountering the CAA leader, Glimcher had never seen anyone with the man's drive for new information, more information, every bit of information—in this case, about the realm of art. Glimcher once confided to *The New Yorker* magazine that dealing with Ovitz and his endless striving for self-improvement could be "exhausting." In 1986, as part of Ovitz's continuing education, Glimcher introduced him to the Manhattan-based, world-renowned architect I. M. Pei.

By now, the structure of CAA had changed. Four years earlier, Mike Rosenfeld had left the agency to go into TV production. Rowland Perkins still worked at CAA but was no longer a managing partner. The new partnership, which included Ovitz, Ron Meyer, Bill Haber, and CAA's chief financial officer, Robert Goldman, was now in charge. In 1986 CAA bought land in Beverly Hills where Little Santa Monica and Wilshire boulevards meet Lasky Drive. Now that Ovitz was ready to give shape and substance to his vision, he did not contact any of the highly qualified, well-known architects in Los Angeles or in any smaller American city. He would no longer do anything that gave the impression of being second-best. He called I. M. Pei and asked him to design his talent agency on the western edge of Beverly Hills. The architect demurred, saying that he appreciated the offer but found the location awkward and had a few other reservations. Ovitz kept calling.

"Mike went to work on him the same way he'd gone to work on a lot of other people," says Rowland Perkins. "He must have spent a hundred hours talking with Pei about why he should do the building and how great it would be. Gradually, the man began to listen."

Ieoh Ming Pei was born in Canton, China, in 1917, but moved to America when he was eighteen. In the mid-1950s, he became a naturalized U.S. citizen; by then he had earned a B.A. in architecture from MIT and an M.A. from Harvard. Over the next several decades, he designed award-winning buildings in, among many other places, Boulder, Colorado (the National Center for Atmospheric Research), Boston (the John Fitzgerald Kennedy Library), Singapore (the Chinese Banking Corporation Center), and Beijing (the Fragrant Hill Hotel) and art museums in Athens and Shiga, Japan. He was a member of many stellar organizations, including the National Institute of Arts and Letters, and had collected a veritable stack of gold medals. By the mid-1980s, as the most celebrated

Ovitz (*seated center*) left the William Morris Agency with four partners to form Creative Artists Agency. At far left is their mentor, Martin Baum. Steve Roth is at far right. Ovitz is flanked by his original partners (*from left*) Bill Haber, Ron Meyer, Mike Rosenfeld, and Rowland Perkins (*Los Angeles Times*)

Michael Ovitz's history of deal-making with Japanese businessmen has become the stuff of both Hollywood and Wall Street legend. He is seen here with Disney chairman Michael Eisner and Tokyo Disneyland head Masatomo Takahashi, as Mickey Mouse looks on (Reuters/Eriko Sugita/Archive Photos)

The new Creative Artists Agency building designed by I. M. Pei
(Joyce Jacques)

MCA chairman Lew Wasserman and president Sidney Sheinberg
(Reuters/Fred Prouser/Archive Photos)

Ovitz and his wife, Judy, chat with Philip Quigley, chairman of the Pacific Telesis Group (AP/Wide World Photos)

Disney chairman Michael Eisner and Capital Cities–ABC chairman Thomas Murphy announce the $19 billion merger of their two companies to make the world's largest entertainment business (AP/Wide World Photos)

Jeffrey Katzenberg, Steven Spielberg, and David Geffen pose at a Los Angeles news conference on October 12, 1994, to announce the creation of their new company, SKG DreamWorks (AP/Wide World Photos)

Edgar Bronfman, president and chief executive of the
Seagram Company and owner of entertainment giant
MCA (AP/Wide World Photos)

Screenwriter Joe Eszterhas with his wife, Naomi, at the opening of
Showgirls. Eszterhas's torrid correspondence with Ovitz became must
reading for everyone in the entertainment business (AP/Wide World
Photos)

Mike Ovitz (*left*) with Disney chairman Michael Eisner during an August 1995 interview (Reuters/Lee Celano/Archive Photos)

Ovitz with *New Yorker* editor Tina Brown at the Bel Air Hotel (Reuters/Fred Prouser/ Archive Photos)

Ovitz at the premier of *Toy Story* in November 1995 (Reuters/Rose Prouser/ Archive Photos)

architect in the nation, if not the world, the seventy-year-old Pei could pick and choose exactly which projects he wanted to do. He was open to suggestions, but his tendency lay in the direction of large public structures that were not located in southern California.

"Mr. Ovitz came to meet me in New York," Pei said one afternoon from his office in Manhattan. "I believe it was in 1986. When he arrived here, he'd done his homework very, very well. He knew as much about my profession as anyone in his position needed to know. He knew what I'd done, and he had a working knowledge of architecture, which surprised and impressed me. He told me why he thought I was the best person for this job.

"I was not convinced that I should do the CAA building. Personally speaking, I have a prejudice against Los Angeles, because of the lack of permanence in buildings there. They build them and then destroy them and then build them again. Michael persuaded me, by being intelligent and earnest, that this was not what he had in mind. He's a wonderful salesman, of course, perhaps the best I ever met.

"At my age, I can spend a lot of time selecting my clients, so that's what I do before I commit to anything. I came out to Los Angeles to see Michael again and to learn more about his organization. I met Robert Goldman, Bill Haber, and Ron Meyer, and I was very impressed with the spirit of CAA. They had a lot of young people in their company, and it was highly professional. I went back to New York and organized a team to come up with a concept for the building. This took three or four months, and it was still not a commitment on my part or their part to do the project. I just wanted to show them my concept and give them the chance to change their mind. I like to test people before we move forward.

"Then I went back to Los Angeles and presented the concept to Michael. He accepted it almost immediately. The most challenging thing about this building was the site, which is at the corner of a busy intersection. The most difficult part for me was placing the entrance to the building. Once I'd resolved that, everything fell into place. The results speak for themselves. I think it was a very good experience for both of us.

"Michael had a lot of his own ideas for the building, which were incorporated into the design. For one thing, he didn't want to emphasize rank within his company; he's particularly sensitive about that. He didn't want his office to be much larger than other people's, and that also impressed me. He wanted the building to be elegant but not Hollywood, not showy or flashy. I was sympathetic to that. He wanted the building to say, 'Here we are,' but say it in a serious way.

"I wanted the building to have a very open feeling and to bring a lot of daylight into the lobby. A dark building in southern California just doesn't feel comfortable or natural. Michael also didn't want people tucked away in cubicles. He wanted them out in the open where they could be seen and see one another. He wanted to emphasize that his company was a family, where the people are open to each other and share information."

Once Ovitz had accepted Pei's design, the next step was the groundbreaking. The architect was on hand for this event, which was unlike anything else Beverly Hills had witnessed. For the occasion, Ovitz brought in white doves, trumpet players, and Chinese priests wearing colorful robes. The priests were there to perform a ritual known as *feng shui*, which is carried out in order to create harmony and good fortune in a specific environment. In essence, *feng shui* applies the Taoist Five Element Theory (water, earth, wood, metal, fire) and the eight trigrams from the Yi-Jing to an office's location, site surroundings, door orientation and to the owner's desk placement (Ovitz's was on the top floor of the three-story building, more or less in the middle of the other offices).

The *feng shui* ceremony puzzled many, but it was a fascinating visual display. "Whatever they did," Rowland Perkins said later about the Chinese priests, "it must have worked."

Feng shui has since become a rather fashionable concept, and one can now buy books on the subject in trendy L.A. bookstores. But it remains perplexing to some people.

"I thought it was very strange to see this ceremony done at the CAA site," says I. M. Pei, "but California is a lot closer to Asia than New York is. Michael is very interested in things Oriental. He's a black belt in aikido, you know, and he's very good at the martial arts. I don't think he selected me to design the building because I was born in China, but he might have. I'm probably less Oriental than Michael is."

13

Ovitz was the product of his own intense self-discipline, which had allowed him to control many things about his life. Yet he could not control everything. Self-discipline had driven him to arise at five A.M. morning after morning so that he could give his body a demanding physical workout before going to the office. Self-discipline had dictated what he would eat and that he restrict his alcohol consumption to a single glass of wine with dinner. Self-discipline had told him which calls to make and which ones to avoid, which meetings to take and which ones to shun. Self-discipline had taught him that there was usually more mystique and power in silence.

Self-discipline had caused him to set aside some days each summer so he could chart his future in one- and three- and half-decade segments. Self-discipline had taught him that he could manage his facial expressions and his emotions, choosing them at will, just as he chose which clothes to wear to CAA each morning. Self-discipline had taught him that he did not need to negotiate from fear but could use the fears of others to his advantage. In earlier times in the entertainment industry, the adage was that if you controlled the talent, you controlled the business. Self-discipline had taught Ovitz that if he could control himself, he had a much better chance of controlling other people.

All that worked exceedingly well for more than a decade at CAA, but then he was presented with a new and disconcerting challenge.

On December 19, 1986, just as Ovitz turned forty, the *Wall Street Journal* ran a front-page story on him. By this time, many people had begun referring to him as "the most powerful man in Hollywood." The label had not only stuck, it had also begun to rankle some studio heads, rival agents, and others in the entertainment business. The *Journal* article, which was the first national piece written about Ovitz, introduced him to the world beyond Los Angeles. It listed his remarkable achievements but also hinted that those accomplishments were generating a growing resentment in others that might one day explode.

The article included producer Edward Feldman's assertion that Ovitz had tried to discourage him from making a movie based on Bob Woodward's book *Wired* about the life and death of John Belushi. The biography had committed the cardinal Hollywood sin of openly mentioning drug use and abuse among some show business heavies. Ovitz was loyal to Belushi's memory, and he was also developing the careers of two of Belushi's friends and former *Saturday Night Live* cohorts, Dan Aykroyd and Bill Murray; in short, the agent did not want the film made. In a community where image is everything, some elements of reality simply cannot be allowed to surface. According to the producer, after he acquired the rights to *Wired*, Ovitz called and told him that pursuing this project "won't be good for your career." Feldman then received a letter from an L.A. attorney that raised the possibility of an invasion-of-privacy suit if the film was ever shot. Feldman went forward anyway, but ten casting directors refused to work with him on the movie. Eventually completed, it had a limited release and soon passed into obscurity.

To many, the efforts to stop *Wired* and intimidate its creators were ominous signs. A level of fear was creeping into the entertainment business, which some of them had never felt before. It was there in the Feldman incident, and there when star actress Debra Winger had walked away from CAA after becoming angry at the way she'd been packaged in *Legal Eagles*. (Winger soon returned to the agency.) Screenwriter Tim McCanlies once told *Spy* magazine that after he informed CAA agent Richard Lovett that he was moving to another company, Lovett warned him that a terrible accident would befall his career. When two CAA agents, Judy Hofflund and David Greenblatt, left and opened InterTalent, Ovitz reportedly threatened to use his clout to prevent them from signing any clients. According to *Spy*, after Tom Strickler, another CAA agent, had breakfast with the rebel Greenblatt, he found himself out of a job. (Hollywood is full of colorful stories about agents who, after being fired, sneaked out of the building with a Rolodex full of phone numbers and addresses of film stars tucked under their shirt, coat, skirt, sweater . . .)

The feeling of fear was there when show business veterans felt compelled to do elaborate mea culpas in front of the media because they'd once dared take on Creative Artists Agency. Back in 1979, Jay Weston, the producer of *Lady Sings the Blues,* had sued CAA over a rights dispute. In the next decade, he produced only three features—*Night of the Juggler, Buddy Buddy,* and *Chu Chu and the Philly Flash*; all of them fell into oblivion. "I regret more than anything else in my business life the mistake of suing CAA," Weston once told the *Los Angeles Times.* "They are the best agency. . . . I have nothing but admiration for them."

CAA had succeeded beyond the biggest dreams of its creators; there was now a new hero—and a new villain—in town. From the mid-1980s on, L.A. would hold two strikingly different views of Michael Ovitz.

"In an age of ever-increasing celebrity," says a former studio vice president, "Ovitz saw that movies would become more and more star-driven. So he went out and rounded up most of the stars. Then he held the studios hostage and bled them for all he could."

"At any given point," says an ex-Hollywood agent, "the studio people could have told Ovitz, 'We're not going to play the game your way, and you're not going to dictate to us what you want. So back off.' But most of them didn't do that. They let their fear control them, and they gave in to him, because they were afraid he would take his clients elsewhere and attempt to keep these studios away from any future projects involving his people. He made the studios think they couldn't live without Robert Redford or Sylvester Stallone or other, smaller names. They could have, but when he made them doubt that, he'd won the battle of wills."

Says another agent, "Ovitz tested people—he's a master at that—and the basic truth is that most movie executives failed his test. He knew exactly where all the buttons in our business are, and he enjoyed pushing them. He saw that there was great power underlying this business, and he believed that if he didn't use that power against the studios, they would use it against him. Mike had just enough paranoia to be wildly successful.

"It's fashionable now to blame Ovitz for the rising costs in the movie industry. He was a catalyst for some of these problems, but he wasn't the root cause. He was negotiating with a lot of undisciplined people, and he knew precisely how to manipulate them. They allowed Ovitz to get away with all this, and then blamed him for showing them their own weakness."

"In the long run," says an independent producer in Brentwood, "Mike was very good for our business, because he got films made, and when he drove up the prices for his people, this eventually made more money for everyone—actors, producers, directors, and screenwriters."

Ovitz could be both kind and ruthless. He was both generous toward and fearsomely possessive of his assets—his talented agents and their even more talented clients. He could seem ego-less when it served his purposes, yet he was fanatical in his pursuit of making his agency the best and most successful in the world. He was modest to a fault in public, but he loved the deference and the glamorous perks of his position: sitting courtside at Los Angeles Laker games in the team's heyday in the mid eighties; eating at posh Beverly Hills restaurants, which had prepared his meals in advance and served them to him when he sat down, in private, like royalty; having a vacation home in Malibu and another one in Aspen; and overseeing CAA's extremely private retreats for its agents, which were held in the spring at resorts outside Los Angeles. What went on at the retreats remained highly secretive, even to the nonagent employees at CAA, although rumors occasionally slipped out that Ovitz like to conclude these events with fiery speeches about the brilliance of the company's future. "No one breathed a word to us about the retreats when they came back to the office," says a former CAA secretary. "I think all this helped create the impression that the agency was a kind of cult and Ovitz was the grand master."

The *Wall Street Journal* article heralded a new era for Ovitz— one that he did not seem to know how to respond to. Sun Tzu had taught him a lot about the psychology of warfare and how it could be applied to the world of modern business, but the Chinese philosopher did not have anything to say about the contemporary

American media and the celebrity machine it had created. Sun Tzu did not write about image maintenance or the fine art of public relations. By 1986, Ovitz's own celebrity was growing, as was his reputation as the most feared man in Hollywood, and he appeared to have a strategy for everything, except coming to terms with himself as a public figure. How does a warrior control his image in the media marketplace?

In Hollywood, individuals are known by the force of their personalities. It is impossible, for example, to watch a movie starring Jack Nicholson without seeing Nicholson first and the character he is portraying second. In a city of extroverts, most people lead with their public personas. Ovitz had developed no public persona, and he seemed to have transcended the notion of personality, at least while in his office, where he'd fashioned his image as the Pure Businessman, the Deal Artist, the man who ate and breathed nothing but Vital Information. The real human being had been kept very well hidden.

But now things were changing. Now he was being criticized in public. Now that he was being called on to respond and reveal himself, what would the warrior do?

The *Wall Street Journal* article set a precedent for how Ovitz would deal with the media in the years ahead, when he was becoming as famous as some of the people he represented. He refused the *Journal*'s request to interview him, claiming that his "little organization" was hardly worthy of such attention. His words conveyed the self-effacing attitude that he often used in public, yet his flat no to the paper was striking. In all of journalism, there is no more straitlaced or respectable organ than the *Wall Street Journal*, and it is, after all, a business publication. Ovitz was known for saying that he viewed himself as a businessman and not a celebrity of any kind, yet when asked for some comments by these sober and responsible editors, he would not speak on the record. He would not answer his critics but ignore them. He would not defend his past actions but plan new ones. He would not slow down for others.

In the future, Ovitz denied almost all requests for interviews and went far beyond this in his efforts to control his public image. He bought up existing photographs of himself—and never wanted to have his picture taken while he was holding a drink. He let it be known to all of his colleagues and many of his clients that he did not want any of them talking about him to the papers or on TV; those acts could get you dismissed from CAA. When the *New York Times Magazine* wrote a story about Ovitz in July 1989, he first refused to talk to that paper's reporter, then changed his mind at the last moment, then agreed to be interviewed, and then wanted to answer only a few specific questions. Even heads of state seldom try to exert this kind of influence over the inquiring minds of journalists; they simply accept them as a necessary evil and talk to them once in a while.

Ovitz had risen to the top by being stealthy; in the years ahead, he would become even more secretive. It was easier to travel through airports to clandestine meetings if people did not recognize you. It was simpler to hold a surreptitious rendezvous in a hotel if no one could identify your face. It was better to use indirection or deception than to confront your attackers head on. He was becoming more myth than man.

"I was having lunch one day in a restaurant," says a screenwriter in West L.A., "when someone bumped into the back of my chair. I turned around and saw Ovitz and Tom Cruise. It was Ovitz who'd run into my chair, and he began apologizing to me profusely. For quite a while, that was my claim to fame in town: Michael Ovitz had apologized to me."

Ovitz's behavior with journalists raises complicated questions with no easy answers. On the one hand, his craving for privacy and his refusal to perform in the modern American celebrity circus is admirable. On the other hand, he helped create that circus, so how can he, of all people, expect to avoid his turn in the center ring? Some people describe him as being painfully shy of publicity and almost terrified in the face of it. Others, including David Geffen, have accused him of blatantly using reporters to plant newspaper leaks that undermine his rivals and further his own goals—and help him get back at those whom he feels have hurt him in the past.

One wonders if Ovitz has any understanding of journalism itself or of the people who practice it. Or does he regard it merely as another tool that can be used to generate additional power and money?

His attitude toward the press may involve a kind of super-subtle riddle that fits in with his entire crypto-Japanese-warrior approach to the movie business: If in Hollywood illusion is reality, and this illusion brings pleasure to millions and riches to some, and keeps many people from having to work at more dismal jobs, then why should anyone be interested in trying to look through the magic mirror? Why should any reporter attempt to expose, behind all those attractive and gifted thespians and all those dramatic or humorous scenes up there on the big screen, a lot of business people sitting in a lot of offices screaming at one another about a lot of money? Why demystify the game when you don't have to?

Or perhaps all of that is much too complicated, and the reality is quite simple. Perhaps, in the words of one CAA employee, "Michael just hates for anyone to know what he's up to."

14

In 1988, *Spy* magazine (which once took great delight in revealing Ovitz's secrets) got hold of the closely guarded CAA client list and published it in its September issue. By this time, Creative Artists had nearly sixty agents and seven hundred people on its talent roster. The list detailed what everyone in the entertainment business already knew: CAA had become the dominant force in Hollywood. Its directors included Richard Attenborough, Peter Bogdanovich, Jonathan Demme, Ron Howard, John Hughes, James Ivory, David Lynch, Rob Reiner, and Oliver Stone. Its catalogue of movie stars was more impressive than ever: Sean Connery, Robert De Niro, Chevy Chase, Danny De Vito, Whoopi Goldberg, Jessica Lange, Glenn Close, Bette Midler, Demi Moore, Michael

Douglas, Robert Downey Jr., Robin Williams, Sally Field, Dennis Hopper, Michael Keaton, Val Kilmer, Sean Penn, Al Pacino, and Sharon Stone, plus up-and-coming actresses Courtney Cox and Elisabeth Shue. The CAA music department, in addition to representing Michael Jackson, Madonna, and Barbra Streisand, had signed Michael Bolton, John Cougar Mellencamp, the Kinks, Joni Mitchell, Roy Orbison, Dolly Parton, Prince, Eric Clapton, and ZZ Top. The agency also repped composer Philip Glass.

Yet the preponderance of clients were not directors or actors or musicians but writers whose names were mostly unfamiliar to those outside the film industry. Roughly 250 of the people on the list fell into this category, and only a few stood out: Jackie Collins, Michael Crichton, William Goldman, Stephen King, and Gore Vidal. The rest stayed busy churning out the scripts that the stars wanted to read first. Ovitz may have never wanted to be a story himself, but he had built his agency on the foundation of those who created original stories, and the other clients had followed.

Ovitz had conquered Hollywood, and rumors were starting to circulate that he was growing increasingly tired of agenting and coddling film stars; he wanted to use his talents on a larger stage. Just as he'd cultivated Marty Baum and Steve Roth a decade earlier before taking CAA into the movie business, and just as he'd sought the help of Barbara Guggenheim and Arnold Glimcher when entering the world of art collecting, he now wanted to know more about high finance and the loftier reaches of entertainment mergers and acquisitions. Naturally, he went looking for the best teacher he could find.

Herbert Allen was the chief executive officer of Allen & Company, an investment banking firm with a Fifth Avenue address. Though not the largest institution of its kind in Manhattan, Allen & Company was deeply respected within the financial community, and Allen himself was acclaimed as the nation's most important fiscal adviser to the communications and entertainment industries. Allen's clients included Rupert Murdoch, the CEO of the News Corporation; Barry Diller, the former chairman of Paramount Pictures and Fox; John Malone, the CEO of Tele-

Communications, Inc., the largest cable company in the world; and Sumner Redstone, whom Allen had helped acquire Viacom in 1987. Allen did not waste words and shunned the spotlight. He was drawn to show biz people, while giving the appearance of breathing more substantial air than they did. He and Ovitz had a lot in common.

A growing number of people in Ovitz's life now referred to him, not in a derogatory manner, as a "sponge," bent on soaking up every drop of information he could on the subject he'd lately turned his attention to. He'd once called Morton Janklow from Los Angeles every week in order to grab the man's attention and convince him to do business with CAA. He'd pestered Arnold Glimcher with arcane questions about art and art history, until he'd worn out the gallery owner. When he began querying Herbert Allen, it wasn't unusual for Ovitz to speak to his new tutor, three thousand miles to the east, every day.

Allen was six years older than Ovitz, and his connections in show business and corporate boardrooms were impeccable. Back in the 1960s, he'd met Ray Stark, a former Hollywood agent who'd turned to producing and was behind such hits as *Funny Girl* and *The Way We Were*. Many of Stark's films had been made for Columbia Pictures, which in the 1970s had a long and distinguished history but was becoming one of the industry's troubled children. In 1973, Stark suggested that Allen invest in Columbia, and Allen not only bought nearly 7 percent of the studio's stock, he also became its chairman of the board. He hired one of his friends, Alan Hirschfield, to run the entire Columbia Corporation, and then hired one of Stark's acquaintances, David Begelman, who had been Barbra Streisand's agent, to run the studio.

In 1977, Allen and Stark were confronted with the fact that Begelman had forged signatures on three Columbia checks worth a total of $40,000. The following year, Begelman was forced out of Columbia, and his behavior and firing created a major scandal (which became the subject of David McClintick's bestselling book *Indecent Exposure*). In the early 1980s, Donald Keough, the president of Coca-Cola, came to Allen and told him that the soft-drink company was interested in getting into the entertainment business. Allen warned Keough of the difficulties outsiders often ran into when they made large investments in the highly unpredictable film industry, but Coca-Cola was determined to take the plunge. In March 1982, Allen sold the studio to the soft-drink empire and became friends with Coke's chief executive officer, Robert Goizueta. Allen then joined the corporation's board of directors, predicting that the marriage of Coke and Columbia would be a great union for all.

The marriage did not last. Half a decade after buying Columbia, Coca-Cola had grown weary of throwing money at the studio and was looking for a buyer for its unruly Hollywood investment. Again, they turned to Allen for advice. By now, Japanese investors were extremely interested in buying their way into show business.

The pioneer in this regard was the Sony Corporation. In 1987, Sony had purchased CBS Records for $2 billion, but its appetite for American entertainment companies was barely whetted. It wanted to own a movie studio. Sony had become successful peddling the "hardware" of the entertainment industry—videocassette recorders, radios, and other electronic devices—and now wanted to sell the more glamorous "software": the music and films themselves.

At this time, the head of CBS Records was Walter Yetnikoff; in his corporate negotiations, Yetnikoff was represented by Michael Ovitz. In 1988, when Sony began making overtures to buy the Columbia/TriStar Studios, Herb Allen was brought in as an adviser to the deal, and, through Yetnikoff, Ovitz was also hired as a consultant. While he did not play a major role in the negotiations that led to Sony's $3.4 billion acquisition of Columbia/TriStar in 1989 (the largest foreign purchase ever of an American corporate entity), Ovitz tirelessly observed the process and filed away his conclusions for future use. He also made a very good impression on the bankers from the Blackstone Group, the investment banking firm that handled the sale, and an even greater impression on the Japanese buyers.

If the bankers were astonished that a Hollywood agent was so knowledgeable about their world, the Sony executives were awed by Ovitz. It wasn't just that, after more than a decade of studying their culture, he understood and respected their manners and mores. It wasn't just that he was drawn to "things Oriental," as I. M. Pei had once said about him. It was also that he was meeting the Japanese at exactly the right moment to wow them. In 1988 *Rain Man*, a film starring CAA clients Tom Cruise and Dustin Hoffman, was released. From its infancy, Ovitz had seen the movie's potential and worked harder than anyone else to hold the project together after several scriptwriters and other film personnel had come and gone. The experience had been tumultuous, but Ovitz had never let it falter. Then, in his final act before *Rain Man* opened, he persuaded MGM, the studio that made the film, to show it in more theaters than they'd planned. This last-minute change in strategy considerably boosted the movie's chances for success.

When Ovitz met with the officials from Sony, he talked with them at length about the creation, promotion, and advertising for *Rain Man*. He told them about his superstar clients who were appearing in the film. He predicted that the picture was going to be a blockbuster—and it was. Ovitz generated the impression, intentionally or not, that the movie business was not very different from the "hardware" enterprise that Sony had already mastered. Perhaps Sony could run a film studio the same way it ran its electronics divisions: carefully, patiently, with an emphasis on research and development, and by consensus. Or could they?

"After a deal is done with the Japanese," says a real estate agent in L.A., "one person in their organization can't make a decision about anything, so business moves forward very slowly. They all have to agree on something before announcing their plans and then implementing them. Americans can't handle this, especially those in the entertainment field, where everything is about change and capitalizing on the latest trends. By the time the Japanese make up their minds about something, one trend has already passed and another one is on the horizon. Their incredible attention to detail has served them very well in the industries they understand, like electronics, but it doesn't translate into some other areas."

Following Sony's purchase of Columbia/TriStar, one thing their leadership quickly reached consensus on was that they wanted Michael Ovitz to run their new studio. And he did not discourage their pursuit. Being romanced by the Japanese owners of a movie studio fit very well into his long-range view of himself. For years, Hollywood insiders had been saying that Ovitz's role model had never been a superagent from the past, like Freddie Fields or Stan Kamen, but a man who'd made an enormously successful transition from agent to studio head, Lew Wasserman, the aging head of MCA/Universal and the most respected name in the entertainment business.

Ovitz, the scuttlebutt had it, wanted to be the next Wasserman—the next show biz godfather. Antitrust laws would keep him from working for a studio and an agency simultaneously, so he would have to leave CAA to realize this dream. Some people said he wasn't ready to make this move—the agency's new headquarters hadn't even been completed—but others said he was itching to make the jump. After all, talent agents, no matter what else they are, are slaves to the needs and desires and whims of their most powerful clients.

Sony's lawyers got busy putting together the paperwork that would have allowed the agent to sell his majority stake in CAA and take over Columbia/TriStar; the code name for Ovitz in the proposals was "Superman." Sony came up with a deal that would have paid the agent an estimated $100 million. Ovitz came back with a reported $200 million counteroffer that would have given him control not only of the movie studio but also of CBS's record division, the cash cow of Sony's U.S. entertainment holdings.

The Japanese, despite their obvious admiration for "Superman," passed.

In 1989, Sony paid $700 million to lure two film executives, Peter Guber and Jon Peters, away from Warner Bros. to run Columbia/TriStar. Peters, a former hairdresser and paramour of Barbra Streisand, was known for his extravagant spending (in 1991, he spent two months in Aspen refurbishing his lodge and stocking the surrounding grounds with reindeer and llamas). Guber eventually grew so paranoid about working for Sony that he believed his employers had bugged his office. Peters and Guber made a series of box-office bombs, including *Gladiator, Lost in Yonkers,* and *Last Action Hero,* yet they also proved that when one reaches a high enough level in certain corporate structures, there is no such thing as failure. In 1991, Peters was forced out of the studio, but his exit was sweetened by a $30 million production deal.

After Sony hired Guber and Peters, Ovitz was annoyed that the corporation had rejected his offer in favor of two people who were flamboyant spendthrifts and far less astute businessmen than he was. He subsequently used his influence in the film industry to dampen Columbia's opportunities for success. CAA and the studio fought over the film project *Mistress of the Seas*, generated by CAA client Geena Davis and her husband, Renny Harlin. It eventually became the disastrous *Cutthroat Island*. And they quarreled over CAA's refusal to let Bill Murray appear in Columbia's *Road to Wellville*, a movie that cost $30 million and grossed a fifth of that amount.

In 1994, Sony finally acknowledged that it had badly overpaid for Columbia/TriStar and took a $2.7 billion write-off and a $150 million operating loss on the property. That was also the year that the studio finally let Guber go, after giving him a $20 million pay-out and a $200 million production deal. In the mid-1990s, Guber and Ovitz were still sniping at one another from a distance, and Guber sometimes intensified the old hard feelings by making a point of inviting the Young Turks at CAA to his retreat in Aspen.

Ovitz took this personally.

15

The year 1989 was one of almost complete triumph for Ovitz. Four films playing at its start—*Rain Man, Scrooged, Mississippi Burning*, and *Twins*—were CAA-driven and would gross almost $400 million. That spring, Ovitz's work on *Rain Man* was repeatedly praised from the stage of the Academy Awards ceremony, where the movie won four Oscars. During their acceptance speeches, the film's producer, Mark Johnson, and its director,

Barry Levinson, expressed their gratitude to the agent for his efforts on the picture's behalf.

In his fumblingly charming way, *Rain Man*'s biggest star, Dustin Hoffman, said, "Thank you. It's a—thank you very much ... I thank the Academy for your support and I—and I also thank Tom Hanks and Max Von Sydow and James Olmos and—and my good friend, Gene Hackman, for their wonderful work, even if they didn't vote for me. I didn't vote for you guys, either ... I thank my agent, Mike Ovitz ... for making this project stick with glue when it was falling apart ..."

Here in the land of fables, where some dreams really do come true, the boy who'd grown up in the Valley and traveled south over the hills, to where the stars lived in big houses, had clearly become the king.

In September 1989, Ovitz, Haber, Meyer, and CFO Robert Goldman obtained the permanent financing for their new building, a $21 million loan from the Equitable Life Assurance Society in New York, and the 57,000-square-foot CAA headquarters was now open for business. It stood as the symbol of Ovitz's preeminence in the talent agency field. The structure was quietly ostentatious, designed to make a statement about success, money, taste, sophistication, and one man's desire to leave his lasting mark on the world of entertainment and Beverly Hills.

"The new building was always Michael's baby," says a CAA employee. "You could just see that in the way he looked at it."

As Ovitz's influence spread throughout show business, he would often be compared to Jay Gatsby, the principal character in *The Great Gatsby*, F. Scott Fitzgerald's classic novel of 1925. The fictional Gatsby, a refugee from the Midwest, has fled the heartland and reinvented himself as a wealthy bon vivant on Long Island. He eventually comes to a bad end in his own swimming pool, but not before impressing any number of people with the grand manner in which he lived.

The comparison between Ovitz and Gatsby is not exact but there are some similarities. Both men placed a premium on style. Ovitz had reinvented the agenting business and was continually in the process of reinventing himself. When his name began appearing in *Who's Who in the World*, he had one of the shortest entries; reading it gave one no idea of where he was born or grew up, for instance. Like Gatsby's, his profound desire to expand his horizons and better himself is both admirable and touching. He clearly wanted to be invited to the biggest and best parties ever held, and he also wanted to invite corporate financiers and politicians into his new building, where they could schmooze the man who schmoozed the stars, seeking endorsements and money from Hollywood's glamor pool.

In 1989, Ovitz chaired a benefit for Senator Bill Bradley and raised $750,000 for the Democrat from New Jersey. A few years later, the invitee would be Bill Clinton, and the ante would go into the millions. Like Dustin Hoffman when he accepted the Academy Award, President Clinton would warmly praise the agent and extend him his gratitude for favors rendered on his behalf.

I. M. Pei had solved his biggest architectural problem at CAA's new home by putting the front door near Lasky Drive, a tree-lined stretch of pavement that diagonally approaches the intersection of Little Santa Monica and Wilshire boulevards. Lasky was relatively quiet and isolated, perfect for the stretch-limousine drivers who could park next to the curb without impeding the flow of traffic and lean calmly against their vehicles while their famous passengers went inside and talked business with their agents.

The building, three stories high with a glass-and-beige-marble exterior, followed the curve of the intersection. At a glance, it conjured up a seashell with black windows. Both the address—9830 Wilshire Boulevard—and the sign reading CREATIVE ARTISTS AGENCY were in such small letters and so discreetly placed that one could easily stroll past without even noticing them. Unlike the boxy William Morris headquarters, just a few blocks to the east, this structure was rounded and feminine, soft in color and surrounded on one side by a bed of geraniums. It resembled a contemporary art museum, which in some ways it would become.

Critics were generally wowed by the new CAA building. Carter Wiseman, the architectural critic for *New York* magazine and the author of *I. M. Pei: A Profile in Architecture*, called it a "three-story gem." The CAA headquarters, he wrote, "generated an assemblage of geometric forms that recalled those of the Kennedy Library [in Boston]. . . . The discrete shapes fitted comfortably into their surroundings, adding considerable elegance to the fragmented neighborhood. The balconies overlooking the atrium of CAA honored the client's request that the architecture encourage interaction among members of the staff, who were used to impromptu encounters."

CAA's entrance was placed well back from the street, and a visitor walked through clean glass doors into a huge lobby. Fifty-seven feet high, it had travertined walls and an atrium letting in streams of light. In one direction was a sprawling ficus tree, and to the right and left were whimsical pieces of modern sculpture, one by John Chamberlain and the other by Joel Shapiro. Hanging in the middle of the lobby, just under the atrium, was a vast painting by Roy Lichtenstein, entitled *Bauhaus Stairway: The Large Version*. The work was twenty-seven feet high and cost a reported $2 million; Lichtenstein and four assistants had worked on the painting, on site, for a month. In this otherwise monochromatically beige environment, the Lichtenstein was bright and bold—an arresting sheet of colorful dots, sharp lines, and geometric shapes, with people climbing uncertainly upward through a deconstructed landscape.

The upstairs walls would eventually hold Japanese calligraphy and modern works by Jim Dine, Chuck Close, and Claes Oldenburg, as well as Andy Warhol's *Marilyn*. The building would feature a painting by Diana Levinson, the wife of director Barry Levinson, a CAA client, and two prints by Don Gummer, the husband of another CAA client, Meryl Streep. The headquarters even had its own curator.

By far the most striking thing about 9830 Wilshire Boulevard was the size and emptiness of the lobby. It took up nearly a third of the entire structure and could be criticized as a colossal waste of exorbitantly priced square footage. But that would miss the point. The lobby provided a remarkable feeling of openness and freedom lacking in most modern buildings. This space reinforced the notion that one was not just entering another enclosed, practical business environment; one was having an aesthetic experience that had been carefully designed down to the very last detail. "Mike was after beauty," says one of Ovitz's associates, "and he made the building so that his employees would want to come there to work each day."

The lobby had two small couches and a glass table holding *Daily Variety* and the *Hollywood Reporter*. While waiting on one of these sofas, a visitor might feel dwarfed by the surroundings, but the scenery was always enjoyable. Fresh flowers sat on the receptionist's desk, and the handsome security personnel walking the floor were superbly tailored. Phones constantly rang and echoed through empty space. In the hallways, well-dressed, well-coiffed, and congenial young people moved in and out of doors, conveying a sense of purpose, confidence, and excitement, bringing to mind a hive where the workers carried not pollen but pieces of information.

The building had valet parking in the basement, and as the day unfolded, the stalls would gradually fill up with BMWs and Mercedeses, most of them dark, like so many horses lined up and anxious to gallop. Agents could get their vehicles washed on the premises just as easily as they could get a haircut or a manicure, while sitting in the office and returning phone calls. A dry-cleaning service picked up and dropped off clothes.

The first floor held a screening room for viewing yet-to-be released movies. It also held an industrial-sized kitchen, complete with a cook and a staff that prepared and served meals for the executives and their guests. Off to one side was CAA's music department, which was considered something of a rebel factory. Its agents were regarded as the bad boys and girls of the company— "the kids of the joint," says a former CAA employee. "They wore shorter skirts, leather jackets, and bigger earrings than anyone else there. They had their own code, and management tended to give them a wider berth."

The more senior agents worked on the second floor, and up above them, appropriately enough, was Ovitz himself. In his sparsely furnished office, he kept a small, beautiful bowl filled with floating rose petals, Japanese-style. When he spoke on the telephone, he wore headphones tightly clamped to his ears and spoke very softly into the mouthpiece, so that no one could hear what either he or the other party was saying.

To understand telephone protocol in Los Angeles is to understand something important about show business. Elaborate computerized logs are kept every day by secretaries, detailing to whom the boss "owes" calls and who "owes" him. It lists who has "returned" and who has thus far failed to call back. It lists the time of each call, the number of occasions on which that person has phoned before, and the subject matter that the caller wants to discuss.

The creation of new phone technology has only made the system more exotic. A Hollywood secretary can now call someone to say that her boss is traveling in his car and that as soon as he gets out of the tunnel he's driving through she will "patch you in" to his vehicle. She might ask you not to reveal certain things during cellular-phone conversations because the technology facilitates electronic eavesdropping. Or she will tell you that her boss is flying over Lake Michigan, but he's in the process of "returning" and, if he has enough time, will certainly get to you before the plane lands.

Hanging up a cellular phone does not always immediately break the connection, and more than one Hollywood executive has insisted that his or her assistant stay on the line following a cellular conversation, in order to determine if the other party is now saying something nasty about the boss.

"I don't think that when the men who run the entertainment business get out of bed in the morning, they feel much more powerful than the rest of us," says a longtime L.A. secretary. "I think they have the same insecurities about themselves that we all do. But then they come into the office and start making calls, one right after the other, and leaving messages. The ability to get others to talk to you, or to get them to call you back, reassures these men that they really are connected to the world and really are important. I don't know what they would do without the phone."

Ovitz's phone manner had become part of his mystique. He not only spoke very quietly but was a fanatically observant listener, usually taking notes in his small, swift handwriting. He tended to ask more questions than he answered. One of his favorite tactics was to tell the other party that he was confused about one thing or another, then seek an explanation for his confusion, which usually resulted in speakers giving away more information than they had ever intended to. The idea, of course, was to get people to solve your problem while they believed they were solving their own.

Ovitz had been honing his phone technique for years. He knew that you had to call some people even when you didn't have a lot to say, just to stay in touch, because the day would come when there would be business on the line, and you couldn't make it look as if the only reason you ever dialed their number was monetary. The phone conquered space and allowed him to sustain hundreds of friendships and relationships, which would be at the heart of many of his future deals.

The big difference these days was that instead of calling across town to learn more about a movie star's business manager or what was taking place that evening at a soundstage at one of the networks, now he was routinely calling New York and reaching across the oceans to financial contacts throughout Europe and to the heads of companies in the Far East. His circle of friends was getting larger all the time, along with his phone bill, but he loved doing business this way.

Up in his office in the new building, sitting next to the rose petals, he was invisible to those he was speaking to, and he could travel around the world at the speed of light.

16

The CAA machine was not only well oiled, but it now had a setting that matched Ovitz's vision of the agency business, and the people who powered it—from mailroom trainees to secretaries to agents to clients—were among the industry's best. Some of the trainees had attended Ivy League universities, but they were still treated like fraternity pledges.

"I got up every weekday at six A.M. and started thinking about my job," says a trainee who was at CAA when the new building opened. "One of my first tasks was to go to Gelson's [a high-toned supermarket near the agency] and buy Pepperidge Farm cookies, Heinekens, and popcorn for my bosses. Each agent had his favorite things to eat and drink, and I bought them these goodies five days a week. I'd spend an hour doing this and arrive at work around eight o'clock. I'd stock their refrigerators and then go down to the mailroom and sort letters for a while. About nine-thirty or ten, the agents would start to roll in. They'd usually been out with stars or other agents the night before.

"I was making four and a half dollars an hour, but getting in a lot of overtime. The pay was shitty, but there were some perks. The first few times you get on an elevator with Kevin Costner, it's a big thrill. After that, it's just normal. One day, David Geffen walked up to my desk and said, 'Tell him [the trainee's boss] I'm here.' He didn't feel any need to say who he was, and he just assumed that I would know. Fortunately, I recognized him, but I thought that was a bit much.

"In the morning, after sorting mail, I would run flowers or champagne all over town. We gave out a lot of gifts. I might deliver cigars to Robin Williams or roses to Whoopi Goldberg. Then I would come back to the office and sort more mail. Sometimes if I was really in the mood to get ahead, I might call up an attractive young woman and tell her to go out with one of my older, hornier bosses. Sometimes she would say yes. Doing these sorts of personal favors for others helped.

"I would eat lunch on the run, wherever I could. Usually it was in my car, which was not a BMW. In the afternoon, I would deliver scripts to actors and actresses or drop things off at the studios. The agents always wanted you to do their personal errands—like paying bills or picking up something outside the building—and the hard part was saying no to them. You would overcommit and then have to work very late. I would usually get home around nine-thirty or ten, unless an agent asked me to go with him to a party. You had to say yes. Then I would get home around midnight and wake up at six A.M. the next morning and start the cycle all over again. Do this for two years and you'll be nuts."

CAA secretaries—who almost never became trainees—sat outside the agents' offices at workstations. A woman who occupied one of them in the late 1980s says, "One afternoon, I had Gore Vidal, Faye Dunaway, and Sidney Sheldon all on hold at the same time. Where else could you do that except Creative Artists Agency? The place always had the feel of controlled pandemonium. It had excellent office managers and was easily the best-run place I've ever worked, but it was very demanding. I'd get there at eight-thirty in the morning and stay until eight-thirty at night, helping the agents return their phone calls while they were driving home and I was sitting in the office doing the dialing.

"Ovitz set the tone in the building, and it was pervasive. It was a very quiet place. People spoke more softly than in most other offices. They kept their desks orderly, and you just didn't see piles of paper stacked up everywhere. Secretaries weren't encouraged to decorate their workstations. If they gave you a plant, they wanted you to put it on the corner of your desk and leave it right there. I didn't even feel comfortable putting my birthday cards on my desk. I always sensed that the neatness police were watching me. If something got broken, like a glass on the floor, it was cleaned up within moments. The swiftness and efficiency of this always amazed me. The bosses just didn't like to see messes or mistakes of any kind. I would get shrieked at for making a typo.

"No one ran in the halls, and there was a very strict unwritten dress code, except for the kids in the music department. The men wore dark suits, and the women had on chic, sophisticated business outfits. I was very careful about my clothing. Everything was very controlled, in that kind of subtle Japanese way. The strangest thing about the place was that they didn't have to spell out any of the behavioral codes I'm talking about. You just got the message."

The woman now works in publishing. "The CAA message was that the people above you are in control of themselves and you'd better be too. When the people you work for are in control of themselves, everything operates better. It was a great place to work, but I like where I am now better. It just feels more human here."

While the machine was running smoothly, the boss was largely free to concentrate on his own agenda. On weekdays, he arose very early, did a lengthy session on his exercise bicycle or performed a martial arts workout, cleaned up, covered himself in Armani, stepped into his BMW, and left the house for a power breakfast at the Hotel Bel Air or one of his other favorite haunts. He made a religion of promptness. If he said he would be somewhere at seven-thirty A.M., he would be there at seven-thirty; if he was two minutes late, he would offer a formal apology.

After arriving at the office, he would make a series of phone calls, unless he had to attend the regular Monday and Wednesday staff meetings. If he was generally very quiet on the telephone, his employees did not always find him so at these biweekly gatherings. Over the years, he and Ron Meyer had put together an effective good cop/bad cop routine, which they occasionally brought forth at the meetings. Sometimes, after a development that appeared to go against CAA, Ovitz would blow up and yell briefly, telling the staff that they'd missed a brilliant opportunity; then he would stomp out of the room. Meyer would gently inform everyone that Mike was just a little upset at the moment and that everything would function more smoothly and everyone would feel a lot better if they could prevent the boss from experiencing any more of these disappointments. No one wanted to see him get any angrier, did they?

But Ovitz was unpredictable. At other times, in nearly identical circumstances, he would tell the troops that in six months what had looked like total failure would evolve into a triumph from another direction; so just keep working and the future might surprise you. Keep making phone calls to your clients and your prospective clients. Keep offering your services. If you think your competitor is making two calls a day on this matter, you make four. Or six. Or more.

Ovitz would eat a power lunch at the Grill or the Bistro Garden or Locanda Veneta, then return to the office for more meetings and phone calls. In the evenings, the power dinner might be at Le Dome or Morton's or Spago. Time management was crucial to him, but not every moment was consumed with work. Some days he left the building early to attend his sons' Little League games or his daughter's school functions. He made a point of being with his children, going to Disneyland and taking family vacations to the Colorado mountains or the Bahamas. He consciously strived for *wa*—for harmony and balance—not just in the building he'd created but in his own life. It was easier to relax when you knew that others were doing what you'd asked them to do.

"When we wanted a client, we didn't just call and call and call." Says a former CAA employee, "We sent gifts and cards. Birthday cards, hand delivered to the other side of town on the weekends, if that's when the birthday fell. We sent gifts to the talent and to their families and children, especially at Christmastime. We sent the kids dolls and ten-speed bikes and beautiful, elaborate toys.

"I'd never seen anything like what happened there during the holiday season. We sent out hundreds and hundreds of presents. Expensive things. Huge boxes of chocolates and twenty-pound containers of brownies. Clothes and incredible flower arrangements and tchotchkes. And the gifts we received. One year Dustin Hoffman sent everyone a basket from Crabtree and Evelyn. It was just unbelievable the amount of money that flowed in and out of that place."

Many clients had never seen anything quite like the new CAA building or like CAA itself, for that matter. Says a screenwriter in Beverly Hills: "Years ago, I came to L.A. from the Midwest. I'd written a couple of scripts and needed an agent to sell them for me. I called a few agencies cold and then went to my first meeting with one. As I'm sitting there talking with this guy, I can hear his partner arguing with one of their clients in the next room. They start yelling at one another, and the client is threatening to kill the agent. They get into a fistfight, and bodies start bouncing off the walls. The man I was talking to didn't seem to notice the brawl next door. This must have gone on all the time there.

"The next agency I went to, an older man welcomed me into his office, but when I began speaking, he continued watching a football game that was being televised on a set above my head. The sound was turned off, but he kept looking at the pictures. As I told him who I was and what I wanted to do, he never said a word and never took his eyes off the game. I felt invisible. I kept talking, and finally I said that one of Jane Fonda's people was interested in something I'd written. He suddenly raised his hand, reached into his desk, pulled out a card, and slid it toward me. 'When you take a meeting with them,' he said, 'tell them I represent you.'

"I eventually signed with ICM. They were much better than anything I'd been involved with in the past, but I felt a little uncomfortable there. Some of the people were screamers, and one of them threw a lacrosse ball against the wall during our meetings. They accused me of not generating enough business for them, but they didn't offer me any real help. And some of their suggestions were not good.

"A couple of years passed, and CAA contacted me. I'm a loyal person and turned them down. Then things started getting worse at ICM. When I'd ask to visit the set during the production of something I'd written, I'd be told, 'You don't want to do that.' Or, 'You don't want to meet so and so.' I'd ask why not and they'd say, 'You just don't.' After a while I figured out that they didn't want me to meet this person because he or she had a better agent than I did.

"Finally, I approached CAA. I called them on a Friday, and we had a meeting the next Monday. They knew more about my career than I did, and we had an agreement in place by the end of that week. I never met Ovitz before signing their papers, but it was almost as if he was there in the halls and the meetings and in the words and expressions of the people who worked for him. You could feel his presence everywhere.

"They wanted me to sign up for two years, but I agreed to only a one-year deal. The way the agreement operates is that if they can't find you work within ninety days, the papers are voided. At the start, they said to me, 'What do you want to do?' I said, 'I'm interested in a miniseries.' Three days later, they had one for me, and it wasn't schlock. It was a quality story for one of the networks. They knew everything about what was available, and they put it right in my hand. I was astounded. They had power, but beyond that they had incredible cooperation among themselves.

"At ICM, I'd worked with one agent. At CAA, they gave me three, and the three were there to help me. They asked me questions and they offered me good advice, not just on money issues but on creative ones as well. They told me what would make something a better script with broader appeal. They told me which meetings to take and which ones were a waste of time. They answered my questions and then set up these meetings for me. The whole thing was seamless.

"When they didn't know something, they made inquiries about it, and they all shared information. The ego was not controlling these people, at least not when they were around me. Maybe at night, when they were having a drink together, that stuff came out, but during working hours we were a team, and they were utterly focused on moving my career ahead. They also had a sense of humor about things and could laugh at the business. In some places in Hollywood, there's a desperation underlying people's feelings, or the sense that everything is going to fall apart with the next phone call. CAA was calm. It was what I'd always thought an agency should be, but I didn't think that such a company existed. They gave me the feeling that I was going to be with them over a period of time and we were both going to make money.

"This will sound strange, but when I think about CAA, I think about ice hockey. In that sport, there's something called a Zamboni machine. It comes out during the intermissions of a game and cleans the ice. It smooths everything out so that the players can skate better and faster and not get hurt. It does the dirty work so the hockey stars can perform their best and get the glory. CAA is like a huge Zamboni."

"Ovitz began with the idea of straightening up a mess," says a long-time CAA watcher. "He does not like to be confused, so he tried to bring clarity to every part of our business. He saw a way to order the chaos around him, and he acted like a magnet for the chaos of others. Actors and writers and performers—people like a David Letterman—were drawn to him because they wanted to feel less chaos in their own lives. If you were confused, he offered you answers. If you were uncertain, he offered you confidence. If you were afraid, he volunteered to manage your fears for you. If you felt disorder within yourself, you wanted someone who could order it for you.

"Many people have tried to do things like this, but they don't possess the inner clarity or discipline that Ovitz does. The secrets at CAA were all about Mike's relationship with Mike. All about not giving in to your fears, not letting them control you, not setting unnecessary limitations on yourself, not letting yourself be defined by the past. He wasn't just building an agency, he was showing people a new way of doing business. He was saying, 'If you think you can make money by being selfish and out of control, let me show you what can do by being a team player and managing yourself better.'

"The reason that Ovitz never comes across in public as having a personality is that he was always sublimating it to serve this larger cause. At home, I'm sure that he's very much of a human being, but at work he functioned more like an idea or a principle. Violate the principle, and you suffered.

"He created the impression that he had all the answers. The fact is that they were the right answers—for him. He found a level of self-management that most of us never achieve, and money just seemed to follow whatever he did. He won't talk about any of this, because basically he's a modest man. You can't tell people, 'I've learned to do things that you haven't even thought about doing.' That's very off-putting, so he just sits there and remains silent."

17

In July 1989, just before the new CAA building opened, Ovitz finally broke his long-standing silence vis-à-vis the media and spoke to the *Los Angeles Times*. He'd heard the ugly rumors going around about his agency: he had "attack teams" that attempted to hurt the careers of those who'd left CAA for another company; that his people were called "secret agents," and CAA was sometimes referred to in Hollywood as "CIA"; he was running a kind of cult factory over on Wilshire Boulevard, turning out samurai clones of himself; ICM and William Morris were deeply resentful toward CAA and even felt that Ovitz was trying to put other agencies out of business; he'd instituted a reign of terror in the entertainment industry, which no one dared criticize or challenge.

Ovitz seemed baffled by such accusations against him and his company. Didn't he try to encourage a family atmosphere with family values inside his business? Wouldn't the new building be enlivened in the afternoons when nannies brought children into the office for visits with their mothers and fathers? Wouldn't there be a huge Christmas tree in the lobby each holiday season, surrounded by presents for these kids? Didn't Ovitz himself make a point of hand-writing a letter to each CAA secretary who decided to leave the company and take another job? Didn't he insist on putting the needs of others first in his business, just as Phil Weltman had taught him to do? Hadn't he done everything possible to ensure that working for his agency would be a pleasant and rewarding experience? Hadn't he given many, many people their start in the entertainment business and helped them achieve vast success and wealth? Why didn't others see his organization as he did?

At the end of his session with the *Times* interviewer, he said that he wanted to add something and then gave an impromptu speech, no doubt the most spontaneous thing he'd ever done in front of a reporter. His words obviously carried some anger and frustration, but they were intriguing mostly because of their simplicity. It was as if at the very center of the man there was almost no complexity or confusion, as if he held a perfectly clear vision of what should be done and how to do it. Results were what mattered, and they were astoundingly good.

This was as close to a statement from the heart about CAA as he'd ever made in public. "We have been accused of being everything under the sun," he told the *Times*. "I read the other day that people say there are 'Moonies' here. The reality is that people here are as individual as any human being you'll ever meet, and they are more interesting than most people you might meet in our business.

"They are really well-rounded people. They are good people. They are people you could have a meal with and whose company you would enjoy. They are people you can trust. They are people if, God forbid, your child was sick, you could call in the middle of the night and they would be there.

"Now, if you were a studio executive, and you had a relationship with somebody like that, I can give you ten people who will tell you that is a bad thing, for a studio executive to call one of the agents in this company because his kid is sick. But you can't not have relationships with people. That is what this business is about. And you cannot have relationships with people [only] when everything is fair weather and great.

"It is like a marriage. And that is what we encourage here. We encourage long-term thinking.

"All of the conversations that take place externally about us, in my opinion, are predicated on the fact that we do not give out information. Yes, we do keep information very quiet. We have such delicate information, and it is not anyone's business. We do not share our clients' business. We just do not. Even between clients we do not share it, unless the client says we want you to tell so and so.

"We function very similarly to a law firm. We have very strong fiduciary obligations. And that makes us very unpopular with the press community. Because they feel we are withholding information. It is not about withholding information. It is about doing what is right.

"One of the pillars of this company is that we like to do what we feel is right and proper. That does not mean that everyone is going to agree with it. The reality is that most people will not, because it is going to get in their way. That is not our intention. Our intention is to service our clients. The clients really are in the limelight of what we do. Therefore, just by deductive reasoning, we should not be.

"All the credit we get for all the other things that we don't do, and all the criticism we get for all the things we do, is a by-product of the nonsense that permeates this community, which is a gossip-oriented community. We run a company that is antithetically opposed to gossip-mongering, so we have a built-in conflict going in the door. We are opposed to the whole nature of chatting up people's lives, whispering in people's ears about somebody's problems or gloating over someone's failures.

"We feel strongly that if people in the entertainment business worked toward each other's success rather than each other's demise, it would be a much better environment for all of us.

"From the day we started in the business, we have never understood this negative philosophy. We have never been able to figure it out, except that I guess it goes to the basic insecurity of everybody. If everyone rooted for each other, and collaborated more with each other, we would make better projects, there would be a wider marketplace."

On another occasion, Ovitz would be asked about the notion that many people regarded him as a "control freak" bent on wielding an iron hand in every corner of his own business and the entertainment industry in general. This time his response was a little sharper: if he were a passenger on an airplane, he said, and he had a choice, he would much prefer that the pilot be a control freak rather than a laid-back airline employee.

Control can be an excellent thing, of course, but without a touch of chaos, there will not be much creativity. And chaos, as Ovitz would soon find out, is always lurking, and sometimes named Joe.

18

From the start, Joe Eszterhas's life was the stuff of legend. He was born in Hungary on a straw bed in 1944, as the Russians were advancing on his family's country. His father, a Hungarian novelist, and his mother, who suffered from mental illness, spent part of World War II in refugee camps in Austria. They came to America when their son was six, and Joe grew up in poverty in Ohio. One day on a playground, he grabbed a baseball bat and clobbered a boy who'd earlier beaten him up. He went to juvenile hall for his troubles, but he'd made his point: he hated bullying and would resort to bullying himself when he felt it was necessary.

As a young man, Eszterhas began working as a reporter for the *Cleveland Plain Dealer.* There he proved himself as a gifted and imaginative journalist—so imaginative that an Ohio family brought an invasion-of-privacy suit against him and the paper after he quoted the mother in a story on flood victims, although she was not present when he conducted his interviews for the article. The *Plain Dealer* ended up paying $60,000 to the family, and Eszterhas soon found himself working at *Rolling Stone* in San Francisco.

It was 1971, and at the magazine the wildly subjective and colorful "gonzo journalism," led by its foremost practitioner, Dr. Hunter S. Thompson, was at its pinnacle. In this looser setting, Eszterhas had room to expand. Everyone at the magazine agreed that he was a gritty and excellent investigative reporter, but some *Rolling Stone* employees found it disconcerting that he liked to stab the conference table with a hunting knife while discussing his work with the editors. He wore a buckskin jacket, had flowing yellow hair, and would later confess that even though he had been married at the time, he had not missed out on the sexual revolution during his years at *Rolling Stone.* Eszterhas wrote superb pieces on bikers and dope, but like countless other young reporters, he wanted to move on to fortune and fame.

He began writing film scripts, one right after another, and finally, in 1978, one got made. *F.I.S.T.* starred Sylvester Stallone as Johnny Kovak, a union organizer passionately committed to helping the downtrodden and given to heated proletarian rhetoric, who inspires his fellow workers to rise up against the powers of management. *F.I.S.T.* got a modest response, but five years later, Eszterhas scored big with *Flashdance,* starring Jennifer Beals. Another working-class epic, *Flashdance* is about a beautiful welder who aspires to be a dancer. In order to finance her dreams, the welder works part-time as a stripper, but in the end she turns her back on the low life and moves on to better things. Eszterhas's general theme had already emerged and would be refined over time: the small guys (or gals) take on the big guys and fight relentlessly for justice.

Next came Eszterhas's courtroom thriller *Jagged Edge*, followed by the war-crime drama *The Music Box* and *Betrayed*, a very ambitious, provocative, and entangled story about the white supremacist movement. By now Eszterhas was a CAA screenwriter, and these three movies had starred, respectively, Glenn Close, Jessica Lange, and Debra Winger, all of them CAA clients. By the late eighties, Eszterhas was a legitimate Hollywood commodity, a prolific scribe who could command a million dollars a script. He not only created compelling screenplays but wrote what the industry calls "star vehicles," featuring the sort of glamorous, dramatic parts that attract big-name talent.

Eszterhas seemed larger than life. Heavyset and barrel-chested, with long, unruly hair, a blondish beard, a rumpled appearance, and a combative face, Eszterhas looked like the sort of man who, on a given afternoon, could either sit down and write elegiac poetry or walk into a biker bar and knock someone out. In America, there is nothing quite so alluring as a sensitive, intelligent person who harbors great wellsprings of violence. (Brando, De Niro, and Bruce Willis have enjoyed careers playing such characters.) All in all, he was a genuine Hollywood character, who got in one studio executive's face after another when fighting to maintain his vision of his scripts and would never go quietly into the mist.

In the 1970s, when he was starting out as a scriptwriter, Eszterhas had been represented by Guy McElwaine, a veteran of the Beverly Hills show business community and something of a character himself. In addition to being married eight times, McElwaine had been a senior vice president at Warner Bros., where he had worked on *All the President's Men*, and a talent agent at ICM, with a client list that included Steven Spielberg and Aaron Spelling. McElwaine had sold one of Eszterhas's early (and still unproduced) scripts, entitled *City Hall*, for the then-gargantuan sum of $500,000. One paycheck for half a million dollars had suddenly given the young writer credibility and helped launch his career. When McElwaine left ICM to go into film production, Eszterhas moved to CAA, and his greatest success had come during his relationship with Ovitz's company.

McElwaine held jobs at Rastar Films, Columbia Pictures, and the Weintraub Entertainment Group before deciding that he wanted to return to agenting at ICM, which he did in mid-1989, and to reunite with the man whose first script he'd sold more than a decade earlier. When Eszterhas learned that McElwaine was going to work at ICM, he decided that he wanted to leave CAA and rejoin his old agent. This set the scene for the most dramatic public confrontation in the recent history of show business.

One of Hollywood's underground classic films is a brief little late eighties comedy called *Business as Usual.* An animated short created by Christopher Guest, it depicts three middle-aged L.A. movie executives who go to lunch and spend a few minutes ordering their meal and making polite small talk. Then one of them mentions a convoluted deal involving the trio, and what follows is a hilarious outburst of profanity and brutal characterizations of some of the people who are holding up the project. Savage remarks are delivered in a matter-of-fact way, which makes them even funnier. Once the men have trashed everyone engaged in the deal, they return to their small talk, and the film comes to an end.

Some people think that *Business as Usual* is pure satire, a grotesque exaggeration of how Hollywood really operates. Others think that Guest got it just about right, and they might well cite what happened between Eszterhas and Ovitz in support of their opinion.

In September 1989, Eszterhas went to CAA headquarters to tell Ovitz he was taking his gifts elsewhere. What happened in that meeting between the two men is in dispute, but a few days later, Eszterhas sat down at his aged typewriter and pounded out a letter that, when it surfaced in the entertainment media, would reveal a side of the business that everyone in it tries assiduously to conceal.

Eszterhas began by saying that two weeks earlier he'd gone to Ovitz's office to tell him that he was quitting CAA and signing with ICM. He wasn't leaving because of CAA's performance on his behalf, but because McElwaine was back in the agency business and this man was his oldest friend in Hollywood. "I knew when I walked in," Eszterhas wrote, "that you wouldn't be happy—no other writer at CAA makes $1.25 million a screenplay—but I was unprepared for the crudity and severity of your response."

According to Eszterhas, Ovitz told him that his "foot soldiers who go up and down Wilshire Boulevard each day will blow your brains out." The agent also said, in Eszterhas's version of events, that he would sue the screenwriter, and that if Eszterhas made him "eat shit," he would make him "eat shit" as well. Ovitz, Eszterhas wrote, said that Hollywood was like a chess game, and ICM wasn't going after a pawn or knight—it was going after a king. "If the king goes," Eszterhas quoted the agent as saying, "the knights and pawns will follow." The screenwriter then claimed that Ovitz had threatened to damage his relationship with Irwin Winkler, who'd produced two of Eszterhas's films, *Betrayed* and *Music Box*, and to harm his relationship with Barry Hirsch, who'd been his attorney for thirteen years.

That night at Jimmy's, a Beverly Hills restaurant near CAA, Rand Holston, another CAA employee, also spoke with Eszterhas about his plans to change agencies. In his letter, Eszterhas wrote that Holston told him that Ovitz was "the best friend anyone could have and the worst enemy." When Eszterhas asked what would happen if he left CAA for ICM, Eszterhas quoted Holston as replying, "Mike's going to put you into the fucking ground." And he added, according to the letter, that no CAA star would play in any of Eszterhas's scripts, no CAA director would direct his work, and Ovitz would go out of his way to speak badly about him to studio executives. "There's no telling what Mike will say when he's angry," Eszterhas quoted Holston as saying in the restaurant. "When I saw him after the meeting with you, the veins were bulging out of his neck."

All of this, Eszterhas contended, amounted to blackmail, and he was "horrified" by it. The role of the agent, he wrote, was to help and encourage his career and creativity. It was not to place him in "personal emotional turmoil. Your role is not to threaten to destroy my family livelihood if I don't do your bidding. I am not an asset; I am a human being. . . . I am not part of a chess set. I am not a piece of meat to be 'traded' for other pieces of meat. . . . This isn't a game. It's my life. . . . I cannot live with myself and continue to be represented by you. I find the threats you and Rand made to be morally repugnant."

He and his family, Eszterhas explained, had spent the past three years searching for a bigger and more expensive home. They'd found one recently and purchased it, but because of Ovitz's "threats and the uncertainty they cast on my future," the screenwriter had decided to sell it.

"I think the biggest reason I can't stay with you has to do with my children," the letter concluded. "I have taught them to fight for what's right. What you did is wrong. I can't teach my children one thing and then, on the most elemental level, do another. I am not that kind of man. So do whatever you want to do, Mike, and fuck you. I have my family and I have my old manual imperfect typewriter and they have always been the things I've treasured the most. . . . [F]rom this date on Guy McElwaine will represent me."

Ovitz immediately responded to Ezsterhas's letter. He wrote back that he was "totally shocked" by it and that his recollection of their conversation "bore no relationship to your recollection." The agent said that this appeared to be a *Rashomon* situation, a reference to Akira Kurosawa's 1951 Oscar-winning film in which each of four people view the same event very differently. Ovitz said that he'd already spoken with Guy McElwaine about the matter and that CAA would do whatever it could to be helpful in Eszterhas's transition to ICM.

"I think that your letter was unfair and unfounded," Ovitz wrote, "but it does not change my respect for your talent. I only hope that in time you will reflect on the true spirit of what I was trying to communicate to you."

Two days later, Eszterhas sent Ovitz another letter that was as heated as the first one. The agent, he wrote, could "quote *Rashomon* as much as you like, but words like 'my foot soldiers . . . will blow your brains out' and 'he'll put you into the fucking ground' leave little room for ambiguity." Eszterhas said that he understood very well "the true spirit" of what Ovitz was trying to communicate to him in the meeting and that he would live his life accordingly. He reiterated that he was selling his new home.

Ovitz hired attorney Seth Hufstedler to represent him in the embarrassing dispute with the Writers Guild of America that grew out of this run-in with Eszterhas. Months later, the Guild released a document, in effect a consent decree, that absolved CAA of responsibility for the substance of Eszterhas's charges in return for the agency's pledge not to behave in such a way toward its clients in the future.

Meanwhile, the letters had become public, first faxed from insider to insider and eventually published in various periodicals. They gave Hollywood something to gossip about for years to come. Many people felt that the blowup between Eszterhas and Ovitz signaled both the end of CAA's dominance and a significant downturn in the screenwriter's career. Neither prediction turned out to be remotely true. Ovitz's agenda would start to widen now, and he would move further away from the world of agenting. While this episode demonstrated that not everything can be controlled all the time, it did nothing to stop Ovitz from thinking about looking in other directions for the next stage of his career.

Eszterhas (who refused to talk about Ovitz for this book) would go on to write *Basic Instinct, Sliver, Jade,* and *Showgirls,* becoming much richer and more famous in the process of penning movies about very dangerous, and often very naked, women. During the making of *Sliver,* in 1993, he split with Geri Javor, his wife of a quarter of a century, and took up with Naomi Baka, whose husband, Bill McDonald, the film's producer, had just left her for Sharon Stone, its star. (In *Showgirls,* Eszterhas named a faithless stripper Nomi after his new wife.)

Piles of money, great notoriety, and new romance provided insufficient balm to Eszterhas's hurt feelings. Still smarting from his breakup with Ovitz, he made a point of flipping off the CAA building every time he drove by.

There were those in Hollywood who found Eszterhas overbearing, but others admired him for his brazenness.

"A lot of people were feeling the things that Eszterhas wrote in those letters to Ovitz," says one screenwriter. "And a lot of people—at the top of studios and in other places—were very tired of reading about 'the most powerful man in show business.' They didn't think that Ovitz had ever deserved that title, and they wanted someone to bust his balloon.

"People in this town are like that. Somebody had to let their sentiments out, and Joe finally did."

PART FOUR

THE LONG GOOD-BYE

Therefore, when I have won a victory I do not repeat my tactics but respond to circumstances in an infinite variety of ways.

—*The Art of War*

19

The Matsushita Electric Industrial Company, headquartered in Osaka, Japan, was generally regarded as more conservative and less "Westernized" than the Sony Corporation, which was based in Tokyo. It was also less well known in the United States; most Americans were familiar with the Sony Walkman, for example, but how many could name a product associated with Matsushita? In spite of this, it was one of the largest manufacturers of electric appliances, such as fans and light bulbs, in the world, and worth $65 billion. In the early 1980s Matsushita had bested Sony by making its own VHS format the videocasette of choice even though Sony's Beta tape was technically superior. Run in a very traditional Japanese manner, it not only had a 250-year business plan—unimaginable to Americans—it also offered "spiritual guidance" classes in the Matsushita philosophy to its employees. The corporation had long been viewed as a hesitant follower of Sony's more innovative path, and true to form, after Sony had purchased the Columbia/TriStar film studio in 1989, Matsushita put out feelers inside the entertainment business that it was interested in a similar acquisition.

This development startled many in the industry, who felt that this Japanese giant was even more unsuited to owning a movie studio than Sony was. Yet it did not surprise Michael Ovitz, whose career had been fashioned by bringing together ideas and people from the East and the West, by perceiving opportunities where others saw only problems, and by discovering new forms of cooperation, which others called "conflict of interest" (wasn't he, after all, now negotiating deals for both movie stars and studio executives?). During his consulting role in the purchase of Columbia/TriStar, for which he was reportedly paid $10 million, Ovitz had impressed the heads of Sony, and his reputation had soon reached the leaders of Matsushita. Now that they were preparing themselves to venture into the entertainment field, he was one of the first Westerners they contacted.

Typically, Ovitz, had already begun doing research on the company and had predicted within CAA that Matsushita was a prime candidate for the next Japanese takeover of a studio. He had put together a team to collect information on the electronics giant, and by the time Matsushita called him, in November 1989, he was well informed on the history, hierarchy, and business philosophy of the corporation. His education included reading several books written by Konosuke Matsushita, who founded the company in 1918. The ninety-four-year-old founder's recent death, in spring 1989, had further convinced Ovitz that the company would be anxious to try new ventures.

As an adviser on the Columbia deal, Ovitz had initially attempted to interest Sony in purchasing the MCA/Universal studio. He had tried to sell them on MCA's long-term potential and on several of its greatest assets, including its magnificent film library, its stellar relationship with America's most acclaimed director, Steven Spielberg, and its overall clout in Hollywood, with Lew Wasserman still at the helm. Sony's financial people were charmed by Ovitz but not swayed by his argument. They felt that MCA was overpriced, at roughly $8 billion, and had been in decline for several years.

While Ovitz had largely stayed on the sidelines during the Sony-Columbia deal, he was determined that this would not happen again. When Matsushita contacted him, he volunteered to guide them and be their teacher through the difficult task of settling upon and then purchasing a Hollywood property. To Ovitz, this endeavor was, in a way, old hat. He'd been putting together puzzles for years—beginning with his TV-packaging deals at William Morris and then expanding into movie packaging at CAA. What was peddling a film studio to a foreign corporation except a bigger, and richer, package deal? What was the difference between selecting Tom Cruise, Dustin Hoffman, and Barry Levinson for *Rain Man* and choosing the investment bankers, attorneys, and public relations experts necessary to sell a multibillion-dollar asset to the Japanese?

"Michael was always fascinated by meshing things from different cultures," says a Hollywood film executive. "He enjoyed doing that in America, by taking his talents and enthusiasms from California to New York, but I think it was a lot more exciting for him to work with people who spoke another language and had other rituals and customs. The big challenge was bridging the differences and just seeing if he could get people to sit down and communicate with each other. Deep down, he's an idealist who believes that common ground can almost always be found."

In November 1989, Ovitz flew to Hawaii and met with Matsushita's executive vice president and director Masahiko Hirata. In his quiet, polite, and insistent way, Ovitz informed Hirata that he would be more than willing to help Matsushita buy a studio, but he felt that too many people had been involved in the Sony-Columbia deal, making the negotiations unduly cumbersome and drawn out. He wanted control over the entire transaction: selecting the participants, coordinating the meetings, and, more than anything else, being the primary communicator with both sides in the negotiations. He would be the one telling the Japanese what the Americans had to say, and vice versa. He did not set a fee for his services, as an investment banker would normally have done in such circumstances, but simply trusted that if things went well he would not be playing the role of international broker for nothing.

While the Matsushita leaders appeared to accept his plan without resistance, Japanese businesspeople rarely give complete trust to a Westerner. In fact, reports would later surface that they assigned their own people to study the numbers once the deal was underway. In the parlance of their own culture, they were using a "shadow team" as well as a visible go-between in the negotiations.

After Matsushita agreed to Ovitz's terms, the corporation sent a group of advisers to Los Angeles, where a small, carefully chosen group of CAA employees gave them a crash course in the history of show business. They taught them about filmmaking, about the different studios, about the stars, about television, music, broadcasting, book publishing, and the theme parks that some of the larger film entities were now building and running. Ovitz spent several months saturating the Japanese with information about Hollywood, then gradually steered them toward three possible acquisition targets: Paramount, Orion, and MCA. In May 1990, the agent flew to Osaka and made a four-hour presentation about which one of the three he was recommending. No one familiar with his view of the entertainment business was shocked to learn that he suggested Matsushita go after MCA, the biggest of the trio and the one with, in Ovitz's opinion, the best future. The buyer did not argue with him.

While consulting with Matsushita, Ovitz hardly neglected the heads of MCA. Far better than most Westerners, he understood that the Japanese do not like unpredictable or obstreperous people, who might embarrass them in public or say things nasty things about them to the media. During the Sony courtship of Columbia, there had been some resistance in the United States—including a congressional hearing on the matter—to a foreign-owned corporation's buying a piece of America's cultural past for $3.4 billion. This time the price tag and the stakes would be even greater, because MCA was a larger and more prestigious organization than Columbia/TriStar. So it was particularly important that, when this second Japanese acquisition of a film studio was undertaken, everything should look as appropriate and unfold as smoothly as possible. And in these circumstances, that could be tricky.

If it was well known inside Hollywood that Lew Wasserman was the most revered name in the business, it was just as well known that his number-two man, Sid Sheinberg, nearly twenty years his junior, could be touchy, if not prickly, in his dealings with others. Wasserman was as elegant as Sheinberg was rough-hewn. The younger man, a native Texan, no doubt suffered from having labored for years in the shadow of his legendary boss, and on occasion he was about as delicate as a Panhandle dust storm. He was just the sort of person who might befuddle or discourage the Japanese.

Ovitz, well attuned to Sheinberg's personality, made a point of going to him early in 1990 and telling him that a deal was being put together and Sheinberg would be an integral part of it. If Matsushita bought MCA, Ovitz assured him, Sheinberg would not lose his job and would be able to negotiate a new and very lucrative management contract with the Japanese.

"I once read that Ovitz was a genius because of the way he treated Sheinberg in the Matsushita deal," says an L.A. entertainment lawyer. "Mike's a smart guy, but come on. It didn't take a rocket scientist to figure out that Sid's a very difficult man and Ovitz had to get him in line before he could do anything else."

"Let's face it," says another Hollywood observer, "Sid's a ball-buster, and Mike didn't want him displaying his talents to the Japanese."

Ovitz was equally solicitous toward Wasserman, and during the first half of 1990 he regularly told the number one and two men at MCA what he was doing and how things were developing. For their part, the MCA chiefs were intrigued with the notion of having Matsushita acquire their studio. Wasserman and Sheinberg were fundamentally interested in two things: seeing their business grow—so it could compete with the other ever-expanding media megacorporations—and keeping their positions at the very top of Hollywood's pecking order. Already in his late seventies, Wasserman was not yet ready to step down, but when that time came, he wanted to play an important role in the leadership transition at the company he'd headed for more than four decades.

Many in Hollywood believed that Ovitz's real aim was to close the deal, then nudge Wasserman aside and take over the studio himself. Ovitz was increasingly ready to move on, the rumormongers kept saying, and running MCA had always been his long-term goal.

"Everyone in town knew that Mike wanted Lew's job," says a Hollywood attorney, "but no one was certain just how bold he would be in going after it. You can only strike once at something like this, and it can't be too soon."

In July and August, Ovitz began hiring people for the upcoming negotiations. To represent Matsushita in the United States, he brought in lawyers from the New York firm of Simpson, Thacher, & Bartlett. For investment banker, to the surprise of none, Ovitz chose Herbert Allen of Allen & Company, and he brought in public relations experts from Adams and Rinehart. All the while, he kept traveling back and forth to Japan, in order to keep Matsushita fully apprised of developments. Ovitz's natural inclination toward secrecy now increased so that he behaved more like a secret agent than a corporate broker.

He flew to Osaka not out of Los Angeles, as he normally would have, but out of San Francisco, so that he would not be recognized at the airport. He told almost no one, including some important members of his CAA staff, where he was going—or he told them that he was going somewhere other than the Far East. Those he did tell were not allowed to enter any information about the deal into the agency's computers; everything had to be handwritten so it could more easily be destroyed. He gave himself a code name: "Mr. Nelson." He held hush-hush meetings with those whom he wanted to be involved in the negotiations. When in Japan, he kept his car parked in the CAA garage in Beverly Hills so that the agency's employees would think he was in L.A. And while in Osaka, he stayed up all night calling his business associates in Hollywood, so that they would think he was in California and operating on Pacific Daylight Time. Regardless of where he was, he kept returning phone calls, no matter how much sleep it cost him.

Matsushita went along with all the people Ovitz had selected for the negotiations but eventually brought in one other player, Robert Strauss, a Washington lawyer, former chairman of the Democratic National Committee, and highly respected veteran on the international political scene. Strauss, who would go on to become the U.S. ambassador to the Soviet Union, was well qualified to speak with leaders on both sides of the table; he knew Wasserman, he knew Herbert Allen, and he knew some of the Matsushita executives. At the eleventh hour, his familiarity with both sides would become crucial.

In late August, Ovitz told MCA's investment banker, Lazard Freres, that Matsushita was interested in buying the entertainment conglomerate. A few weeks later in Manhattan, Ovitz met with Sheinberg and Felix Rohatyn of Lazard Freres and told them that Matsushita was preparing to make an offer for the studio that would come in between $75 and $90 dollars a share. At this time, MCA's stock was trading at only $36 dollars a share, so this appeared to be a very generous offer indeed. Yet there were complications. Six weeks earlier, on August 2, Iraq's Saddam Hussein had invaded Kuwait and set the entire world and all its financial markets on edge. The New York Stock Exchange was down, and the price of many offerings, including MCA's, had been deflated. If the United States now went to war against Iraq, as was being contemplated in Washington, this would make all the markets more unstable and all international negotiations more delicate.

Thus far, Ovitz had managed to keep his dealings with Matsushita and MCA quiet, but on September 25, the *Wall Street Journal* reported that the two corporations were talking with one another about Matsushita's buying MCA for between $80 and $90 a share. A great deal of speculation about who had leaked this story to the paper ensued. Some people felt that Ovitz himself had done it, in order to push the negotiations ahead and prevent the kind of months-long stalling Japanese dealmakers were known for. Other people said that MCA officials had leaked the information because the price per share quoted in the article looked so favorable to their company and its shareholders; it would be inappropriate now, went this line of thinking, for the Japanese to make a low-ball offer. And still other people said that the source was music mogul David Geffen, who may have had several reasons to slip this story to the *Journal*. The people who thought Geffen was the culprit believed that he had a long and unforgiving memory.

Ten years earlier, Geffen had produced the film *Personal Best*, a story of a lesbian love affair between two track stars. It was also the directing debut of Robert Towne, who'd gained fame in Hollywood as the screenwriter of *Chinatown*. While *Personal Best* was being shot for Warner Bros., the Screen Actors Guild called a strike, and Warners, already nervous about the movie's subject matter, decided to dump the picture.

Geffen went to Barry Diller, who was then running Paramount, and asked him to pick up the movie. Diller wanted to see what had already been filmed, but Geffen balked at this request. Then Ovitz, who was Towne's agent, went to Diller and asked for more money for the director. In the end, Paramount rejected the film, and Geffen later claimed that this decision had cost him millions of dollars. Lawsuits followed, and Warners eventually agreed to take back the movie, but Geffen neither forgot nor forgave the damage he

felt Ovitz had caused him. Some people were convinced that he
would get even with the agent when the opportunity arose.

Geffen may have had another, more practical reason for leaking the information: MCA had bought out Geffen Records, and he
owned ten million shares of MCA stock. Because of this, he may
have wanted to force Matsushita's hand. If the deal quickly closed
and he cashed his shares out at around $90 each, he stood to gain
nearly a billion dollars.

No matter who was the source of the leak, Matsushita's people
did not appreciate having their secret business trumpeted in the
Wall Street Journal. They would not be easily intimidated or hurried
into making a buy of this magnitude, and some observers believed
that one more such leak would bury the deal. While this indiscretion had given both Matsushita and MCA the jitters, it had also
pushed up the price of the studio's shares from $36 to $61 apiece.

Until the early autumn of 1990, the leaders on each side had regularly been hearing about what their counterparts on the other
shore of the Pacific were doing, but they'd never actually met.
Ovitz had orchestrated this strategy too, and many people felt that
keeping them apart as much as possible was particularly shrewd. If
the two groups had come together for any period of time, they
might have realized just how different their cultural and business
backgrounds really were.

Matsushita was old-school Japanese, profoundly conservative,
built on the foundation of manufacturing and distributing electronic products that could be developed slowly and marketed
worldwide, with relatively predictable results. It traded in and understood electrical "hardware." MCA created entertainment, a
commodity Hollywood sometimes refers to as "software." Wall
Street has another name for the products of the movie industry:
"vaporware," because films are such unpredictable and fleeting
creatures. Both MCA and Matsushita were very good at what they
did, but in every way they remained worlds apart.

"I think it's absolutely amazing," says a business executive in
L.A., "that Ovitz could get these old-line Japanese to come to
America and offer billions of dollars for something they were com-

pletely ignorant about. Running a fancy American hotel or a golf course is one thing. Running a film studio is something else. Anyone who knows anything about the history of Hollywood knows that outsiders get fleeced in the movie business. It's just too small a world, and too specialized, for most Americans to penetrate or make sense of, let alone most foreigners. I think Ovitz has something to answer for here. He had to know what the Japanese were getting into, even if they didn't."

20

The parties met for the first time in Lew Wasserman's home in Los Angeles on October 7, 1990. On this occasion, Ovitz brought the head of MCA and Sid Sheinberg together with Masahiko Hirata, the executive vice president of Matsushita, and Keiya Toyonaga, the corporation's managing director. Little more than pleasantries were exchanged at Wasserman's residence, and the electronic company's leaders soon returned to Osaka. During the next month, reports of what Matsushita might be willing to pay for MCA—between $60 and $65 dollars a share—began surfacing in the Japanese media. This was a far lower price than MCA wanted, and when these numbers were publicized in the United States, the studio's stock fell to $50 a share.

By the start of November, Wasserman and Sheinberg were increasingly displeased. If the heads of Matsushita had earlier felt that the film studio was using the media to raise the price of its shares, the MCA executives now felt that the Japanese executives were using the press to produce exactly the opposite effect. Because the two groups had no direct contact with one another, they were left to guess at what the other side was actually willing to pay, or accept as payment, in order to close the deal. Then reports began appearing in the Japanese media that if an agreement could not be arrived at soon, the deal would fall apart.

In mid-November, both sides, fearing the collapse of the sale, decided to fly to New York and begin formal negotiations. Wasserman, Sheinberg, and several of Matsushita's leading executives met on Sunday evening, November 18, at Manhattan's La Regence, a restaurant in the Plaza Athenee Hotel. Once again, the evening was devoted largely to social banter, conducted through interpreters, and serious talks did not begin until the next day, when Ovitz intensified his role as the deal's chief go-between. He told the MCA people that Matsushita was now willing to pay $60 a share, plus $3 a share for an equity stake in an MCA-owned television station, WWOR. This number remained, of course, a very long way from the $90 a share that had been reported in the *Wall Street Journal* back in September.

The studio heads had been expecting a better offer, but Ovitz explained to them that during the past two months, threats of war in the Persian Gulf and the drop in MCA's price per share had significantly reduced the value of their stock. Some followers of the negotiations felt that Matsushita had never intended to pay anything like $90 a share but had simply been using Ovitz to bring MCA to the bargaining table. Matsushita had recently hired its own financial adviser, Nomura Wasserstein Perella, a mergers-and-acquisitions specialist based in Japan and staffed with Japanese; when it came to crunching numbers, the corporation wanted its own people to be handling the calculators. Bankers from Nomura Wasserstein Perella had also flown to New York and were staying on the same floor as the Matsushita executives in the Waldorf-Astoria Hotel.

On Monday, November 19, Ovitz began traveling back and forth between the law offices of Simpson, Thacher, & Bartlett, where the Japanese buyers were encamped during the day, and Wachtell, Lipton, Rosen, & Katz, where the American sellers were based. The Simpson headquarters were on Lexington Avenue between 43rd and 44th streets, while the Wachtell office was on Park Avenue in the 50s, so Ovitz had roughly ten blocks to cover each time he went from one group to the other.

"Michael literally began moving faster during this time," says someone who followed the negotiations closely. "The whole process energized him to a new level, and he looked more lean and alert than ever. I don't think he'd ever been as happy as he was now."

The studio heads quickly rejected the offer of $60 a share; a day later, they said no to sixty-four. Ovitz was in the ticklish position of trying to explain to Matsushita why he believed that MCA would accept a figure in this range and simultaneously attempting to mollify the feelings of Wasserman and Sheinberg, who'd been led to expect a much higher bid. By Wednesday, November 21, Matsushita had not raised its number, MCA had not made a counteroffer, and it appeared that the deal might be dead. The next day was Thanksgiving.

On Wednesday, to the astonishment of many, Ovitz decided to fly back to Los Angeles and spend the holiday with his wife and children. This, like many other things he'd done, would become the subject of multiple interpretations. Some people said that he left because he'd played out the role he'd created for himself and there wasn't much more he could accomplish. Others believed that he calculated that leaving now would bring the participants together and cause them to start talking with one another.

During the next twenty-four hours, Robert Strauss and Herbert Allen, two veterans of international relations and financial negotiations, stepped forward and brought the talks back to life. Strauss, in particular, now assumed the role of go-between. With him representing Matsushita and Allen representing MCA, both sides were able to achieve a level of communication that had thus far been missing. On Thanksgiving Day, the Japanese raised their offer by $2 a share, a difference of about $200 million if the deal were to be consummated. With this offer on the table, Ovitz called both Hirata and Sheinberg from Los Angeles, saying that if the parties met now, they could reach a resolution. A short while later, Hirata walked out of his room at the Waldorf-Astoria and strolled across Park Avenue to the offices of Wachtell, Lipton, Rosen, & Katz, where the MCA people were awaiting his arrival.

By that evening, they had reached an agreement on the price: $66 a share, plus $3-per-share equity position in WWOR. During the next few days, the two sides battled over a number of lesser issues, and by Monday, November 26, the deal was set to close. This was an extraordinarily swift conclusion to a negotiation involving Japanese participants, who would have normally flown back to their own country and held numerous meetings before reaching a consensus opinion and moving forward. At nine A.M., the papers were signed. Matsushita had purchased MCA/Universal for $6.6 billion.

While the participants celebrated in New York, half a world away in Osaka the mood was more sober. Akio Tanii, the president of Matsushita, was asked during a televised news conference what the company would do if MCA made a film depicting the late Emperor Hirohito as a war criminal. Tanii first said that Matsushita would use "appropriate judgment" in these matters; then, when pushed, he stated that "such movies will never be produced." This was not, of course, what the studio, or Hollywood's film community, or the U.S. Congress, or even some people in Japan had wanted or expected to hear. A few days later Tanii backpedaled, saying publicly that Matsushita had "no intention of becoming involved in decisions regarding the subject or content of creative products of MCA."

That statement notwithstanding, the Japanese corporation began sending its own people to Los Angeles to keep a close eye on the studio and on Sheinberg and Wasserman, who were still running it; these "shadows" reported back to Osaka on a regular basis. If this made some Americans in the entertainment industry a little nervous, their concerns were not allayed when it became known that the heads of Matsushita and of Sony had been in communication with one another during the negotiations that had led to the purchase of MCA. After the sale was finalized, Sony's CEO, Norio Ohga, publicly declared that he was very much in favor of the deal. "The decision," he said, "means there will be two Japanese companies controlling both hardware and programs in the audiovisual field."

If the Japanese corporate honchos were delighted and optimistic because of their recent acquisitions, their euphoria would be short-lived. In the past, many American outsiders, like Coca-

Cola, had come to L.A. with the intention of getting rich in the film business—and soon been faced with the reality of overseeing a dream factory. Now it was Matsushita's turn to discover the difference between wanting something that looked very glamorous from afar and managing that property on a daily basis. It was also Wasserman and Sheinberg's turn to discover what it felt like to be an employee of a vast and distant corporation.

In the winter of 1991, the two men flew to Osaka for a budget review, and when the Japanese did not move as quickly as they wanted them to on decision making, or even on smaller matters, like attending meetings on time, the two aging and much deferred-to Americans were said to be miffed. The MCA duo were anxious for their company to expand, especially now that the fabulously wealthy Matsushita owned them, but the new owner was cautiously examining all of its options. Matsushita had, after all, just laid down $6.6 billion for MCA; now they wanted to make some money before spending any more. For the time being, Wasserman and Sheinberg decided to hold their tongues and hope for the best. But Sheinberg, people said, would not keep still forever.

Ovitz, for his part, expressed no public concern over any of these issues.

"Mike is a dealmaker first and last," says an agent in Beverly Hills. "To him, this was just another deal, and he loved bringing it off. He was selling the Japanese a piece of the future, just like it was a piece of real estate. He was always selling people the future. That was his gift. The strange thing is that when the future arrived, he was usually off doing something else."

By March 1991, Ovitz had gone back to running CAA and was working on new projects. He was also awaiting that spring's Academy Awards (in the event, one of his recent signees, Kevin Costner, would win Best Director for *Dances With Wolves*; the film won seven Academy Awards in all). Ovitz had never been more prominent or richer, and the past couple of years had truly been a remarkable time for him. He'd not only brokered the largest sale of a studio in Hollywood history—and convinced most people that his stepping aside at the end of the negotiations had been a brilliant stroke that had helped seal the deal—he'd also picked up a tidy fee for his efforts. The exact amount was never made public, but reports ranged from a whopping $40 million to the more modest figure of $8 million.

The sale of MCA was now the highlight of his career. He'd taken his skills as a negotiator/teacher/student-of-other-cultures/cooperator/dealmaker/catalyst to a level never before seen in the talent agency business and had become, in effect, an investment banker. He was being written about in publications all over the country, as well as in Japan, and some journalists were describing him as an "economic samurai." East had met West in the person of Ovitz, and he, more than anyone else, appeared to be the beneficiary of all these transactions. While the Matsushita and MCA officials were left with the sticky task of getting to know one another and forging a good working arrangement, Ovitz began putting together new consulting deals that would eventually include Coca-Cola, Apple Computer, Nike, and several other corporations, looking for his next coup.

"Ovitz is very bright and extremely focused," says Porter Bibb, of the New York brokerage house, Ladenburg, Thalmann, & Co., "and his primary skill is knowing how to parlay his connections into something more. He knows how to leverage his contacts in the entertainment business and how to intimidate others. Early on, the film studios should have been able to say no to him, but he was able to pull off what he did by being single-minded and always holding to his plan."

"When he brokered the MCA-Matsushita deal, he generated some resentment on the East Coast among the investment banking houses that are traditionally involved in transactions this large. People on Wall Street and people up in Boston looked at him and said, 'Who the hell is this guy from California? He has no financial grounding, but he's out there doing our deals.' Ovitz has made some enemies, but so far nothing he's done has hurt him."

If many on Wall Street were taken aback at Ovitz's triumphant maneuverings in 1990, people in another wealthy and highly competitive segment of East Coast society would be equally stunned by something the agent achieved in 1991. Through Morton Janklow and Arnold Glimcher, Ovitz had gotten to know David Rockefeller, who invited him to join the Chairman's Council of New York's Museum of Modern Art. High finance and high culture, like East and West before them, had come together in the leader of CAA.

What other realms were left to conquer?

Plenty of folks out in L.A. still said that despite all his accomplishments, more than anything else Ovitz wanted Lew Wasserman's job, but he'd have to wait a few more years for the old lion to retire.

These people may have been underestimating Ovitz's ambitions. After he'd joined the board of MOMA, *Vanity Fair* magazine, in a piece about art collecting, questioned one of its sources about rumors that the talent agent wanted to be president of the museum. The source laughed and said, "He wants to be president of the world."

21

While Ovitz was moving ahead in several different directions, the film industry was going through a slump. Profits were falling all over town—20 to 30 percent at some studios—or were nonexistent. MGM was in serious trouble, Orion would soon go into bankruptcy, Carolco was losing millions of dollars on high-budget flops, and independent producers were dropping out of the business. Sony, after a couple of years of bullish spending at Columbia under Guber and Peters, was rethinking its strategy. Disney, which had never been known for parting easily with cash, was clamping down even further. Not enough work was being generated for all the writers, producers, actors, and directors in Hollywood, and because of this, some of the talent agencies were suffering.

CAA, on the contrary, was thriving, despite a costly, ill-advised investment in QSound, a new audio technology that was supposed to sweep away the competition but did not, and an equally bad $6 million investment in Mercantile National Bank, whose stock then plunged by half. Not every decision Ovitz made about the direction of CAA was right, of course, but these losses barely made the newspapers, while the MCA-Matsushita deal was known from coast to coast. And besides, a couple of bad investments had little effect on the overall financial stability of the agency.

CAA was still far ahead of its Hollywood competition. With its long-term TV packages in place; with its 1990 signing of Steven Spielberg, who had previously worked without an agent, but decided that CAA could do things for him that he could not do alone; with its recent inking of another star, Tom Hanks, who would soon catapult into megafame; and with its plan for luring away from William Morris the rising director Tim Burton, who'd made *Beetlejuice* and *Batman*, about to pay off, CAA was as healthy as it had ever been. If all this made for good business, it also made for hard feelings, which had been building against the agency for years. A recession in the movie industry did nothing to soften these emotions.

CAA had lately been squabbling with various studios over money, but most of its recent struggles had involved the Walt Disney Company. The agency and Disney had quarreled over *Billy Bathgate*, a gangster movie featuring Dustin Hoffman, after Disney accused CAA of attempting to renegotiate Hoffman's contract and bilk the Mickey Mouse empire for additional millions. Disney's point man in this confrontation was studio chairman Jeffrey Katzenberg, a formidable opponent in any battle.

Inside the industry, Katzenberg was sometimes compared to Ovitz in terms of his relentless drive, his resourcefulness, and his dedication to his company. Two of his work habits had become legendary in Hollywood. The first was that, to keep all his contacts on full alert, he would regularly make a hundred calls a day, most of them lasting a minute or less. Second, he was known for getting to work before sunrise, and he expected his minions to show the same level of commitment to Disney—if not more. There were tales of Katzenberg driving into the corporate parking lot at dawn and seeing the cars of his subordinates already lined up. Still not satisfied, he would feel the hoods, taking the temperature of each one. If the metal was warm, the employee who owned it was suspect. But if it was cold, the driver had been at work for quite some time, and Katzenberg knew he could trust this fellow fanatic when things got tough.

During the *Billy Bathgate* dispute, Ovitz and Katzenberg had gotten into a minor flap over the phone, but this was only the initial salvo in an ongoing conflict. They fought over the terms for using Robin Williams's voice for the genie in the animated feature *Aladdin*, and they skirmished again over the Muppets. In 1989, Disney had agreed to purchase some of the Muppet characters, but negotiations went on for months and were thrown into turmoil when Jim Henson, the creator of the Muppets, died in May 1990. The following year, the legal problems surrounding the sale went to court, after Henson's heirs charged that Disney had in effect stolen some of the Muppets. This was not at all, of course, what the upstanding, family-oriented studio wanted to read about itself in the papers.

The Disney leaders, including studio head Katzenberg and CEO Michael Eisner, were well aware that CAA had consulted for Henson in this dispute on some of the issues that had led to the lawsuit. Because of all this, Ovitz got another call from Disney over the Muppet flare-up—this time from Eisner himself.

Twenty years earlier, when Eisner was a vice president of comedy development at ABC, he had been instrumental in buying some of the first CAA television packages. He'd helped the five William Morris renegades launch their business and had been both a friend and an ally of Ovitz's for two decades. In 1984, when Eisner was hired to run the Disney organization, the studio was in the doldrums both creatively and financially, but during the next few years he and Katzenberg had resurrected the empire and made its products both vigorous and enormously profitable. From the mid-1980s onward, there were no greater success stories in Hollywood than those associated with the entity often referred to in the entertainment press as "the two Michaels": Eisner and Ovitz.

When the head of Disney telephoned the head of CAA about the Muppet lawsuit, he reportedly called the Ovitz-supported language in the Henson estate's legal brief "disgusting" and asked that the talent agency apologize to the film studio. What happened next remains cloudy, but there is no record of any public mea culpas coming out of 9830 Wilshire Boulevard.

These contretemps were indicative of something more than an argument over who owned the Muppets. By the early 1990s, movies had become more and more expensive to produce, the film business was losing money, the industry was coming under increasing criticism for the sex-and-violence content of some of its products, and the overall mood in the business was foul. While Ovitz and CAA had become rich entertainment gurus who acted as if they could do no wrong, they also evolved into natural targets for the disappointments and bile of others.

At a 1991 meeting of the Motion Picture Association of America, one studio executive told an audience that the real problem in their industry was named Michael Ovitz. While others quickly came to the agent's defense and said that blaming any one person for a new and complicated reality was unfair, the executive's words had been publicly spoken, and the harsh feelings would not go away.

Despite all the sniping that was taking place around it, CAA had always positioned itself on the high road, and it would not change now. When reporters came to the agency and asked for responses to the criticism, the few people who were allowed to speak answered with platitudes: "We don't really have that much power"; and "We're just trying to make everyone in our industry more successful"; "It's a misperception that we control the business."

The skeptics were unconvinced.

22

Back in 1982, while brokering Coca-Cola's sale of the Columbia studio to Sony, New York investment banker Herbert Allen had become friends with Coke's chairman, Robert Goizueta. The banker was soon named a director of the soft-drink empire. Through Allen and other contacts, Ovitz had met the leadership of Coke and nurtured his own relationships inside the corporation. He made a lot of calls to the Coca-Cola people, and they were as impressed with him as the Matsushita execs and the Sony execs before them had been. By the early 1990s, Ovitz had let the soft-drink company know that if it ever needed advice or any connections with the talent pool in Hollywood, for its TV commercials or other ventures, he would be more than willing to help.

In September 1991, CAA once again startled the media and shook up Madison Avenue when Coke's Atlanta headquarters announced that it had hired Creative Artists as its worldwide media and communications consultant. CAA was being brought in to advise Coca-Cola on everything from advertising to the use of actors in its commercials. A team from the talent agency would be offering assistance to the corporation that controlled nearly half of the $47-billion-a-year worldwide soft-drink market. Pepsi had only 15 percent.

Domestically, however, the numbers were closer; Pepsi had 33.2 percent of the market and its rival 40.9 percent. And Coke had lately fallen behind Pepsi in terms of the innovation and creativity of its ad campaigns. Pepsi had Michael Jackson peddling its product, while Coke had recently lost basketball superstar Michael Jordan to Gatorade. Coke's "It's the Real Thing" slogan was now widely perceived as old and flat. Three TV viewers to one preferred Pepsi ads to Coke commercials. Coke was searching for a new image. Where better to turn for the hottest trends than the agency that was attached to some of the biggest names in show business.

"California sets the cultural agenda for the world," Peter Sealey, Coke's director of global marketing, told the *L.A. Times* on the day of the announcement. "CAA knows what songs we'll be singing next year and what motion pictures we'll be seeing in December 1992." According to Sealey, the CAA team, led by Bill Haber, movie department co-head Jack Rapke, and agent Paula Wagner, had already submitted more than fifty ideas for improving the advertising and marketing strategies of the soft-drink corporation.

While the deal was perceived as another stunning victory for Ovitz and his people, it was also seen as a direct affront to the two giant New York ad agencies that had represented Coca-Cola for years: McCann-Erickson Worldwide and Lintas: Worldwide, which handled Coke and Diet Coke, respectively. Never before had an international conglomerate like Coca-Cola hired someone other than an ad agency to produce a marketing campaign. Because Coke spent more than $350 million a year on its domestic advertising alone, the CAA consulting agreement was not merely an emotional shock but also a financial blow to the ad agencies. Madison Avenue, like Wall Street in 1990 and the Hollywood studios back in the eighties, had suddenly learned that while others were conducting business as usual, Ovitz was encamped in his office in L.A., headphones clamped over his ears, working the telephones and leveraging his way into new realms.

Naturally, the new deal unleashed more accusations. As soon as the Coke-CAA arrangement was announced, Ovitz's critics began charging that he had created another unseemly conflict of interest. The next thing you knew, some industry people were saying, Ovitz would be insisting that CAA-driven movies include scenes of big-name actors drinking Coca-Cola (something that did not come to pass). The agency's response to these charges was the same as it had always been: the critics be damned! CAA was going forward, as Ovitz liked to tell his employees at the end of their springtime retreats. The agency was moving into uncharted territory, and those who were not prepared for the speed and the unpredictability of the ride might as well get off now.

When the Coke-CAA agreement was first revealed, it appeared that the agency would do little more than act as a strategic adviser and suggest new concepts to the soft-drink company. But a year later, CAA's role expanded when it hired Len Fink, a creative executive from the advertising power Chiat/Day/Mojo, and Shelly Hochron, a former marketing executive with Columbia Pictures. In October 1992, CAA rocked the ad world again when two of its clients, Joshua Brand and John Falsey, who had created and produced the hit TV series *Northern Exposure*, were brought in to write and direct a Coke commercial. Fears that a commercial product would be piggybacked onto an artistic one were raised, but Brand and Falsey's ads did not feature *NE*'s Dr. Joel Fleischman chugging the soft drink.

CAA's twin goals were to create novel ads and to develop a single concept for the Coke brand worldwide, in the United States and 191 other countries. The result was a new slogan and theme song—"Always Coca-Cola"—and a series of animated TV spots featuring big, friendly looking polar bears drinking bottles of Coke, then smiling ecstatically. The ads were generally liked by the public but received mixed reviews from Madison Avenue executives, some of whom said that the commercials were "ineffective" and "unfocused." The numbers, however, were not debatable. After CAA had produced more than a score of TV ads, Coke sales grew by 500 million cases a year, an increase of 8 percent. The rest of the industry was growing at about half that rate.

While 1991 was a standout year for CAA, it ended with an event that most people initially perceived as a tragedy. Ovitz had long been a basketball fan, and had taken on the Los Angeles Lakers' Magic Johnson as a client. Ovitz not only admired Johnson's remarkable abilities on the court but also liked to use Johnson as an example when exhorting his CAA troops to employ more teamwork. Magic, he was quick to point out, was not the highest scorer on the Lakers when they were winning five NBA championships in the 1980s, but he led them in another category—"assists," passing the ball to a player who then scored—which was at least as important as making baskets. He was, in fact, their all-time assists leader.

In Ovitz's cryptic and overly modest comments to reporters about the agency's accomplishments—which sometimes took on the qualities of haiku—he would occasionally say that all he really did at CAA was "give the ball to the open man." And in some of his speeches to his colleagues, Ovitz would ask them to be more like Magic Johnson and more concerned with functioning as team players than with chasing personal glory.

In early November 1991, Johnson told the world that he had tested positive for H.I.V., the AIDS virus. The fear of the disease and the confusion surrounding it were so great that his revelation led many to believe that he was near death; he felt compelled to retire from the NBA in part because other players were now afraid to share the court with him. Before speaking to the media about his test results, Johnson had gone to Ovitz and sought his advice. Inside the agency, Ovitz had long been known as someone who simply refused to put a negative spin on anything and said that what at first looked like a terrible thing might one day be viewed in a very different light. He told Johnson that while AIDS was a horrible illness, the basketball player was now being given the opportunity to educate millions of people about the disease. Because he was the most prominent person yet to have tested positive for the virus, he might be able to dispel some of the fear and ignorance surrounding the issue.

Johnson went out and courageously faced the media. He would later say that hearing Ovitz's words at that time had greatly helped him go forward.

Magic Johnson, of course, did not immediately die or even deteriorate physically. He went on to compete in the 1992 Olympic Games and made a triumphant return to the NBA early in 1996. His experience and his example did quell some of the paranoia that swirled around AIDS, and he became a symbol of what was possible for others who also tested positive.

In 1994, Johnson came back to Ovitz and told him that he was interested in owning some movie theaters; he was looking for financial backing and wanted the agent to represent him in this endeavor. Ovitz just stared at Johnson for a while, saying nothing. Then he brushed him off, telling Magic that the problem with most athletes was that they were not any good at thinking about or planning their economic futures. He doubted that Magic was serious about wanting to be in the theater business, and under these circumstances Ovitz didn't want to waste his time discussing the subject.

He suggested that if Johnson really wanted to talk about the matter, he should go do some homework. Then Ovitz ended the meeting. Johnson later told the *New York Times* that he had gone into the agent's office standing six feet, nine inches, but he came out of it feeling "five-foot-two."

He was discouraged but not defeated. He asked for another meeting with Ovitz, and on this occasion the agent gave him a pile of business magazines to read. Consuming all that material and more, Johnson became versed in the rudiments of running a movie theater. Once he was able to talk intelligently about the possibilities and challenges facing anyone going into this field (just as Ovitz had been when approaching I. M. Pei about architecture), Ovitz had time for him, and advised him at length.

Johnson eventually opened a twelve-screen movie complex in L.A.'s mostly black South Central neighborhood, and after six months of operation it ranked in the top five in gross revenue among 21,800 theaters in the nation.

23

In the winter of 1992, Ovitz delivered one of his last blows to the William Morris agency. For months, he'd been interested in signing the young director Tim Burton, a Morris client, but Burton had resisted his initial efforts. In a very rare maneuver, Ovitz decided to invite him to his home in Brentwood, where they could meet in a more relaxed and informal setting. Normally, Ovitz kept business and his domestic life separate, but these were unusual circumstances, and he wanted his children to meet the director who could create such fanciful movies as *Edward Scissorhands* and *The Nightmare Before Christmas.*

Burton arrived one chilly evening and was let in through the wrought-iron security gate and made his way up the long driveway to Ovitz's residence, which has been described as "modern colonial." Ovitz, who knew that Burton had once studied art, took great pleasure in showing him his private array of modern canvasses, Ming furniture, and African treasures. Burton was awestruck by both the man's collection and his knowledge of painting and sculpture.

Ovitz also knew that the young man was intrigued by new entertainment technology, and the agent himself had spent years investigating future investment possibilities in this area. That gave the two of them something else to discuss when the art tour had been concluded. By the time the evening was finished, Ovitz had also described what sort of future his agency could provide for Burton, and the director could not say no.

He soon made the move to CAA, proving to Hollywood that Ovitz had not lost his touch for personally romancing prospective clients. Burton's defection left the William Morris film division, which had already been gutted by CAA, just a little more angry and depleted.

In the spring of 1992, Jeffrey Katzenberg, the chairman of Walt Disney Studios, appeared in New York along with several other film executives at a conference that had been sponsored by the entertainment trade paper *Variety.* One hot topic at the gathering was the changing economics in the movie business, and Katzenberg told the conference that the leverage Hollywood talent agents now had was an important cause of the ever-rising costs of producing movies. He did not mention any agencies by name, but those familiar with the industry knew whom he was talking about. A short while later, at an impromptu luncheon with some reporters who were covering the conference, Katzenberg increased his attacks on those who represented film talent.

When word of this got back to CAA, Ovitz was said to be livid.

He phoned the Disney executive in order to express his feelings, and although there is no record of the language the men actually used, the Hollywood gossip mill was soon reporting that the conversation had not been entirely gracious, on either side.

Katzenberg's sentiments were being echoed elsewhere. In a *Los Angeles Times Magazine* article published three months after the conference in New York, producer Ray Stark and David Geffen lined up behind the Disney executive. In the same story, an unidentified "studio chief" called Ovitz's negotiating tactics "gangsterish," and an unnamed senior Disney exec put the sharpest point on what all of them were feeling. "CAA still has the eighties mentality," this person said. "With them, it's just kill, kill, kill, and Ovitz has done nothing to rein his agents in."

Another hot topic was also starting to emerge. Studio heads, agents, directors, screenwriters, and the media had lately begun talking about "interactive"—the new buzzword in entertainment. According to industry prophets, who were everywhere at the start of the 1990s, the computer and other forms of high technology were about to dramatically alter the nature of their business. It was widely publicized that within a few years kids everywhere, instead of passively watching TV or videos, would be interacting with their personal computers, writing and directing stories featuring the animated characters the software provided. If they wanted a tale with a sad ending, they could create that on the screen; if they wanted one with a happy conclusion, they could have that too. Instead of just consuming movies, they would, in effect, make their own.

As untested ideas that might have unlimited market potential often do, this one generated immense speculation (along with at least one wonderful new word: the marriage of "Silicon Valley" and "Hollywood" produced "Siliwood"). Not only would your kid be the next Steven Spielberg, your household would have access to thousands of TV channels, and your local cable outlet or telephone company would deliver movies on demand: just dial up the Bell System, ask for *Ghostbusters* or *Citizen Kane*, then flip on the television and watch the credits roll.

Interactive was still in its formative stages, but for years Ovitz and CAA had been conducting research into it and looking at the fledgling companies that might play a significant role in this coming new age. As usual, CAA was out in front of the other agencies in this regard, laying the groundwork to sign up the people who were creating this new form of entertainment.

Ovitz and his team had also been doing significant legwork on video-on-demand. One of his key lieutenants, Sandy Climan, had gone to Harvard with someone who was now a senior executive at Microsoft, and this led Ovitz into a relationship with Bill Gates, the founder of Microsoft and the billionaire guru of the personal computing industry. CAA employees were soon talking with Silicon Valley and AT&T. Early in 1992, after Ovitz learned that telephone companies were interested in delivering home entertainment via their phone wires, a group of CAA people created a plan for the seven Baby Bells to bring movies into American living rooms. The plan was called "Project Interconnect" and was detailed in a 150-page business proposal. CAA cast itself in the role of strategic adviser, and the Tele-TV concept, as it was now being called, lurched forward into the unknown.

Despite resentment and recession in film land, it was a time of virtually unmitigated triumph at CAA.

The year 1993 began auspiciously. In January, Ovitz became David Letterman's agent and started negotiating with the networks for the comedian to have a new deal for his late-night talk show. Letterman had not been represented by an agent until now and was even known for making disparaging remarks about the agency business. But he knew Ovitz through his reputation and was at least willing to sit down and talk with him; maybe Ovitz could tell him something he hadn't heard countless times before.

Using all of his smoothness, savvy, charm, and mastery of information, Ovitz outlined to Letterman exactly what leverage the agency could give the comedian, who was under contract at NBC and wanted to stay there but was angry because the network had offered the prestigious *Tonight Show* to his rival Jay Leno. When Ovitz succinctly laid out Letterman's past accomplishments, present dilemma, and long-range goals, the chronically self-critical and insecure comic was not merely impressed but overwhelmed. This agent had all the answers before Letterman could even pose the questions. He signed up, and CAA went to work.

First, Ovitz invited to Creative Artists representatives from networks other than NBC, so they could make Letterman better offers than he was getting from the Peacock. Then Ovitz persuaded Robert Wright, the chief executive of NBC, to allow him to start negotiating with the other networks, in exchange for letting NBC have more time to decide whether or not to renew Letterman's contract, which was about to run out.

Even after he was presented with a phenomenally lucrative deal from CBS, Letterman still inclined toward staying at NBC, so Ovitz lured some of that network's representatives out to L.A. for more discussions. He had no intention of accepting their offer; he just needed to buy a couple of days for Letterman to consider the CBS deal. That was all it took for the comic to change his mind and agree to CBS's $12.5 million contract.

Three months after closing the Letterman deal, Ovitz inspired yet another Hollywood tempest. The agency announced that France's Credit Lyonnais, the world's eighth largest bank, had just become its client. CAA had agreed to help manage the bank's $3 billion worth of entertainment loans, which included financial arrangements with Carolco, MGM (in which Credit Lyonnais had a 98.5 percent controlling interest), and United Artists. CAA had steered the bank toward lending United Artists $250 million and offering MGM more monetary support. The latter studio, which had given the world *The Wizard of Oz* and *Gone With the Wind*, was now reportedly losing $300,000 a day.

As soon as this announcement was made, more cries of "conflict of interest" flew at CAA, and this time Jeff Berg, the head of Hollywood's huge ICM agency, was leading the charge. He feared that by advising Credit Lyonnais CAA would gain an obvious and unfair advantage in getting its clients work at MGM. Ovitz's people dismissed the accusation, saying that CAA would be doing nothing more than speaking about financial matters with bankers in Paris.

Some inside the industry felt that anything that helped MGM and United Artists would also help the entire movie business, but others echoed Berg. The three major talent guilds—representing actors, directors, and writers—were called in to examine the arrangement between the agency and Credit Lyonnais, and Berg himself threatened to ask the Federal Trade Commission to investigate CAA for violations of antitrust laws. In the end, the agreement between the bank and the agency stood, and Jeff Berg was left to wonder what Ovitz would do next. He got his answer when Ovitz helped install Mike Marcus, one of his own agents, as the head of the MGM studio.

CAA's year ended on an extraordinarily high note. In December, President Clinton came to Los Angeles for a fund-raising excursion, and one leg of this venture took him to the CAA lobby on a Saturday evening. With four-hundred show biz celebrities or near-celebrities looking on—including Dustin Hoffman, Whoopi Goldberg, Warren Beatty, Sally Field, and Michael Eisner—Ovitz introduced the President of the United States to the shimmering, glimmering crowd of superstars and dealmakers. Standing on a raised platform in front of the huge Lichtenstein canvas, the chief executive warmly thanked Ovitz, Ron Meyer, Bill Haber, and the "entire CAA family" for hosting the event. He noted Hollywood's efforts to fight against world hunger and for world peace, and he made a few perfunctory remarks about the need to curb portrayals of violence in movies and television.

Most of the guests had paid a thousand dollars to come to the I. M. Pei building, but the truly select, like Hoffman and Michael Eisner, had paid an extra fifteen hundred to sit and chat with President Clinton in an upstairs conference room. As the gala affair came to an end and the guests departed the agency, they were given a navy blue coffee mug with the presidential seal and Bill Clinton's gold autograph on one side. On the other was the CAA logo, also pressed in gold.

The presidential visit to CAA headquarters generated nearly as great an uproar in Hollywood as had the sale of two movie studios to Japanese buyers and the recent consulting agreement between

CAA and Credit Lyonnais. People were either outraged because they'd been left off the guest list (which was top-heavy with CAA clients) or enraged because the secretive Ovitz and his company had pulled off another stunning move and won personal kudos from the leader of the free world.

That evening was, in a sense, the last of CAA's long-running series of triumphs. The world of Hollywood was about to change and CAA would not emerge from this period of transition as the same company, with the same fearsome clout. While it's hard to say exactly when something commences or finishes, some people believed that the end had really begun five or six years earlier, when Ovitz became involved in the sale of Columbia to Sony and let it be known that he might be available to run that studio. Others said that his departure from CAA was inevitable after 1990, when he brokered the purchase of MCA by Matsushita. And others insisted that his urge to leave had been building only in the past few months, because of his desire to move on to something new and to avoid the mounting criticism that had been hurled in his direction. Yet it was something apart from all those things that became the real catalyst for closing this era of CAA's history.

Frank Wells was the much-admired president and chief operating officer of the Walt Disney Company, situated below CEO Michael Eisner but above studio head Jeffrey Katzenberg in the Disney chain of command. Over the past ten years, the troika had brought the fabled studio out of a slump and back into prominence and riches. In *Vanity Fair*, Wells was once described by an industry insider as "the highest of the high goyim"—and Hollywood offers no finer praise than that. On April 3, 1994, to the shock and dismay of those who knew him, Wells was killed in a helicopter accident. His death left a vacuum at the heart of the Disney empire.

24

Almost a year before Wells's death, during a Disney retreat in Aspen, Colorado, Eisner made a remark that left Katzenberg, the studio head at Disney, convinced that when Wells eventually stepped down as president and chief operating officer of the corporation, Katzenberg would take over his job. The issue of his ascension in the Disney hierarchy was never put into writing, but as far as Katzenberg was concerned, it didn't need to be formalized: Eisner was a man of his word, and the deal was done.

For the past several years, tension had been gathering between the two men. Katzenberg had written a notorious memo criticizing Disney's film division, claiming that the company spent too much money on big-budget productions, such as *Dick Tracy* and *Billy Bathgate*. The memo, like many other things in Hollywood, soon found its way outside the walls of Disney and into the hands of the press and the gossip mavens. Eisner was not happy about this.

In the summer of 1994, several months after Wells died, Katzenberg attacked rival studio MCA/Universal at a video industry convention in Las Vegas, excoriating the Lew Wasserman-led company for selling videos at McDonald's. In his speech, one video he cited was *An American Tail: Fievel Goes West.* In Katzenberg's opinion, peddling videos cheaply at a burger joint would make the public less willing to rent or buy them at higher prices at another venue. The whole business would suffer, Katzenberg said, if people could just "walk across the street for a Big Mac with Fievel and fries." Neither Eisner nor Wasserman was taken with this example of Hollywood wit.

In mid-July 1994, Eisner attended a conference for corporate leaders at Sun Valley, Idaho, sponsored by Herbert Allen. On July 15 at two A.M., he awoke with pain running up and down his arms.

When it intensified, he left his bed and went to a local clinic, where he was given an electrocardiogram. The pain subsided, and medical exams seemed to indicate that the crisis had passed. The next day he returned to L.A. for more testing, and doctors had him walk at different speeds on a treadmill. The results were alarming, and Eisner was rushed into emergency quadruple-bypass surgery. The operation was successful, and he spent the next few weeks recuperating.

When Eisner went in for his surgery, no decision had yet been made about who would eventually replace Wells as the president of the company. Despite Katzenberg's unflagging devotion to the Disney studio and his significant role in such hits as *Who Framed Roger Rabbit?*, *Beauty and the Beast*, and *The Lion King*, many on the corporation's board were not comfortable with him assuming the top spot in their organization. He was outspoken and somewhat unpredictable, traits not highly valued in a business aimed at families with small children. And some people felt that he was just a bit too ambitious for Disney's good. Eisner himself may have tipped his hand on the matter when he told the *Los Angeles Times* that Katzenberg was "the best golden retriever I ever had"—not exactly the sort of praise one bestows on presidential material.

Following the surgery, no one from Eisner's family or from Disney called Katzenberg to tell him that the man running their company had just had a quadruple bypass. Katzenberg only learned of it when he called Eisner's home the weekend after the operation. During Eisner's convalescence, when Katzenberg began to sense that he was no longer the choice for the president's job, he asked for a meeting with his boss. He went to see Eisner, prepared to resign as the head of the studio, but the recovering patient surprised him by telling him to prepare a memo detailing his plans for improving the Disney empire.

Back in his office by the last week in August, Eisner summoned Katzenberg, who thought he was being called in to show Eisner his memo. But Eisner had prepared his own document, which he was about to release, stating that Jeffrey Katzenberg was no longer with the company.

It was the kind of firing that rocked Hollywood and burned up the phones and fax machines. For the past decade, "Eisner and

Katzenberg" had been synonymous with the rebirth of the Disney studio and its string of phenomenally successful animated films. "Eisner and Katzenberg" were like "Wasserman and Sheinberg" or "Ovitz and Meyer." These were long-term, stable professional marriages in Hollywood, and they defined the entertainment business as an ongoing, enduring, productive set of relationships that served not only their own interests, but those of the industry as a whole. Now this partnership was suddenly over.

Some of the biggest names in Los Angeles were openly critical of the axing. David Geffen, who'd sniped at Disney in the past, immediately came to Katzenberg's defense. Steven Spielberg told the *Los Angeles Times* that Katzenberg's dismissal from Disney was Eisner's "Machiavellian loss." Others wondered if the boss was going to fire Mickey Mouse next. While the controversy was still white-hot, Katzenberg consulted with entertainment lawyers about how much severance pay he could wring out of Disney. Rumors had him going after $100 million, but that figure was low. In April 1996, he sued Disney for $250 million.

In the aftermath of the breakup, Eisner hired Joe Roth to replace Katzenberg. Roth, who'd been working at Caravan Pictures—where he produced *The Three Musketeers, I Love Trouble,* and *Angels in the Outfield*—had earlier been at 20th Century–Fox. His agent was Michael Ovitz.

In the fall of 1994, Creative Artists was having disturbances of its own. The previous summer had seen a megasmash, *Forrest Gump,* directed by Robert Zemeckis, a CAA client, and which starred CAA's Tom Hanks, who'd gotten off the mat of movie schlockdom (in *Joe Versus the Volcano*) and appeared in *Sleepless in Seattle* before becoming this season's heavyweight champ. *Forrest Gump* also featured CAA actors Sally Field, Gary Sinise, and Robin Wright, CAA producer Wendy Finerman, and CAA writer Eric Roth. *Gump* was not just a wildly successful movie; it soon became a cathartic emotional experience for viewers all over the world. Mama Gump's sayings "Life is like a box of chocolates, you never know what you're going to get" and "Stupid is as stupid does" were quoted in bedrooms and boardrooms everywhere.

While *Gump* was generating warm feelings—not to mention hundreds of millions of dollars—in theaters, the old guard at CAA was feeling something else entirely. In years past, there had been minor defections from Ovitz's company. CAA agents had gone on to form InterTalent and Endeavor, but these were mere annoyances to the men who ran Creative Artists.

Now a different movement was afoot at 9830 Wilshire, and it was strangely reminiscent of something that had occurred almost exactly twenty years earlier at William Morris. Five young CAA agents had been talking among themselves about wanting either to have a bigger stake in the agency or to start a company of their own. As word spread of their discontent, they began to be regarded as a group of serious comers, a threat that was growing more powerful all the time. They were all males in their thirties, and their collective name was "the Young Turks."

Richard Lovett, Jay Moloney, David "Doc" O'Connor, Kevin Huvane, and Bryan Lourd were well-positioned and well-heeled young men. Lovett, people at CAA said, was being groomed for an eventual leadership position at the company; O'Connor and Moloney had been Ovitz's personal assistants; and Huvane and Lourd had been lured away from William Morris a few years back by Ovitz himself, then quickly promoted over more senior CAA agents. When the five looked up the agency ladder now, they saw not only a lot of bodies in front of them, but also—as Mike Rosenfeld had said about the situation at the Morris office back in the mid-seventies—too many diners in the restaurant and not enough tables.

This is not to suggest that CAA's leaders were anything like the aging Morris executives of that era, Nat Lefkowitz and Sam Weisbord. Ovitz and his partners were keenly, even painfully, aware of the ambitions that some young men harbor and of the craving they often feel for older men's jobs. No one needed to remind the CAA founders of the underlying dynamics of this situation, and no one had to tell them that they did not want to see a repeat of the Morris rebellion. Ovitz and his lieutenants heard the footsteps coming down the hallway and the voices whispering in the elevators.

As a result of all this, Ovitz took action. He was instrumental in getting three key people, who were all older than the Turks, out of their way. After becoming a consultant to the French bank Credit Lyonnais and getting Mike Marcus his job as head of MGM, Ovitz also got Rosalie Swedlin, a major force in CAA's motion picture department, a lucrative production deal at Universal, and he encouraged Paula Wagner, who'd been part of the CAA Coke advertising campaign, to enter into a production partnership with her erstwhile client Tom Cruise.

Ovitz was also steering more and bigger clients the Turks' way. Jay Moloney, the youngest at age thirty, was now handling such stars as David Letterman, Bill Murray, Dustin Hoffman, Martin Scorsese, and Steven Spielberg. Richard Lovett, thirty-five, was largely being given the credit in-house for helping Tom Hanks ignite his career after leaving William Morris and coming to CAA. For his efforts on Hanks's behalf, Lovett was said to have received a million-dollar bonus from the boss.

Doc O'Connor, who'd once dated Helen Hunt, star of the hit TV show *Mad About You*, brought to the Turks a little more maturity—he was the oldest, at thirty-seven—and a client list that included Robert Redford, Michael Douglas, and Sean Connery. Kevin Huvane, thirty-five, had built his reputation at the agency by helping bring in younger talent like Julia Ormond, Linda Fiorentino, Ralph Fiennes, and Brad Pitt. The fifth Turk, Bryan Lourd, had gained instant and unwelcome notoriety in 1994, when gossip columnist Liz Smith reported an allegation that the thirty-four-year-old agent, who was then living with actress-author Carrie Fisher and had fathered her child, had attempted to steal the boyfriend of an openly gay Hollywood producer named Sandy Gallin. When these allegations evaporated, Lourd was still plugging away at the agency and representing Woody Harrelson and Ethan Hawke.

In trying to placate the Turks by giving them more clout and more glamorous clients, Ovitz had also given them enough leverage to start a powerhouse company of their own—if they could convince their stars to come with them. The rumors moving around CAA in the autumn of 1994 said that the five young men were thinking of doing just that unless Ovitz divvied up a piece of the business (he owned 55 percent of the agency; Meyer and Haber had the rest). While Ovitz had done much to keep the Turks happy, he was not ready to relinquish ownership to the upstarts.

The quintet were growing more restless—and more rebellious. When they took vacations together in the Caribbean, and when they hung out in Hollywood with some of their star clients, and when they visited the Aspen ranch of Peter Guber, whose conflict with Ovitz over the Columbia studio had never been fully healed, they talked about what to do next. People said they were preparing to make an all-for-one, one-for-all pact, so that when the showdown finally came, they would stay at CAA or they would go as a unit, five young men ready to take on the world of Hollywood.

"Try to imagine a place where one man sets the tone for everyone and everything," says a former CAA employee. "A place where that man tells—or shows—people how to dress, how to talk on the phone, or not talk, how to negotiate, how to carry yourself, how to instill fear in others, and what is and is not permissible. Try to imagine a place where someone has complete control and power over a group of people, and all of them are living in fear of his disapproval. Imagine a place where one individual has dictated all the details of a working environment—from the ceiling down to the parking garage. Imagine a place where everyone believes that this is the most important person in one's career and financial future.

"The strange thing is that Mike deserved that kind of respect and deference, if anyone in Hollywood ever did. He was good to his people, and they knew if they stayed with him, they would have success and be rewarded for it. But he pervaded everything there, and he was always going to be controlling the terms of your success. Some people can live with that better than others.

"Working at CAA was a constant confrontation with the notion that someone was more organized than you were, and more disciplined, more attuned to details, more ambitious, more calculating, and more driven. If you could accept that, you were in a great position, the best in Hollywood. If you couldn't, it was going to be more difficult for you in subtle ways. You were living inside one man's vision, and you felt that every day."

On October 12, 1994, Jeffrey Katzenberg, Steven Spielberg, and David Geffen announced at a press conference the formation of

their new film studio, SKG DreamWorks, which would bring together three of Hollywood's biggest players and start turning out
pictures in the next few years. But the world already knew about
their plans because the story had been leaked to the *Los Angeles
Times* a few days earlier. Katzenberg, whose feuds with Ovitz had
long been a matter of public record, and Geffen, who'd done his
share of carping about Ovitz in recent years, both believed that
CAA was the source of the leak. It was payback time, in their opinion, for Ovitz's conviction that Geffen had given some details of
the MCA-Matsushita deal to the *Wall Street Journal* more than four
years earlier. Ovitz denied this accusation but it was one more reminder that he was increasingly open to public criticism.

He was not only busy denying rumors and quelling the Turks'
rebellion inside his own building, he was also moving the Tele-TV
concept forward. In October 1994, three of the Baby Bells came
up with the $300 million needed for startup money for this proj-
ect, and Ovitz soon invited some entertainment heavies to CAA for
a strategy session. Along with several telephone company executives, author Michael Crichton, director Ivan Reitman, producer
Aaron Spelling, and actor Warren Beatty all met at the agency to
talk about how the Baby Bells could best deliver movies and other
show business properties to American households.

Ovitz also contacted Howard Stringer, the head of CBS Television, whom he had gotten to know while helping negotiate David
Letterman's leap to CBS. A Welshman who'd spent the past three
decades working for CBS, Stringer had long been known for his
ambition, his intelligence, his rather highbrow taste in entertainment, and his disdain for most of the breathless talk that had lately
been swirling around interactive media. In Stringer's view, a number of these big ideas would soon be roadkill.

Then Ovitz called and asked him if he would be interested in
leaving CBS to run a new venture in which the phone companies
would bypass both cable and broadcast networks by transmitting
entertainment directly through their own wires. The cost of
launching Tele-TV nationwide had been estimated at $150 billion,
and no one had quite figured out where the money would come
from. That could be worked out later.

Combining his enthusiasm for new technology, his belief in the need to create new media, and his natural gifts as a salesman, Ovitz was able to get Stringer's attention—and keep it. In February 1995, the head of CBS walked away from the Tiffany Network and threw in his lot with the Baby Bells and CAA.

25

In the first week of November 1994, Herbert Allen received a call from Matsushita president Yoichi Morishita, asking him to come to Japan and talk with the heads of the electronics giant about selling MCA. As many had suspected as early as 1990, Matsushita's marriage with the studio and its other assets—including Universal Pictures and Putnam Publishing—had not worked out. Sid Sheinberg had kept quiet for as long as he could, but lately he'd been talking publicly about the frustration of dealing with his Japanese bosses half a world away. Knowledgeable observers felt that virtually everything he said also reflected Lew Wasserman's feelings.

Wasserman and Sheinberg had tried to convince Matsushita that MCA needed to grow. They proposed buying the massively successful Virgin Records. Osaka said no. The two Americans then attempted to interest the leaders of Matsushita in cable or broadcasting properties; the answer was no again. Morishita had come to power at the electronics behemoth soon after the extremely expensive recall of some flawed Matsushita refrigerators, and he was not in the mood to buy anything.

In October 1994, Wasserman and Sheinberg had flown to Osaka to meet with Morishita and present their plan for MCA and ITT to purchase CBS from Laurence Tisch, a deal that would cost Matsushita in the neighborhood of $5 billion. At Morishita's office, the two Hollywood veterans were left waiting for hours before the Matsushita official would even come out and talk to them. The Americans flew home livid.

"It was a typical Japanese power play," says a Beverly Hills real estate agent. "They made the Americans angry, just to keep them off balance and to show them where they stood in the pecking order."

Back in the States, Sheinberg fired off a blistering letter to Matsushita, demanding an apology to Wasserman. He also called for a meeting with the Matsushita brass, so that he could present them with a hard-edged choice: either let the men run MCA and make their own investments, or they would quit. It was at this point, in early November, that Matsushita contacted Herbert Allen, who agreed to fly to Osaka and discuss the company's options.

Among other things, Morishita asked Allen how much MCA would sell for; he was given an answer of between $7 and $8 billion. Then Allen flew home and began evaluating the situation in more depth. Soon Allen & Company employees, representatives of the New York investment banking house of Goldman Sachs, and advisers from the Manhattan law firm of Simpson, Thacher, & Barlett, were all working on behalf of Matsushita, studying the financial aspects of a potential sale. In December, Allen made plans to fly back to Osaka and present the electronics conglomerate with a financial analysis of MCA, but on this occasion he did not want to travel alone. He wanted Ovitz to go with him.

Matsushita executives were reluctant to include the agent in these hush-hush talks. Because Ovitz represented Steven Spielberg, who was very close to Sheinberg, they feared that word of the meeting would leak back to MCA. If Sheinberg found out that Ovitz was engaged in secret negotiations for another sale of MCA—without his or Wasserman's knowledge or involvement— there was no telling what fireworks might ensue. "The first time around," says a Hollywood entertainment executive, "Ovitz had been able to control things and do them his way, but this time it was too big and unwieldy. This time Sid and Lew were out of the loop, and that was potentially dangerous."

In the end, Allen's high opinion of the agent's ability to work with the Japanese swayed the Matsushita executives. Ovitz came to Osaka, but with the understanding that he could not tell the MCA people what he was doing.

At this meeting, Allen's second with the Japanese, he was asked why Wasserman and Sheinberg were saying harsh things about MCA's owners to the American media. This wasn't the way things were done in the Far East, wasn't the behavior of team players, and wasn't something the leaders of Matsushita could understand or condone. Allen, known for his terseness, replied that if the electronics company didn't like the reality it now found itself immersed in, it could either sell MCA, keep it and get rid of the management, or keep Wasserman and Sheinberg and give the men what they wanted. Other than that, there was little to be gained by discussing the matter further. The Matsushita people thanked him for his views and, in effect, said they would think about it. Ovitz and Allen flew home, maintaining their vows of silence.

In January 1995, whatever unsettling feelings there were between MCA, Ovitz, and SKG DreamWorks were all put aside, at least for one evening, when Ovitz, Spielberg, Katzenberg, and Geffen all got together to attend Sheinberg's sixtieth birthday party at Spago. Everyone had fun, but when it was time for Sheinberg to blow out the candles, he bent too far forward over the table and got cake on his tie.

Early in the new year, Ovitz told some of his colleagues that he had a strong intuition that 1995 was going to be tumultuous and would bring about changes that the entertainment world had not yet imagined. When asked by one reporter what this meant, Ovitz's response was vague; he didn't have a crystal ball, of course, just a feeling, and he sensed that a storm was coming, which would blow through Hollywood and rearrange everything.

Ovitz, a longtime snow skier and a good all-around athlete, had now taken up golf, a game perhaps even more subtle and harder to master than the entertainment business. In the winter of 1995, Ovitz was occasionally sighted on the fairways of Bel Air Country Club, hacking away. Playing by himself or with his son, Chris, Ovitz seemed a lonely man who'd found a new way to get some exercise and to teach himself more about humility.

The first squall in the storm that Ovitz was predicting came in January, when Wasserman and Sheinberg went back to Japan, met with the Matsushita execs, and were told that Ovitz would soon be arriving to assess their value to MCA. Between them, Wasserman and Sheinberg had spent almost eight decades at MCA, and the older man in particular was incensed that he was now being judged and evaluated by a talent agent not much more than half his age—an agent who'd never devoted ten minutes to running a company like his. Despite his protestations, a short while later Ovitz came to Osaka and gave the Matsushita brass his opinions of the venerable duo. After delivering his views and telling the Japanese the names of some potential MCA buyers (the short list included Seagram's, the Montreal-based spirits-and-beverage giant), Ovitz flew back to L.A.

The next day an earthquake shattered Osaka, killing more than five thousand people. If someone else had made this return flight, on precisely this schedule, it would have been seen as a remarkably lucky coincidence. Because Ovitz did this, it only added to his aura as the man whose timing was perfect and who could do nothing wrong.

One thing Ovitz had done exceedingly right was sustain his friendships and business contacts over long periods of time, and one such contact was Edgar Bronfman Jr. At the end of the nineteenth century, Edgar's grandfather Samuel Bronfman (the last name means "whiskey man" in Yiddish) had come to Canada from Eastern Europe, started out in the hotel business, and soon moved into selling whiskey. Sam Bronfman eventually merged his business with Joseph E. Seagram and Sons. He himself had four children, including the handsome Edgar Bronfman the First, who went on to become quite a ladies' man, marrying a quartet of women, and one of them—Georgina Webb, whose father ran a pub in England called Ye Olde Nosebag—twice. Edgar's second oldest son, Edgar Junior, became estranged from his father, in part because of the older man's series of marriages and divorces. In young manhood, Edgar Junior made his way to Hollywood, where he tried to establish a career as a film producer (he also wrote very romantic songs and penned a tune, "Whisper in the Dark," that would eventually be recorded by Dionne Warwick). In 1982, he saw one of his efforts, *The Border*, starring Jack Nicholson, reach the screen, but it was not a hit. By then, he was approaching thirty and thinking that he might be better off assuming the multibillion-dollar reins of the family empire rather than attempting to conquer the quirky field of entertainment.

After making something of a reconciliation with his father, he learned about the liquor business by serving training periods in London and New York, and in 1989, he became the president of House of Seagram. Under Edgar Junior, the company would branch out from its "brown" drinks and begin selling Martell cognac, Absolut vodka, and Tropicana fruit juices. It also spent $2.2 billion to get Edgar back into the entertainment field, purchasing approximately 15 percent of Time Warner.

Bronfman then wanted to deepen his involvement in the entertainment industry by holding a seat or two on that company's board, but Time Warner's chairman, Gerald Levin, spurned his offer, causing Bronfman to start looking in other directions. Gradually, he turned his attention to film studios.

When he assumed the presidency of Seagram's, Bronfman made Stephen Banner, a fifty-three-year-old former head of corporate law at the New York firm of Simpson, Thacher, & Bartlett, his special assistant. In January 1995, Banner spoke to a Matsushita official and said that his company was in an acquisitive mode. By now, Matsushita was putting out its own feelers, indicating that it had a Hollywood property that might be for sale. Banner informed Bronfman that one of Matsushita's attorneys, Kaoru Takada, would soon be in New York and was interested in pursuing the matter further. Bronfman was intrigued and began gathering information on Matsushita and MCA. In late February, he began making preparations to go to Japan to initiate his campaign to purchase MCA.

In the first week of March, Bronfman flew alone to Kyoto in a Gulfstream IV jet. On the flight, he pondered whether or not to divest virtually all of Seagram's 163 million shares of E. I. du Pont de Nemours and Company, which the spirits corporation had acquired in 1981. Since Seagram's had bought those shares, their value had tripled to $9 billion. For Bronfman to accomplish in Japan what he intended, he needed cash. Just on the verge of turning forty, he'd boarded the jet in an aggressive, optimistic mood. Unloading the shares and pursuing MCA seemed worth the risk.

In Osaka, Bronfman met with Yoichi Morishita, the newly appointed president of Matsushita, and they spoke through an interpreter at some length about their respective businesses. It was strikingly unusual for Bronfman to have made this trip and gone to this meeting alone, but he wanted to establish a personal connection between himself and Morishita. He also wanted to show the Japanese executive that he did not stand on ceremony and did not expect any form of deference from Matsushita, as Wasserman and Sheinberg had. Finally, he was very interested in doing this deal quietly and quickly, without attracting media attention or letting other buyers know that MCA was available. He did not want a bidding war; he wanted MCA.

During their first talk, the men did not discuss the amount of money that MCA might bring, but rumors had Matsushita looking to sell the property for around $10 billion. Bronfman and Morishita spoke again the next day, and then the American flew back to the States, ready to put together a formal proposal on what Seagram's was willing to offer Matsushita. In order to avoid publicity, the prospect of a bidding war, and the potentially explosive reactions of the heads of MCA, both sides were committed to keeping these developments hidden from Wasserman and Sheinberg.

Three weeks later, on March 26, Bronfman flew back to Japan, once again by himself; Ovitz, who had regularly been consulting Bronfman as a friend and cultural adviser, had strongly recommended that the head of Seagram's return to Osaka alone. Bronfman had dinner with Morishita and then offered Matsushita $7 billion for MCA. Morishita said the figure was too low.

Back in the United States, word was leaking out that Seagram's was about to sell off its 163 million shares of du Pont. To astute observers of high finance, this could mean only one thing: Edgar Bronfman was getting ready to buy something big, and MCA was reputedly up for sale. This news could alert other suitors for the studio, exactly what Bronfman didn't want, so now the deal, at least on Seagram's side, took on an air of urgency.

Matsushita, which seemed as interested as Bronfman in doing something fast, countered with an offer of its own: it would sell 80 percent of MCA to Seagram's and thereby generate a huge amount of operating capital ($5.7 billion) and perform an important function both in its own culture and internationally. By retaining 20 percent of the entertainment company, it would save the corporation's face. This arrangement would also give Seagram's an important outlet in the Far East for selling and distributing its own beverages, as well as MCA's "software." At the end of March, as word of the deal began to break in the press, media pundits compared it to the Japanese surrender aboard the battleship *Missouri* at the end of the World War II.

On Sunday morning, April 9, two Gulfstream IV jets took off from suburban New York City and headed west. On board were Edgar Bronfman Jr. and several members of his staff. Another Gulfstream IV took off from an airfield in Virginia; this one held Edgar Bronfman the First. By mid-afternoon, the three planes had landed in southern California, and various attorneys, corporate executives, investment bankers, and one talent agent all made their way to the downtown Los Angeles law offices of Shearman & Sterling. They went to a conference room on the twenty-first floor. Herb Allen had flown in from his Wyoming ranch and was wearing cowboy boots.

When Yoichi Morishita and his people arrived at Shearman & Sterling, Ovitz welcomed them in the lobby and escorted them upstairs. Once the parties were ready to sit down at the oversized conference table, where the deal would be consummated and the papers signed, there was a moment's hesitation on Ovitz's part, while he studied the situation and decided which side of the table to be on. In a sense, the moment symbolized his whole career. Did he belong with the Matshusita officials, whom he'd been advising, off and on, for more than half a decade and whom he'd led into the purchase of MCA? Or did he belong with his longtime friend

Edgar Bronfman, whom he'd been advising on this deal for the past several months? Or did he belong somewhere in the middle of the table, with one eye cast in each direction?

Ovitz sat down next to Bronfman and smiled politely across the table at the Matsushita representatives. A few minutes later, Bronfman and Morishita put their names on the documents, and then congratulations were in the air and champagne was being poured.

Afterwards, a number of media critics and others in Hollywood said that Ovitz (who once again reportedly picked up a multimillion-dollar fee for his part in this transaction) had had very little to do with the deal and that all the credit belonged to Herb Allen and the lawyers from Simpson, Thacher. While the agent's role was much more limited than it had been in 1990, he was undeniably at the center of things when key strategies were being planned.

Porter Bibb, a New York investment banker who was writing a book about the House of Seagram, had known Edgar Bronfman for twenty years and followed the 1995 purchase of MCA closely. "The amazing thing about Ovitz," he says, "is that when he initially sold Matsushita on MCA, the Japanese bought a sow's ear instead of a silk purse. You'd think that Ovitz would have been the last one they would have wanted to deal with after that, but this wasn't the case. He was still welcome in Osaka and at the negotiating table. That says a lot about his ability to maintain relationships and trust over long periods of time. He always stayed in touch with the Japanese, even when money wasn't changing hands, just to keep the communication going. It's all about contacts and cooperation and getting people to believe that you can help them. The force of Ovitz's personality did just that.

"The Seagram deal happened because Ovitz had a personal connection with Edgar Bronfman and they spent a lot of time talking about how to interact with the Japanese, how to be humble and show your respect. Ovitz was like a mentor to him, especially in instructing him on how to behave and how to bow in front of the Japanese.

"Edgar was very smart not to put a lot of pressure on the Japanese during the negotiations, and letting them keep 20 percent of

MCA was exactly the right thing to do. For a young man, Edgar has a lot of patience, and the Japanese like that. The other reason the sale happened is because Edgar went to Japan by himself and literally knelt before the heads of Matsushita. He showered them with his respect and obeisance. Other companies came forward and made offers to the Japanese, but no one else did what Edgar had done."

26

The tumult of 1995 had only just begun. In early March, a high-ranking Disney executive, Michael Frank, suddenly quit his job. Like Frank Wells and Jeffrey Katzenberg, Frank had been considered a possible successor to Michael Eisner. Now he was gone. Also in March, David Letterman appeared as host of the 1995 Oscar ceremony—a gig Ovitz had helped his client get. In one of the comic's first gags on the stage of the Dorothy Chandler Pavilion in downtown Los Angeles, Letterman presided over a 'stupid pet trick,' as he was famous for doing on his late-night program. A dog came out in front of all of Hollywood's biggest names and chased his tail around and around, while music swelled in the background. This was widely regarded as a lousy joke—and something worse than that.

Show business is a very tricky thing. What might play beautifully on late-night TV was now viewed, at least in some quarters, as a sign of disrespect toward the Oscar ceremony and the entertainment community itself. Hollywood is notoriously thin-skinned; you can make fun of it, but not too much fun, and Letterman had fired wide of the mark. He bombed, and this in turn reflected badly on his agent.

For Ovitz, this was a small moment in a very large career, but perception is everything in Hollywood, and the pundits are quick and nasty. Ovitz had done so many things right for so long, and had had so many public victories that it took only one slip to bring out the naysayers. By April, they were gossiping that he was at fault for Letterman's performance; that he didn't deserve kudos for his part in the Seagram-Matsushita deal, although he'd walked away with big money; that the Young Turks were finally getting to him, causing him to lose his perfect grip on CAA and the rest of the business; and that he was thinking too much about finally making a play for Lew Wasserman's job, now that the older man was going to be moved aside under Edgar Bronfman's new leadership. Maybe, just maybe, people were saying, CAA's long run as the dominant force in town was nearing its end.

In L.A., if people like to see you rise, they love to see you fall. By May, a few members of the media were beginning to question Ovitz's infallibility, and several comedians were even daring to throw barbs at him in nightclubs around the city. It's a town where you can make your name and earn your paycheck by being the very first to spot a trend in music, film, TV, fashion, or language. The *Los Angeles Times Magazine* carries a column on the buzzwords created in southern California, including those used in the film business—"to ankle," for example, means to leave a location or a job—and salting your conversation with them before other people do gives you a certain cachet. If something that small can attract attention, anyone predicting or providing evidence that the reigning king of show business was starting to slide was certain to find an audience. Writers for magazines like *Los Angeles* and *Buzz* were watching closely for the slightest signals of Ovitz's descent.

By mid-May, the rumors of a major career move for Ovitz were reaching a crescendo. With Seagram's purchase of MCA, Wasserman was being elevated to the position of chairman emeritus (meaning he was being gracefully retired, with huge benefits). And Sheinberg, also laden with benefits, was making plans to leave MCA and start his own production company, which would carry the felicitous name of the Bubble Factory.

Now that Bronfman had paid nearly $6 billion for MCA, he needed someone very good to run it. Time was passing, and he wanted to make the hire soon. He had already mentioned the position to Barry Diller, but with negative results; Diller wanted Seagram's to buy CBS as part of his management deal, and Bronfman declined. Virtually every qualified observer now believed that Ovitz was the top name on his list. The moment was ripe and the situation perfect: Ovitz was, as he'd been so many times before, exactly the right man in the right place for the right position at the right time. And beyond all that, many industry people were certain, he was finally ready to make a move and leave his agency behind. What more was left for him to accomplish at CAA?

If he needed a hard reminder that he'd grown weary of the agency business and of trying to understand and placate the egos of the talent, he received one in early May when his old nemesis, Joe Eszterhas, contacted CAA to ask for representation. Eszterhas felt that CAA could now do more for him than Guy McElwaine was doing over at ICM, and he thought that a reconciliation with Ovitz, accompanied by written statements, would put their past differences neatly behind them. After giving the matter careful consideration, Ovitz decided that despite the screenwriter's ever-increasing income, he did not want Eszterhas back. Eszterhas went over to William Morris.

By late May, CAA was filled with palpable expectation—and apprehension. Because the sale of MCA to Seagram's had been such a heavily publicized event, and because it was well known that Bronfman was looking in the direction of CAA for a leader for his new company, Ovitz could not keep his interaction with Seagram's quiet. Everyone knew that they'd been talking since April and that the talking had now become serious. The visibility of these conversations went against everything in the agent's nature, but this was more than even he could control. It was inevitable that his employees would whisper in the halls and wonder what the boss was up to. For years, he'd been omnipotent at CAA. His people had grown accustomed not just to success but to feeling a certain level of security because he was in command. But now no one knew quite what to think, and as the Memorial Day weekend approached, the sense of uncertainty was growing untenable.

Ovitz's older lieutenants—Jack Rapke and Rick Nicita, for example—wanted to know what he planned to do. If he stayed at CAA, would they be given more power at the agency? Or would the reins be handed to the Young Turks? After all, Ovitz had lately let Richard Lovett run the weekly staff meetings. When rumors began mounting that Ovitz was going over to MCA, senior CAA agents started receiving job offers. Several studios and other agencies were interested in them and wanted to know if they were available. Should they take these positions, because they didn't want to be at CAA with Ovitz gone, or should they turn them down, because Ovitz was never going to leave the business he'd started and still controlled? They needed some answers.

On the Memorial Day weekend, the four unmarried Young Turks—Lourd, Moloney, O'Connor, and Lovett—had gone to the Caribbean with Warner Bros. executive Tom Lassally, Columbia honcho Barry Josephson, and Peter Guber. Before this excursion, the Turks' phones had been steadily ringing with advice from industry insiders: Ovitz is vulnerable, so this is the time to ratchet up your demands; Ovitz is weakened, so now is the time to start your own company; Ovitz is leaving anyway, so take control of the situation now and get what you want from him before he leaves. In the Caribbean, the Turks affirmed that they were all in this together. Regardless of what they did, they were going to do it as a unit, because five men moving in unison were more powerful than any one or two of them acting alone.

"Ovitz had taught his people some very valuable things," says an entertainment exec in L.A. "He'd taught them to do things in groups, and now they were ready to turn this against him. He'd taught them when negotiating a deal, someone out there would always give them what they wanted. If you can't get it here, look over there. Act as if you have leverage, and you do. If Ovitz wouldn't meet their demands, someone else would. The Turks had learned all this from the master, and now they were using their knowledge on him."

Over the Memorial Day weekend, Spielberg, Katzenberg, and Geffen were also trying to decide what they would do if Ovitz assumed control at MCA. Lew Wasserman had let it be known that if the agent took over his old office, he was saying good-bye to the company, and the new owners could have his chairman emeritus title and do with it what they would; he was finished. Ovitz's behavior during the Seagram purchase had miffed the eighty-two-year-old gentleman, and he hadn't forgiven Ovitz for his behind-the-back play. More significantly, SKG DreamWorks was about to sign a ten-year distribution deal with MCA, but the three partners in the new studio were seriously thinking about pulling out of this and taking their business to Warner Bros.—if Ovitz was put in charge of MCA. The SKG men were good friends with the co-chairs of Warners, Bob Daly and Terry Semel, and Warners was reportedly prepared to make them a better offer than the one they had at MCA.

This was also the weekend that Senator Bob Dole, the Republican from Kansas who everyone knew was going to make a run for the presidency in 1996, was laying plans to deliver a blistering attack on the entertainment industry. In early June, he would unleash his wrath on the current state of movies and television shows, referring to them as "nightmares of depravity" because of their explicit language, sexual content, and violence. Police yourself, the senator was saying, before the government does it to you.

"Bob Dole," says one show-biz veteran, "knows absolutely nothing about the film industry. No picture was ever made because some writers sat around a table and said, 'Let's put some more sex or violence in right there.' Movies are made because stars are willing to commit to scripts and then money can be raised to shoot the film. That guy doesn't know what he's talking about."

Maybe not, but his words—coming from a powerful man in Washington, who had at least some chance of becoming the next chief executive—sent a chill through Hollywood.

And finally, this was also the weekend that Ovitz's people began gathering in New York for negotiations with Bronfman's aides, to see if they could reach an agreement that would make the agent the new head of MCA. The meetings took place at the offices of Simpson, Thacher, & Bartlett. L.A. attorney Ron Olson appeared on Ovitz's behalf, while Kenneth Edgar of Simpson, Thacher represented Seagram's. With the talks in their preliminary stages, Ovitz remained in southern California, keeping mum about the situation and managing the daily affairs of CAA.

"A business strategist always tries to assess what he can and can't control," says a longtime Ovitz-watcher. "What is manageable and what is outside the realm of your influence? You don't want to react out of fear, and you want to scrutinize all your choices. In May of 1995, MCA had some problems and everyone in Hollywood knew it. Kevin Costner's $180 million movie, *Waterworld*, was about to come out, and this was going to cost the studio a bundle. Some people thought it would be the biggest failure in film history. MCA's movie division was having difficulties—the whole motion picture business was—and Mike would have been expected to turn this around. He certainly couldn't have done this without Spielberg, who was the studio's greatest asset. So he had a lot of questions to ponder.

"What were his strengths and weaknesses in this situation? What were his opportunities and risks? How much of a challenge was he looking for? Did he want to answer to superiors, something he hadn't done for two decades, or did he want to remain self-employed and always able to slip away when the deal was done and move on to something new? Did he want to remain unaccountable to anyone else? He was contending with all of the basic issues an executive faces when it comes to changing jobs.

"How much more could CAA grow? How much longer could he control the Young Turks? There is something in young testosterone that always wants to overthrow the king. You see this in animals as well as in humans. In nature, it's all oriented toward killing the patriarch and getting the females, taking control of the families. Show business is especially vulnerable to these kinds of dynamics. It's not built on really solid corporate structures, and it's not held together by trade secrets or technologies that will guarantee continuity of management and keep a business going through times of transition. The head of Coca-Cola dies, the company keeps turning out the product. The entertainment business is held together only by relationships, and they can change very quickly.

"Given the ugliness of some of the criticism and gossip that surrounds the industry, Ovitz had to feel that if he slipped just a notch or two, it would be hard to recover and get back on top. He sensed the vulnerability of what he'd created and how it was being threatened not so much by external forces as by internal ones. And once you start to slip, there's usually a high revenge factor. All your allies can easily turn into jackals, especially in Hollywood. There's a certain delight in tearing apart someone who's been so successful for so long.

"Ovitz must have sensed a buildup in the pressure of the business and thought that it might whiplash back on him. Once the word got out that he was thinking about going to MCA, no one inside his own organization felt they could absolutely trust him anymore. Not the agents or the actors or the other people whom CAA represented. Things became more fragile, and these kinds of weaknesses will always be exploited by others."

27

In Manhattan, the negotiations between the Ovitz and Seagram's factions continued for ten days, amidst rumors of every kind. People said Ovitz had already taken the MCA position and these meetings in New York were just a formality. Some said the talks were edging toward collapse because Ovitz's demands were too high and the SKG partners had decided to bolt MCA. Others said the agent had finally approached his Rubicon and didn't know what to do; the man who'd always been three or four steps ahead of everyone else had now gotten too far out in front of himself. He'd let it become public knowledge that he was seeking this job, and if he didn't get Wasserman's chair now, it would look like a colossal failure.

Despite all the gossip, very few people had a sense of what was actually taking place at Simpson, Thacher. And until Ovitz held the meeting with his assembled staff at nine-thirty on Monday morning, June 5, almost no one knew what had been resolved.

One person at that meeting was Mike Rosenfeld Jr., the son of one of the five founding partners of CAA. As a teenager young Rosenfeld had hung around the office when his father, Rowland Perkins, Bill Haber, Ron Meyer, and Ovitz had been working with used furniture and hustling for every dollar. He'd seen CAA's humble beginnings and knew the fierce determination and loyalty that the partners had brought to their cause.

As a young adult, the junior Rosenfeld had tried a few other jobs before coming to CAA as an employee in 1984, when it was located in Century City, and after his father had gone into television production. Like virtually all others who approached CAA with the ambition of becoming an agent, he started in the mailroom. The handsome Rosenfeld, who resembled a less intense-looking Al Pacino, labored as hard as anyone to advance inside the company.

In 1987, he became a TV literary agent; five years later, he was made a TV-packaging agent. He liked to tell people that working for Ovitz, Meyer, and Haber was akin to playing on the basketball "Dream Team." In recent years, his clients had included Paul Simms, the creator of *News Radio*, Winnie Holzman, the creator of *My So-Called Life*, Kevin Abbott, the executive producer of *Grace Under Fire*, Mike Saltzman, the executive producer of *Murphy Brown*, Carol Leifer, the coproducer of *Seinfeld*, Howard Gould, the executive producer of *Cybill*, and Bill Maher, the comedian who was host of *Politically Incorrect*. Rosenfeld's father was very proud of him.

As the meeting commenced in the CAA screening room, young Rosenfeld was reminded of something that he'd heard Ovitz say many times. History repeats itself, the head of the agency liked to tell his employees; things came around again and again, always presenting new opportunities. At the moment, "History repeats itself" meant to Rosenfeld that Lew Wasserman had begun his career as an agent and had then made the transition to running a studio and a corporate empire. Ovitz wanted to repeat his pattern, and if he assumed Wasserman's position now, prophecies would be fulfilled. All things would be in order, and Ovitz would have controlled his destiny just as he'd controlled the agency business for all these years.

But history wasn't quite that manageable or cooperative.

At a few minutes past nine-thirty, Ovitz came forward and told his staff that he was not taking the MCA job but would stay at CAA and run the business as he'd been doing for the past two decades. Many of Rosenfeld's cohorts hugged each other or broke into applause or tears, but his own response was subdued.

"I felt in my heart," he said months later, "that because this whole episode had been played out in public, things were never going to be the same at the agency. If people hadn't known about all this, it might have been different, but the negotiations were media-driven, and that made the situation uncomfortable. At that meeting in early June, I had a very, very strange feeling. I just sensed that, sooner or later, something had to give."

After the deal fell apart, word leaked out that Ovitz had wanted a quarter of a billion dollars to leave CAA and move over to Wasserman's office in the Valley. In its August 1995 issue, *Los Angeles* magazine reported that the agent had been considering a $360 million deal: $285 million in MCA stock, $25 million in Seagram stock, and $50 million in salary over a decade. Spin masters on all sides now jumped up and said whatever served their agenda: that Seagram's had not wanted to part with that amount, not even for Michael Ovitz; or that the agent himself had walked away from this package because he could not quite bring himself to leave CAA and go to work for someone else; or that both parties had amicably agreed that they could not find a way to close the deal.

In Manhattan, Porter Bibb had watched the negotiations from his position as a longtime investment banker and acquaintance of Edgar Bronfman. His view of the situation leaves little room for ambiguity. "The MCA job didn't happen," he says, "because Ovitz wanted the store and Edgar wasn't giving it up. Ovitz wanted him to pay for his equity in CAA, plus giving him a huge compensation, plus giving him a sizable share of Seagram's, and that was never going to happen. Ovitz and Edgar had been friends for a long time, and I think it came as a shock to Ovitz when Edgar said no. He was older than Edgar, he'd acted as something of a teacher to him in the past, when it came to the entertainment business. I think he felt that he was shrewder than the younger man. Edgar is nice, but he's also tough.

"In Hollywood, the studio heads had not stood up to Ovitz because they'd always felt that they needed him for their survival. Edgar never felt that way. He definitely did not need this man for his survival."

Ovitz continued with his duties at the agency, but people said he was no longer quite the same man. He was spending more time at the office than usual, walking the halls and making his presence known. He was talking more openly with his employees now, asking them questions about what they needed or wanted, working harder to ensure that they were contented with their jobs. He was much more solicitous than in the past, shaking more hands at CAA, even touching people gently on the shoulders and backs and arms, wanting to know how they were feeling and if there was anything he could do to make their situation better.

He also showed up at a film opening or two around town, schmoozing with his clients and others in the business, doing the sorts of things that agents normally do but that he hadn't felt much need to do in recent years. People said that he'd long ago grown tired of being seen with movie stars at parties and running for a drink for them in public, the way agents often do, but now he found himself in special circumstances. He had to let everyone know that he was minding the shop once again and that things at his agency were decidedly under control. In spite of all his efforts, the gossipmongers around L.A. insisted that Ovitz had lost his edge. A power shift of huge proportions, they said, was taking place just beneath the surface of Hollywood.

A month after the MCA deal fell through, when things had just begun to quiet down on the rumor front, another shock wave hit

CAA. On July 10, Edgar Bronfman announced that he had hired Ron Meyer to run MCA. Ovitz had apparently not even been aware that his two old friends had been speaking about the job, let alone that Meyer had flown to New York and gone to dinner with Bronfman. The media had not been privy to these negotiations, either, because they did not follow Meyer nearly as closely as they did the head of CAA. The announcement took everyone by surprise.

Before their dinner was finished, Bronfman and Meyer had reached an understanding, and the former agent was now the head of Seagram's new studio. His compensation was reported to be a fraction—perhaps a third—of what Ovitz had been seeking. As Meyer left the restaurant that evening, he called his wife, the model Kelly Chapman, and then phoned Ovitz to give him the news. The boss, who in the past was the one who surprised people, was now said to be stunned by Meyer's sudden departure.

First the Turks had tried to revolt, then Letterman had bombed at the Oscars, then Ovitz's talks with Bronfman's people had collapsed, and now this. The stormy year the agent had predicted had become much more tumultuous than even he had expected. Hollywood had just seen its third long-term business marriage dissolve. First, Eisner and Katzenberg had divorced; then Wasserman and Sheinberg; now Meyer was leaving Ovitz and CAA. Instability was the order of the day. In addition, Hollywood insiders were anticipating that 1995 would be an ugly year at the box office. Although MCA had just released the hit film *Apollo 13*, featuring two CAA stars, director Ron Howard and Tom Hanks, many other high-budget pictures, most notably Kevin Costner's *Waterworld*, were expected to lose money, and this trend would worsen as the year continued.

Naturally, a few spinmeisters in the media came forward and suggested that Ovitz himself had orchestrated Meyer's move over to MCA. Under this scenario, Ovitz would now not only have one of his former agents running a studio—Mike Marcus at MGM— he would also have his oldest and best lieutenant heading MCA/Universal. This rumor was given some credence when one of Meyer's first acts at MCA was to sign CAA client Sylvester Stallone to a $60 million three-picture deal. According to this theory,

Ovitz was attempting to help out the struggling industry by planting his own people in the highest places. Therefore, he hadn't actually lost power in Hollywood, rather he had gained some. To many observers, it barely seemed possible that Ovitz could not be in charge of something as large as the defection of his oldest business ally.

"It's always amazed me," says Porter Bibb, "that some people in the media saw Ovitz not taking the MCA job as a failure for Edgar Bronfman. In my opinion, this was not a defeat for him at all. In Ron Meyer, he got what amounted to an almost mirror-image of Ovitz and at a much more reasonable price. I think this was a great victory for Edgar, and I really don't believe he could have handled this much better than he did."

28

By 1995, Mike Rosenfeld Sr. had been gone from CAA for thirteen years. Rowland Perkins had departed the agency in 1994 to start his own production company in Beverly Hills. Now Meyer was also gone, and Ovitz remained in the building with Bill Haber, the one partner who'd challenged his leadership of CAA in the past. The two men held different visions for the agency, and Ovitz's had prevailed, and the tension this had created had carried over into the present atmosphere of the company.

Since the late 1970s, Ovitz had aggressively moved the agency into the film business, while Haber had consolidated its power in television. Over the past decade and a half, CAA had become known as a movie-driven agency. Despite this perception, CAA's television business produced anywhere from 40 to 60 percent of the agency's revenues, and this inevitably generated some strong feelings inside the organization. No matter what they accomplished or how much money they brought in, some highly successful TV agents at 9830 Wilshire felt they never received the level of respect they deserved.

It was no coincidence that the Young Turks were all film agents with glowing client lists made up of motion picture stars. For that matter, it was no coincidence that the agents who were competing most heatedly with the Turks within CAA, men like Rick Nicita and Jack Rapke and Fred Specktor, were also film agents. For decades, TV packaging and syndication had brought the agenting business vast amounts of cash, but never shared the glamor associated with the big screen.

There were other points of contention between Ovitz and Haber. Ron Meyer had always been Ovitz's main ally within the company when it came to planning and executing a long-term strategy for dominating the film business. It was Ovitz and Meyer, with his softer touch, who'd approached Sylvester Stallone back in the early eighties, when he was lying on a beach in Hawaii, pondering his future. It was Ovitz and Meyer who'd gone after, and landed, most of the other big names that were connected to the agency. And it was Meyer who could regularly be seen at the Grill in Beverly Hills eating lunch with his famous clients. When Meyer left CAA in 1995 his client list included Stallone, Michael Douglas, Jessica Lange, Demi Moore, Whoopi Goldberg, Barbra Streisand, and Tom Cruise. Meyer had given the agency something that Ovitz himself could not: a certain physical glamor that came with his clothes, his fashionable hairdo, and his toney glasses. He *looked* like an agent to the stars.

Now the high school dropout from a tough West L.A. neighborhood had moved on, leaving a vacuum in his place. In years past, Meyer had on occasion kept Ovitz and Haber from quarreling when they disagreed over how things should be done at CAA. He often played "the good cop" in negotiations, to Ovitz's "bad cop." He was the nicest man around, everyone said, and even secretaries and mailroom trainees found themselves referring to him as Ronnie. Without him to act as a buffer, the atmosphere at the agency instantly became more contentious.

Compared to Meyer, Haber had always been rough around the edges, and occasionally volatile. With Meyer gone, Haber and

Ovitz were thrown back on one another, left to run the agency together, and they were unprepared for that. The past few months had caught everyone off guard, and now the two remaining figureheads had to decide what they were going to do with the agency, with the Turks, with the older agents who were still clamoring to become partners, with each other, and with themselves. Rumors coming out of CAA in July 1995 claimed that the two men were not communicating better as a result of all this, but were barely speaking to one another.

Ovitz was said to be in hibernation, closed up, looking more uncertain and down than his employees had ever seen him. He'd stopped walking the halls and touching arms, stopped talking so openly to his staff. He was spending more time in his office now, by himself or on the phone, wondering what might happen next.

The year, after all, was only half over, and the storm was not finished. As July came to an end, the U.S. House of Representatives was about to pass a sweeping telecommunications bill that some people felt would lead to even greater upheaval in the business. Beginning in the 1930s, the legislative branch of the federal government had put in place a series of laws designed to keep individual media outlets from becoming too powerful. The number of newspapers and radio or television stations any one outlet could own were limited so none could develop a monopoly on information distribution in its market.

By 1995, this arrangement was generally seen as no longer relevant to the modern communications industry. If it had been devised, for example, to keep a William Randolph Hearst from gobbling up papers and imposing his views on huge readerships, Hearst was long since dead, and his empire was no longer run by a single individual with absolute control over his product. Because of the evolution of the media, many lawmakers now believed, there was no longer a need to prevent TV networks from owning more local stations or to keep the networks from owning their own programming. A few quiet voices disagreed with the new bill and still felt that too much concentrated power in media ownership was a threat to the republic, but a majority in Congress was prepared to move forward and deregulate the industry.

On the final day of July, Michael Eisner announced that the Walt Disney Company had just purchased (subject to government approval) Capital Cities/ABC Inc. At eleven-thirty A.M., Eisner appeared at a press conference in New York with Cap Cities chairman Thomas Murphy, and the men fielded questions about the $19 billion acquisition—the second largest corporate takeover in American history. Their words were broadcast not just nationwide but worldwide through satellite transmission. Disney/Cap Cities was now the biggest entertainment conglomerate on earth.

Disney was already a global business, of course, and ABC possessed a network, cable stations, magazines, and a myriad of international investments. The annual revenues of the two corporations combined was $19.3 billion, the cash flow was $4.6 billion, and together they employed eighty-five thousand people. Some of their assets included Walt Disney Pictures, Touchstone Pictures, ABC Productions, eleven TV stations, 228 TV affiliates, twenty-one radio stations, and the cable networks ESPN, A&E, Lifetime, and the Disney Channel. They owned newspapers in thirteen states. Together, they were worth $24.4 billion.

A few days later, Westinghouse Electric Corporation made a $5.4 billion bid for CBS Inc. This seemed like a minor event, an anticlimax to what Disney and ABC had just announced. Yet it was one more sign that vast companies were getting vaster and that passage of the telecommunications bill (which came in early 1996) would only mean more mergers and acquisitions throughout the entertainment business. Everything big was growing bigger and more diversified, more international and richer.

NBC was also reportedly for sale, and a few weeks after CBS and ABC were purchased, Time Warner and the Turner Broadcasting Network also joined forces. Media properties had become the hottest commodities around, and entertainment was the fastest-growing industry in the country, with Americans spending $400 billion a year on fun.

The impetus behind all this change was straightforward: huge distribution companies wanted to have more programming con-

tent to deliver through their systems. Rupert Murdoch, owner of
the Fox Network, had been the innovator in this arena. He had
used his satellite delivery systems in Asia and Europe to broadcast
Fox TV shows across the oceans, and these programs had become
the most lucrative of all his U.S. holdings. Time Warner and Viacom were building TV networks for the same reason: so they could
sell their own content through these new outlets. And once Disney
had purchased ABC and ESPN, it could deliver these networks'
products all over the world.

By 1995, Disney's reach, even before the merger with ABC, was
truly astounding. It made the old Octopus—as MCA had been
called in decades past—look like a baby squid. Mickey Mouse was
known as Topolino in Italy, as El Raton in Spain, and as Mee-La-
Shoo in China (where he was seen by 200,000,000 people every
week). Disney's audience for *The Lion King*, which had produced a
billion dollars for the company, now included kids in almost every
village on the globe with electricity. Each seven days on earth, 395
million people watched a Disney TV show, 212 million danced to
Disney music, and 270 million bought Disney-licensed merchandise
in fifty different nations. Every year, in Disney theme parks in California, Florida, Paris, and Tokyo, more than 50 million people
walked through the turnstiles. And while EuroDisney had initially
been a disaster, costing the company $500 million, these losses had
not squelched Eisner's desire for more expansion. After closing the
Cap Cities/ABC deal, he began negotiating for an aquatic theme
park in Japan. These days, the sun never set on Eisner's empire.

Led by Disney and the other show-biz behemoths, the entertainment industry was fantastically good to the United States.
While Americans produced only 10 percent of the earth's films,
these movies grossed 65 percent of the worldwide box office receipts. Entertainment was now generating the second largest
American trade surplus, next to the aerospace industry, with the
rest of the planet.

As the Eszterhas-Ovitz saga had proven, in Hollywood, no blowup
is ever final, and no one can ever predict who will be lying down
with whom in the future—when money and work are on the table.

After Disney bought Cap Cities/ABC, Michael Eisner again became, in the roundabout way that these things work in L.A., Jeffrey Katzenberg's boss. SKG DreamWorks, which had signed a ten-year distribution arrangement with MCA after Ovitz did not take over the studio, also had a $200 million production agreement with ABC. Deals, especially of this magnitude, are bigger than any individual spats. On August 3, three days after the forces of Disney came together with those of ABC Inc., Eisner and Katzenberg met and made up in public, proving to themselves and to others that the world of entertainment is very small, that it's bad form to hold grudges for long, and that SKG's relationship with Disney was more important than anyone's feelings. Yet Katzenberg would still sue Disney for a quarter billion dollars.

With his new purchases in hand, Eisner was now intensely interested in broadening his foreign contacts and building more distribution outlets overseas. The Far East intrigued him—Japan in particular. The person in Hollywood who was most familiar with how the Japanese did business was not working at Disney, of course, but over at CAA. Maybe it was time for Eisner's longtime friend to get stunned again.

On Friday, July 28, three days before Disney and Cap Cities/ABC announced their merger, Eisner called Ovitz at four P.M. The men had intended to get together at Ovitz's Malibu beach house that evening, but Eisner wanted the agent to come to his home in Bel Air right now. Immediately, Ovitz was worried. He'd known the head of Disney for more than twenty years; back when the Manhattan-bred Eisner had first visited California, Ovitz had been his guide around Disneyland. The agent had closely followed Eisner's 1994 quadruple-bypass surgery and his recovery. Despite their occasional disagreements in the past, they were long-term friends who'd spent most of their careers pursuing the same goal of expanding the entertainment business. When Ovitz received the call, his first thought was that Eisner was going to tell him that he was ill again—or something worse. Ovitz raised this concern on the phone, but Eisner told him not to worry, it was nothing bad, he just wanted to talk.

Ovitz drove to Eisner's hilltop home, and Eisner laid out the deal he'd just done with Thomas Murphy and Cap Cities/ABC.

The Disney chief told Ovitz that he was now presiding over a media giant, the biggest in the world, and it might be time for the agent to consider making a change. The number-two job was waiting for him at Disney, the same presidency job that Frank Wells had held when he died, the same one that had never been offered to Jeffrey Katzenberg. Ovitz didn't have to respond today. He could think about it over the weekend, and they would talk again.

According to Eisner, Ovitz left his home in shock.

29

O n Sunday evening, August 6, David Begelman, the former agent and head of Columbia Pictures, checked into the Century Plaza Hotel in Century City, just a block or so from where CAA had once had its offices. Since his fall from grace after the check-forging controversy in the late 1970s, he'd been one of those creatures that Hollywood specializes in: the aging figure who'd once been at the apex of the business but was now looking for anyone who could open the door just a little and invite him back into the game.

Outgoing, cheery, and well dressed, Begelman was superb at keeping up appearances. Regardless of the circumstances, he picked up the check for dinner, and he held delightful, intimate soirees at his home in Beverly Hills. Yet throughout 1995, the facade had been crumbling as he slid further into debt and depression. He couldn't shake his gambling habit, which had haunted him for years. He was asking friends for loans and telling them that he just needed a break, just one, and he could reemerge as a power in the industry. But it hadn't come, and on this Sunday evening in the first week of August, in his hotel room in Century City, he sat down on the bed, loaded a gun, and took his own life.

In Hollywood, a notable—or notorious—person's death rever-berates with a larger effect than one might imagine. Old enemies as well as friends come forward to offer warm reminiscences and praise. The show business community puts aside its sniping for a few days, forgives old transgressions, and offers its heartfelt condo-lences and prayers. This had happened back in the mid-eighties, when William Morris's old guard was dying, and it had happened in April 1994, when Frank Wells perished in a helicopter crash. By the summer of 1995, David Begelman hadn't been a real player in the industry for a long time, but his death touched people all over the city and stood as a symbol for what everyone in the busi-ness knows: no one can stay on top forever—no studio head, no actor or actress, no producer or director, no screenwriter, and no agent. The business is fragile, and another storm is always building.

Phil Weltman knew that as well as anyone. Two days after Begel-man's death, he went to work as he always did, entering his office at the rear of a small building with a green-and-black marble fa-cade, just at the southern edge of Beverly Hills. Weltman was past eighty now, but he came in every day, although he had only one client left on his roster: the comic actor Tim Conway, for whom he had landed a role on *McHale's Navy*, the TV hit of the 1960s. Like Weltman, Conway was more or less retired, but neither one of them was quite ready to quit for good, and if work came along for Conway, he would always need a good agent to smooth out the business details.

More than two decades had passed since Weltman had been put in the William Morris computer and found wanting, but the old soldier was still fighting. At the drop of two words—"Sam Weis-bord"—he would start cursing the man who'd fired him, the agency where he'd labored for thirty-five years, and computers in general.

Weltman was precisely what he appeared to be: a tough old agent, a little hard of hearing now, a little slow of movement, but his heavy-lidded eyes were alert, and his hair was cropped, just as it had always been. He fought his battles and won the most important ones, by outliving almost all of his former colleagues.

His office was dank and dark-paneled; he kept it very hot. He also kept it full of the memorabilia he'd accumulated over a lifetime behind the scenes in show business. In the corner was a director's chair, which the founders of CAA had given him; on its blue back were the words "Phil Weltman the Godfather." On one wall was the plaque the CAA men had given him at his farewell luncheon, following his dismissal from William Morris back in December 1974. The walls also held a framed *Los Angeles Times* article on Creative Artists, and one of the agency's founders had written on it that without Weltman, this would be a blank page.

The old man proudly recalled some of his famous former clients, but when he came to Tallulah Bankhead, he fell silent and stared off into space, dumbstruck by her presence half a century after working with her. "Boy," he said after a few moments, "was she a star."

He talked about once getting $45,000 for Vivian Vance for her role on the *I Love Lucy* show and about getting $10,000 a week for Tim Conway for his part in a film version of *McHale's Navy*. "In thirty-three years as his agent," Weltman said, "Tim and I have never had a disagreement. I told him lately maybe he should think about getting a younger agent. It was like I gave him a devastating blow."

Even more proudly, he spoke of the men he'd trained at William Morris who'd gone on to run film studios: Joe Wizan, Barry Diller, and Bob Shapiro.

More proudly still, he began talking about the five fellows who'd created CAA, and how they'd treated him over the past two decades. As he spoke, Weltman leaned back in his chair and looked more relaxed, his words becoming more passionate.

"The manifestation of love and affection for me from these men," he said, "is unbelievable. These are honest, decent men, every one of them. My men were top rank, impeccable. My boys were so good to me, and they still are."

He said that when the quintet founded CAA, they'd invited him to some of their meetings and even offered him an office in the Hong Kong Bank Building, but he turned them down. "I told them I wanted my privacy," he said.

They'd put a bust of Weltman in the new building in Beverly Hills, and he came to their Christmas parties every year, but one part of the festivities made him uncomfortable. Ovitz would stand before the staff and tout the old man's virtues to such an extent that it embarrassed him. "One time," Weltman recalled, "I said to him, 'Christ, Mike, why don't you stop that?' But he didn't want to."

Weltman said that three of the original five partners remained in very close touch with him. Bill Haber kept inviting him to come to his château in France, but he didn't travel anymore and always turned the younger man down. Six weeks earlier, Ron Meyer had come to him seeking his advice on a ticklish and very important matter: should he take the position as the head of the MCA/Universal studio and leave Ovitz and CAA behind, or should he stay at the agency where he'd found so much success? "Ronnie visited me when I was recovering from a problem in the hospital," Weltman said. "He was sitting beside my bed and asked me what to do. I said, 'Look, if it's what you want, go after it.' "

Weltman was asked about Ovitz's future. He shifted in his chair, as if he were not so anxious to discuss what the head of CAA might do next, although he'd been very forthcoming in his praise of the man and his past accomplishments. Weltman seemed in awe of Ovitz's brokering the sale of film studios to Japanese buyers. "My generation never thought about doing anything like that," he said.

In the past, Weltman had on occasion told Ovitz that he might want to think about slowing down a bit, just taking it a little easier and enjoying his enormous success, but the CAA leader had never seemed to pay much attention to these suggestions. He was still hungry, and there were still so many frontiers he wanted to explore, the Tele-TV venture with the Baby Bells and Howard Stringer being only one of them.

Did Weltman think that Ovitz would stay at CAA much longer or would he make a change? The old man shrugged, a noncommittal gesture. Then he appeared to shake his head. "This is a very sensitive time for Mike," he said.

When asked to elaborate, he glanced down at the floor and repeated, "A very sensitive time."

What exactly did that mean?

He shook his head again.

30

O n this same afternoon in early August, the mood at Digital Planet was somber. Music by the Grateful Dead traveled from a radio and through the halls of the warehouse in Culver City, which served as the company's headquarters. Jerry Garcia, the Dead's lead guitarist, had passed away the night before, and the news had saddened many of the young people who worked here. As they went about their day, they sang along with the songs being broadcast, reminisced about the legendary Bay Area band, and talked about the memorial services for Garcia that were being planned around L.A.

Digital Planet was only ten months old, but it already employed thirty-six people, who were involved in creating computerized interactive entertainment and advertising. In the front of the warehouse were executives whose jobs included looking for new business and for venture capital to help the company expand. In-house there were also writers and directors who were capable of generating original, animated, interactive stories for the personal computer market. In the back of the warehouse were the computers themselves and members of that new class of human beings who appear to hold some of the precious secrets of our time: the young people who'd actually mastered computer technology and could make the machines do whatever they wanted them to do. These were the techno-geeks, and the general public was not allowed to see them at work.

The Internet, the internationally linked computer system that had initially been built by the U.S. government to keep American computers working during a nuclear attack, now had many other functions, yet it was still much like a big library. Most of what currently appeared on the Net, which had around twenty-five million patrons, was still two-dimensional text. Digital Planet's technology would allow it to create moving images presented in a 3-D format.

Using this technology, the company generated trailers on the World Wide Web for two of 1995's biggest summer hits: *Apollo 13* and *Casper.*

Digital Planet also created interactive corporate ads for the Web. Their AT&T spot, for example, involved having the computer user answer a series of questions about the telephone while absorbing the AT&T advertisement. Digital Planet's long-range goal was to turn out its own interactive forms of entertainment, which might then be distributed by one of the large studios. Viewers would no longer passively watch the plot unfold: they would have the freedom to alter the course of the narrative and the behavior of the characters. This was a whole new way of going to the movies, and you didn't even have to leave home.

For months, CAA had been following the progress and expansion of Digital Planet's contacts, as the fledgling company began working for the film studios and several major American corporations. Ovitz himself had not been out to the Culver City warehouse to talk with Josh Greer, the founder of the business, but his associates had met Greer and reported back to the boss that DP was exploding with activity and wildly alive with young people and new ideas.

The walls at Digital Planet held no art or even cheap posters, the furniture was secondhand and there were not enough chairs to go around. When guests arrived, a mad scramble ensued among the employees to see who would get to attend the meeting sitting down. Lately, good words were spreading across Los Angeles about the company, and some of the recent visitors to the warehouse had been from major media outlets, including *Premiere* magazine and the *Wall Street Journal.*

What put Digital Planet on the cutting edge of new technology was that it was a full-production facility, capable of creating original stories and doing all the technical work that would bring those stories to one's personal computer screen. To borrow a word from show business's past, Digital Planet was interested in "packaging" and selling interactive products: bringing together the writers, directors, and technical people who could generate new material for the entertainment market. But their package would not appear on television, as the CAA founders' had once done. It would be featured on computers. The very machine that a generation earlier had put Phil Weltman out of a job would, according to some industry observers, create vast new entertainment revenues in the not-too-distant future.

Ovitz, who'd spent years tracking growth opportunities for his agency, had his eye on Digital Planet—and the young company was understandably ecstatic about this. Twenty-something Josh Greer, the head man at the warehouse, had been playing with computers since age five and selling them since age twelve. Extremely intelligent and articulate, he spoke faster than most people, freely used arcane high-tech terms, and sometimes made his listeners feel quite old and badly out of date. Greer was a fireball of enthusiasm.

"The computer," he said on this August afternoon, "is the new television. People just haven't realized that yet, but they will. At Digital Planet, we're not concerned with the container, the computer itself, but with what's in the container—with the content of the stories we can deliver. All of the media of the past have been one-way. Ours will be two-way, and you will get involved in it and play an active role. This is a new genre of entertainment and the most important communication tool for the next millennium.

"CAA wants a piece of us in the future, but right now, they're helping us get venture capital. Ovitz will have a great entertainment delivery system with the Baby Bells. He's already connected to a great talent pool, and we have the production facilities he's looking for. Once our relationship gets further along, I think he'll come see us.

"I have a lot of respect for him. He's taken the best of Japanese business culture and combined it with the best of American business practices. He's done it without establishing a hierarchical structure and by having his employees work in teams. We work in teams here, too, just like CAA. I love the way Ovitz looks at the big picture. When you're around him, you have to wear sunglasses, the glow is so great."

Down the hall from Greer was Tom Lakeman, a Digital Planet vice president who had once been a speechwriter for Tom Pollock, the vice chairman of MCA. Lakeman could talk even faster than Greer, and one of his favorite subjects was the notion of creating original myths for this new form of entertainment.

"Show business keeps growing out from what it already is," he said. "Vaudeville evolved into radio. Radio evolved into TV. Interactive games on the computer are just an extension of the games that were once played in an arcade. But they cause you to become more conscious of the choices you're making as you play the games."

Lakeman wanted to use the computer to tell stories that would teach children how to behave more civilly. He wanted to help them develop their imaginations, have stronger values, and understand how to share and how to "make nice" with one another. He envisioned a game in which a youngster would have the choice of killing one of the animated characters inside the computer, but the character would beg the player to spare his life. This way, the child would see and feel the cost of violence and the suffering it creates. "When someone is pleading with you to let him live, you have a very hard choice to make," Lakeman said. "Now that's interactive.

"Society needs something that will connect people to one another. Neighborhoods and schools are failing. Computerized interaction is part of the answer. You can sit at home now and talk to millions of people through your computer. Typesetting came along in human history when hand-printing wasn't cutting it anymore. Now we need more communication tools to reach out to an exploding population. In five years, I think Digital Planet will either be seen as a pioneering organization filled with gurus or we'll be out of business."

On the computer screen on his desk, a series of phrases appeared and disappeared in a hypnotic rhythm: "Belching is not a constitutional right" and "I will not trade underwear."

"Ovitz is to our industry what the sun is to California," Lakeman said. "He reinvented the movie business in the post-studio era. He's known for packaging, and interactive is the only art form that hasn't been packaged yet. So it's natural for him to be interested in what we're doing. He's positioning himself right now for the entertainment future.

"He's so powerful in Hollywood that you almost can't talk about him. He's so big that he's been stripped of all personality. Kind of like George Washington. Mike invented the CAA agent as a martial arts master who arises at five A.M., practices aikido, eats algae for breakfast, lives by the survival-through-paranoia mentality, and closes every deal. He pervades everything in this town."

Several hours later, as the sun's rays were setting brilliantly across the face of the Pacific Ocean in a sheen of black and pink and purple and gold and blue, a successful screenwriter sat in a tavern in Santa Monica, sipping beer and speaking angrily. The bar was funky: sports posters on the walls, cigarette butts on the floor, waitresses wearing short skirts and black cowboy boots. Nostalgic rock 'n' roll played overhead, and a baseball game unfolded on several different TV screens. The front door was open, and cars shot past on the boulevard, blurs of color and sound against the damp California evening. The tavern was nearly empty, except for a couple of older men who looked as if they came here every evening and took the same stool at the bar.

"What does it say about our business," the screenwriter said, "when the agent is king? What does it say about us that everyone you meet is afraid to talk about Ovitz? What more do you need to know about what has gone on in Hollywood for the past ten or fifteen years? Show business executives used to be associated with great films. Like Darryl Zanuck with *Gentleman's Agreement* or David O. Selznick with *Gone With the Wind*. But these men today are far too big and too grand for anything like that. Now they're associated with corporate mergers and international deals and merchandising and theme parks. Everything in the business now is about getting bigger and bigger and richer and richer—at least for the few who are on top. But is any of it any better than it was in the past?"

He sipped his beer and glanced up at the ball game.

"If you haven't been a CAA client in this town lately," he said, "you've been excluded, and it's been harder to get work and be a part of things. Ovitz has priced movies beyond what is reasonable. Films that might have cost ten million a few years ago cost fifty million now, because of the so-called talent. He is the most powerful man in Hollywood, and he decides what happens and what doesn't happen. The Ovitz regime has affected working people all over Hollywood. When stars get millions and millions of dollars, there is less money for others. Having Ron Meyer over at MCA will start to change our business for the better."

He took another sip.

"It's been like a totalitarian state around here, with people afraid to say one negative word about the dictator."

31

In another part of town, not far from the tavern, Michael Ovitz was making plans for a weekend trip with his wife, Judy, and their three children to his vacation home in Aspen. He had a number of things to think about.

"Get out of town and get a fresh perspective" is a cliché, of course, but when you're breathing at ten thousand feet above sea level, things look clearer somehow. You feel you have far more choices on the slopes of the Rockies than in L.A.'s rush-hour traffic.

Michael Eisner and his wife, Jane, were visiting their own vacation home in Aspen that weekend. On Friday, August 11, the Eisners and the Ovitz family took a hike that carried them toward the summit of Independence Pass and up to an elevation well above ten thousand feet. Independence Pass is about the closest thing to the top of the world that the Western Hemisphere has to offer. Standing up there and taking in the view, your chest seems to open as your vision is enlarged. In one direction there are peaks that never lose their snow cover, and in another there are vast acres of evergreens. On the horizon the sky is transparently blue, and in the distance aspen groves shake in the breeze and send twirls of sunlight off the edges of their leaves. Nearly two miles below the pass are deep-green valleys full of winding silver streams. Running alongside the water are narrow lines of asphalt that bring cars and bicycles up to the zenith of the Continental Divide.

On their walk, Eisner and Ovitz drifted away from the others for a while, and the Disney chief raised the same issue he had two weeks earlier, when the agent came to visit him at his home in Bel Air. The men spoke about it in greater depth this time, with more details and possibilities floating in and around their conversation. According to Ovitz, there was one subtle change from their last discussion: this time, Eisner said "please."

For years the Disney leader had been tracking Ovitz's progress through Hollywood and beyond. Eisner had watched Ovitz as a young packaging agent at William Morris, watched him become the head of the most powerful agency in town, and watched him broker international deals. More than once he'd thought about trying to hire him away from the agency business, but the timing had never been right, or not as right as it was on this Friday morning above Aspen.

"The business strategist," says a film executive in L.A., "is always looking for something with a long-term future, where he can exert the most power over an extended period of years. I think when Eisner and Ovitz were up on that mountain, Eisner must have reminded him that he could never have been the number-one man at MCA. Edgar Bronfman would have always been standing in front of him, but at Disney the situation was different. The path there was clear.

"Eisner had had his heart surgery and received his wake-up call. He was fifty-three years old, five years older than Ovitz, and he would be moving on in a few more years. Then Ovitz would have the keys to the kingdom. He would become the head man, sitting at the helm of the largest entertainment company on earth, with vast production capabilities and distribution resources. Or maybe Eisner didn't even have to say these things, because they were obvious. Maybe he just looked at him and said, 'Mike, don't you think it's time to come in out of the rain?' "

Ovitz gave no answer on the walk, but the next day, the men spoke again. Following this discussion, Eisner began calling other executives at Disney and telling them what was unfolding in the mountains. On Sunday, more conversations ensued, and then Ovitz and Eisner flew back to Los Angeles. On Monday morning, August 14, at ten A.M., Ovitz called his staff into the screening room.

As the CAA employees gathered to listen to Ovitz's announcement, many of them now shared Mike Rosenfeld's feeling that something had to give. Ovitz would later describe the atmosphere in the screening room to a journalist from *Daily Variety*: "It's as though we were all sitting on this quiet beach and we're not aware of the huge breakers that are about to come down upon us."

He told the CAA staff that he was leaving them to become the president of the Walt Disney Company. There was no spontaneous applause this time, no standing and cheering, only hugs and tears and a pervasive feeling that a permanent vacuum now existed at the center of their business. Even CAA's building no longer seemed the same.

On August 14, 1995, Disney's stock rose $2.50 a share, up to fifty-nine dollars. The next day, Ovitz's departure from CAA was front-page news in the *Los Angeles Times*, and a photo captured him and Eisner standing together for the announcement of his new job. Eisner looked delighted, and Ovitz looked humbled by his good fortune, yet aggressively ready to take on a new challenge; a bit surprised at his sudden deliverance from an increasingly uncomfortable situation at CAA; and like a youngster who's won a long-coveted prize but doesn't want to gloat in front of others.

The *Times* had elicited comments from many show business heavies around town regarding the latest development in this year of great changes. Almost no one, not even Joe Eszterhas, had anything bad to say about the agent, and Hollywood talent manager Keith Addis declared, "They're celebrating in the halls of ICM and UTA like it's New Year's Eve."

Harvey Weinstein, the head of Disney-owned Miramax Films, said, "The other studios might just as well throw in the towel. At this point, why bother? Stay on vacation. We've got the greatest lineup in the history of the entertainment industry."

The lone dissenting voice came from Archie Kleingartner, a professor from UCLA, who'd once headed that school's arts and entertainment management program.

"Two big egos," the professor observed, "can work together, but not forever."

Details of the deal would not be made known until November, when Disney, a publicly owned company, filed its papers with the Securities and Exchange Commission in connection with its purchase of Cap Cities/ABC. In the interim, trying to fathom Ovitz's compensation package at Disney became something of a Hollywood parlor game. Most everyone felt that he'd taken less money to work for Eisner than he'd wanted from Edgar Bronfman. The cynics said that he'd settled for second best, but others believed he'd done just fine.

When the numbers were announced, they revealed that Ovitz had signed a five-year contract with a base salary in the neighborhood of a million dollars a year. But he also had an option for five million shares of Disney common stock, and if the company continued to grow as it had in recent years, his compensation had the potential to surpass the MCA deal. The lowest figure quoted for the package, based on a 10 percent annual expansion at Disney, was around $178 million, and the highest figure, based upon greater growth, was just about half a billion dollars.

In the weeks after he left CAA, the big breakers continued to roll in, yet most of them were hitting not Ovitz but Creative Artists Agency. Before he left and officially began his new job on October 1, Ovitz established a ruling body of nine agents. Bill Haber, who was making his own plans to leave, was not among them. All nine were men, and only one, Lee Gabler, was associated with the TV business. They included Jack Rapke, Rick Nicita, Gabler, Tom Ross, and the five Young Turks. Richard Lovett, the thirty-five-year-old Turk, became the new president of CAA. This group of nine would buy out Ovitz's 55 percent of the business, not immediately but over time, in order to ease CAA's own financial transition with its leader gone. And no one, at least at the start, moved into Ovitz's office, which some CAA insiders said would eventually become a conference room.

Without Ovitz's involvement, the $300 million Tele-TV deal suddenly faltered. Howard Stringer, who had left his very lucrative job as the head of CBS to join up with Ovitz and the telephone companies, was left in the lurch. He was said to be something on the far side of disappointed. The phone companies were angry too, but what choices did they have? Without Ovitz at the center of this enterprise, using his connections and clout, no one felt that it would go forward soon.

In November, Coca-Cola ended its relationship with CAA and took its business to Disney. The French bank Credit Lyonnais also moved on from its involvement with Creative Artists Agency, and months after Ovitz had left his old company behind, Digital Planet was still looking for venture capital.

All of these things were minor blows to CAA compared to the departure of star clients from the agency. Steven Seagal left. So did Alec Baldwin, Kevin Costner, Sylvester Stallone, and Barbra Streisand. In upcoming months, Madonna, Winona Ryder, Liam Neeson, Whoopi Goldberg, and directors John Hughes and Joel Schumacher would also depart Creative Artists. While this was not the mass exodus that some inside the agency had feared, it was the most significant change since CAA's founding. The center was holding, but the walls were showing fissures. A few big-name clients, including Anthony Hopkins and TV star Jennifer Aniston, of the hit show *Friends*, had joined CAA in recent weeks, and the agency had some huge film packages coming out in the fall and winter: *The American President, Nixon, Jumanji,* and *Heat.* Plenty of money was still flowing into 9830 Wilshire Boulevard, but the hot rumor around town was that the other agencies were now calling CAA's clients and offering to cut their commissions to lure them away.

On the TV side, CAA quickly lost, among others, Bruce Paltrow, the creator of *St. Elsewhere*; Carol Leifer, the co-producer of *Seinfeld*; Michael Saltzman, the executive producer of *Murphy Brown*; David Kelly and Nick Harding, respectively the creator and supervising producer of *Picket Fences*; Julie Martin, the producer of

Homicide; Roz Moore, the co–executive producer of *Home Improvement*; and Bonnie and Terry Turner, the executive producers of *3rd Rock From the Sun*. They also lost TV agent Marty Adelstein, who left for Endeavor and took several important clients with him. Adelstein was responsible for more than half of CAA's new packages for 1995–96, including *The Single Guy*, a hit for NBC.

Mike Rosenfeld Jr. was also looking at his options. "In the transition period after Ovitz went to Disney," he says, "some of the people at the agency were disheartened and mad at Mike for leaving. But he had done so much for all of them. He paid them 15 percent more than they would have gotten somewhere else, and if they didn't like CAA, they should have just left. You have to be responsible for yourself."

With Ovitz gone, the Young Turks began to loosen up a bit and have some fun (the new joke in Hollywood was that in years past, to advance at CAA you needed to get married and act married, just like Ovitz; to get ahead now, you needed to party with the Turks). According to the November 1995 issue of *Vanity Fair*, one evening President Lovett got ensnared in a scavenger hunt, involving approximately two dozen "bachelorettes," and a couple of the women took a picture of the CAA leader naked. *Entertainment Weekly* reported that Jay Moloney underwent open-heart surgery in August and then checked into a drug rehabilitation center in Oregon. CAA had clearly entered a new phase.

In the February 1996 issue of *Los Angeles* magazine, Joe Eszterhas wrote a satirical column pleading with Ovitz to come back to CAA because he missed the good old days when his former adversary was passing out copies of *The Art of War* and "Japanese techno-gadgets" to his employees.

"When you were around," Eszterhas wrote, "there was this mad, amok buzz all the time about the skullduggery that was either going on, thought to be going on or hoped to be going on. It was the kind of power-breakfast gossip that must have gone on around the Borgias—deals and conspiracies and turnarounds and buyouts and princes in and out of favor. . . . Conspiring with Michael Eisner can't have the same jolt as conspiring with Ron Meyer at CAA. You and Ronnie went after the world. You and Michael Eisner are going after the cash. . . . Come on, man, gather the foot soldiers and grab the guns. I miss the sound of gunfire in the night. I miss the smoke in the air. . . . Come on back and kick ass, Michael. . . . That's the difference. You kicked it. Richard Lovett shows it."

By September, Ovitz had started dressing differently for working hours, exchanging his Armani suits for slacks and polo shirts. He was spending part of his day at CAA and the other part at Disney, although he'd not yet assumed his full duties there. During this period, he kiddingly told people that he was now a seller in the morning and a buyer in the afternoon, and he intended to keep it this way. He and Disney were reportedly looking into bringing a new pro-football team to L.A., since the Rams had just left for St. Louis, and he would soon fly to Tokyo, where Disney was planning an aquatic theme park.

People were saying that Ovitz actually looked relaxed now, although on one occasion, during his first days at Disney, he couldn't help but wince. One evening in September, at a premiere party for the film *Unstrung Heroes*, a photographer wanted a group shot of Eisner, Ovitz, and Disney studio head Joe Roth (the former agent's former client). Ovitz, who'd never much liked having his picture taken, tried to duck out of the shot, but his new boss told him to get in front of the camera and smile. So he did.

A few months into his new job, Ovitz set off his first controversy at Disney, when NBC executive Jamie McDermott asked her employers if she could be released from her two-year contract with that network in order to go to ABC. Don Ohlmeyer, the president of NBC West Coast, accused Ovitz of surreptitiously luring McDermott away from NBC, which had lately been defeating ABC in the ratings, and violating the rules of Hollywood etiquette by not calling McDermott's bosses before starting to negotiate with her. Ovitz and Disney denied any involvement in the matter, but Ohlmeyer was furious. In *Time* magazine, he referred to Ovitz as "the Antichrist, and you can quote me on that." Then in the April 9, 1996, *Los Angeles Times*, Ohlmeyer said, "Ovitz has been spreading rumors with the sole intention of destabilizing NBC and my position here. It's been open warfare for a month. We will take them on like we take on all our competitors, but now there's added incentive for making that $18 billion purchase [of ABC] as worthless as possible."

The former agent had not escaped the nastiness, after all, and at least one TV executive was no longer afraid to attack him in public.

While Ovitz was adjusting to his new life as an employee of a huge corporation, his former partners at CAA began to look back on what all of them had achieved at the agency. "We knew we had something good," Rowland Perkins said one morning, while sitting in his production company office in Beverly Hills, "but we didn't know it would be this good." Half-jokingly, he added, "Now that I'm on the other side of the business and work as a buyer and deal with talent agencies, I sometimes wonder if we made agents too powerful."

"What happened at CAA," Bill Haber said one morning from Connecticut, "is that five extraordinarily gifted people came together and did something that had never been done before and will never be done again. We helped shift the balance of power in Hollywood, by making the on-camera talent more equal to the people who run the business. Now there will be a new spring and a new beginning, just as there should be."

"The creation of CAA," Mike Rosenfeld Sr. said one afternoon, while eating lunch at the Santa Rosa, California, airport, "is a unique story about five guys who were not powerhouse agents when they left William Morris. Back then, we didn't represent one big-name star, but very quickly we became the number one agency in the field. I think this is the most significant thing that has happened in show business in the past twenty years."

By late October of 1995, Haber was the only founding partner left at CAA, and one day he called the staff together and announced that he too was departing the agency to join Save the Children, an organization that had spent the past six decades working with families and communities in the United States and abroad to improve their economic circumstances, health, and educational opportunities. Haber would be dividing his time between this job in Westport, Connecticut, and living at his château in

France, where he was known for giving luxurious parties and then having his guests fly over the countryside in hot-air balloons. Haber's farewell address at CAA was, predictably, more emotional than either Meyer's or Ovitz's.

"Bill gave the most eloquent speech I'd ever heard," says Mike Rosenfeld Jr., who would announce the very next month that he was also leaving CAA for a senior vice presidency at ABC. "He thanked everyone and praised everyone from the heart for all their hard work at the agency. Being an agent is a tough, tough job, and Haber understood that and really appreciated what we'd done. He said that he would miss all of us, and then he said good-bye. There were a lot of tears flowing, and it was a reflective moment for all of us.

"I went back into my office and closed the door and sat down and cried. The last page had been turned. I knew my time at CAA was over and this was the end of the CAA I'd known. I'd been there at the beginning, when my father and the other men were starting the business, and I'd seen it grow and grow. I'd been lucky enough to work with Michael Ovitz and learn from him.

"I remembered how he would tell us to call our clients during the Christmas season more than the rest of the year, because the holidays were a very hard time for people, especially if they weren't working. He said that our competitors would be calling their clients once over Christmas, so we were to call them three times. Ovitz didn't just want to be better than our competition and to beat them. He wanted to beat them three times."

There were people who once worked for CAA who said that even when Ovitz was in New York or Japan they could sense him watching them in the office. His presence was that strong. The CAA building was still curvaceous and beautiful without him, but it seemed smaller somehow, and the air within it less charged. Agenting in Hollywood had gone back to being just a business, and the feeling around the intersection of Wilshire Boulevard and Lasky Drive was no longer crackling with tension and fear. Beverly Hills lost something when Ovitz moved to the Valley—some rush of money and adrenaline. The door was open for new warriors.

ACKNOWLEDGEMENTS AND SOURCES

I would first like to thank Reid Boates, my agent, who initiated this project because of his longtime fascination with Michael Ovitz. Both Reid and my editor at Carol Publishing, Bruce Shostak, were very supportive and helpful with their suggestions throughout the research and writing of this book. Also, Jerry Leider, my Hollywood mentor, proved to be invaluable, as did his assistant, John Martin. Finally, my wife, Joyce, spent many hours digging up facts and details at the Academy of Motion Picture Arts and Sciences Library in Los Angeles, while I was busy interviewing people and writing. She answered an abundance of questions about the entertainment business and was a terrific partner from the beginning.

During my legwork for *Power to Burn*, I basically absorbed everything I could find out about Ovitz and Creative Artists Agency. He'd been written about extensively in periodicals, and I read stories on him (and on the Walt Disney Company) in *Time, Newsweek*, the *New Yorker, Vanity Fair, Esquire, Entertainment Weekly, Los Angeles* magazine, *Premiere, Business Week, L.A. Weekly, Advertising Age, Buzz*, the *Los Angeles Times*, the *New York Times*, the *Wall Street Journal, Daily Variety*, the *Hollywood Reporter*, the Associated Press, *Wired, ComputerLink, New York* magazine, the *New York Times Magazine*, the *L.A. Times Magazine, Spy*, and *National Perspectives Quarterly*.

Contrariwise, Ovitz had not been written about much in books, with two notable exceptions: Frank Rose's "The Agency" and Bill Carter's "The Late Shift." Both of these were well-worn companions by the end of my involvement in this project. I read other books that were essentially reference works for the City of Los Angeles, the field of entertainment, and the philosophy of Ovitz himself. These included Mike Davis's *The City of Quartz*, Fritjof Capra's *The Tao of Physics*, Sun Tzu's *The Art of War*, Neal Gabler's *An Empire of Their Own: How the Jews Invented Hollywood*, Kenneth Anger's *Hollywood Babylon*, David McClintick's *Indecent Exposure: A True Story of Hollywood and Wall Street*, Peter C. Newman's *King of the Castle, the Making of a Dynasty: Seagram's and the Bronfman Empire*, plus a handful of books about successful athletes and sports franchises.

Reading was an important part of my research, but talking was probably even more important. I spoke with hundreds of people in L.A. about Ovitz and never stopped asking them questions. I interviewed everyone from film and network executives to those who'd catered parties at CAA and swept out the lobby of the agency after the bigwigs had all gone home. The most interesting thing I found was that some of the more perceptive comments about the industry or about Michael Ovitz came not from those at the top of the movie business but from those who did the trench-work for the entertainment field, the secretaries and assistants and mailroom trainees, who not only had a lot to say but were often more willing to say it than were those above them on Hollywood's power chain. An offhand remark here and there or a sentence that fell out casually in conversation seemed to illuminate as much about the business and about Ovitz as anything else.

By the end of writing this book, I'd relearned what I always learn doing these things. A combination of voices makes up what we call reality, and each opinion holds something of value. Everyone has his or her own truth, and you just try to get their words right.

INDEX